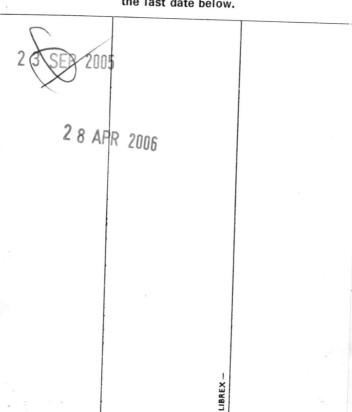

Gender and Knowledge
Elements of a Postmodern Feminism

SUSAN J. HEKMAN

Polity Press

Copyright © Susan J. Hekman 1990

First published 1990 by Polity Press
in association with Blackwell Publishers Ltd
First published in paperback 1992

Reprinted 1995

Editorial office:
Polity Press, 65 Bridge Street,
Cambridge CB2 1UR, UK

Marketing and production:
Blackwell Publishers
108 Cowley Road, Oxford OX4 1JF, UK

A CIP catalogue record for this book is available from the British Library.

ISBN 0 7456 0653 9
ISBN 0 7456 1048 X (pbk)

Printed on acid-free paper

Typeset in 10½ on 12 pt Bembo
by Colset Private Ltd, Singapore
Printed in Great Britain by
T. J. Press, Padstow, Cornwall

Contents

Acknowledgments

Writing a book on an aspect of feminism is quite different from writing a book on any other topic. In the course of researching and writing this book I was on numerous occasions amazed and gratified by the extent of the support that I received from the feminist community, even by those who disagreed with me. In particular, the feminist community at the University of Texas at Arlington, the Arlington Ladies Sewing Circle and Terrorist Society, encouraged me at every stage of the project, offering both scholarly and emotional support. As I was finishing the project, the feminist community at the University of Washington provided a congenial atmosphere in which to do feminist scholarship.

A number of people read all or portions of earlier drafts of the manuscript and offered valuable advice. Linda Nicholson read the entire manuscript at an early stage and supplied insightful comments that aided in my task of rewriting. Christine Di Stefano helped me iron out the thorny problems of the feminine subject over endless cups of espresso. Jan Swearingen offered both moral and scholarly support during the difficult times in which the manuscript was written. And Evan Anders uncomplainingly suffered through tortured discussions of Derridean epistemology that would have tried a lesser individual. I offer my heartfelt thanks to all of them. I only hope that I can repay the favor someday.

1

Modernism, Postmodernism, and Feminism

Contemporary intellectuals in a wide range of different disciplines frequently proclaim the current "crisis" of western thought. This crisis is defined in many different ways, but in recent years it is usually cast in terms of the opposition between modernism and postmodernism. Although many critics argue that the debate is unresolvable because the participants cannot agree on precise definitions of either "modern" or "postmodern," the broad themes of the dispute are nevertheless clear. Most of the participants agree that the dispute assumed its current form with the work of Nietzsche. Nietzsche's questioning of the Enlightenment–humanist legacy that is the hallmark of modernity set the stage for the contemporary dispute.[1] Following Nietzsche postmoderns question the foundationalism and absolutism of modernism and propose instead a non-dualistic, non-unitary approach to knowledge. "Postmodern" is not the only label that describes this critique. "Antifoundational" and "poststructural" are also used to characterize the attack on modernism. But however it is defined it is not an exaggeration to say that the entire spectrum of intellectual thought has been profoundly affected by this fundamental dispute.[2]

One of the most influential and radical movements of the second half of the twentieth century, contemporary feminism, occupies an anomalous position with regard to the modernism/postmodernism debate. On one hand feminism seems to have much in common with postmodernism. Like postmodernism, feminism is a radical movement that challenges the fundamental assumptions of the modernist legacy. Both feminism and postmodernism challenge the epistemological foundations of western thought and argue that the epistemology that is definitive of Enlightenment humanism, if not all of western philosophy, is fundamentally misconceived. Both assert, consequently, that this epistemology must be displaced, that a different way of describing human knowledge and its acquisition must be found. Feminism, like postmodernism, poses a challenge to modern thought in every discipline from philosophy to physics, but the cutting edge of both critiques is to be found in those disciplines that study "man." Both feminism and postmodernism are especially concerned to challenge one of the defining characteristics of modernism: the anthropocentric definition of knowledge. Since the Enlightenment, knowledge has been defined in terms of "man," the subject, and espouses an epistemology that is radically homocentric. Feminist and postmodern critiques have converged in their attack on this homocentrism and, consequently, have devoted particular attention to the sciences of "man."

Despite the similarities between the two movements, however, there is at best an uneasy relationship between postmodernists and feminists. Few feminists are willing to label themselves postmodernists and, similarly, many postmodernists are profoundly skeptical of the feminist movement. This is partly due to the fact that there is not one "feminist" position but, rather, many "feminisms." But there is a more fundamental reason for the uneasiness between postmodernism and feminism: the profound ambiguity in the feminist heritage. On one hand, feminism, because it challenges the modernist, Enlightenment epistemology, is an intellectual ally of postmodernism. On the other hand, however, contemporary feminism is both historically and theoretically a modernist movement. The eighteenth- and nineteenth-century roots of the feminist movement lie in liberal-humanism, a movement that is one of the primary objects of the postmodernist challenge. Although Marxist/socialist feminism is an independent movement that rejects liberal feminism, it, too, has modernist roots. From both of these directions feminism inherits a legacy that is thoroughly modernist, a legacy rooted in the emancipatory impulse of liberal-humanism and Marxism. This legacy, furthermore, is not just an irrelevant historical fact. Modernist values are very much a part of contemporary feminist positions. The contradiction between these values and the postmodern themes of much of contemporary feminism thwarts attempts neatly to categorize feminism as modernist or postmodernist.

The anomalous position of feminism *vis-à-vis* the modernist-postmodernist debate is of enormous importance for the future of the feminist enterprise. The issues at stake are far from trivial. Postmodernism is challenging, among other things, the fundamental dichotomies of Enlightenment thought, dichotomies such as rational/irrational and subject/object. It is questioning the homocentricity of Enlightenment knowledge and even the status of "man" himself. These are not issues on which feminism can be ambiguous. If all the "feminisms" have anything in common it is a challenge to the masculine/feminine dichotomy as it is defined in western thought. It is this dichotomy that informs all the dichotomies the postmoderns are attacking, even though they do not always make this explicit. Similarly, challenging the priority of "man" in the modern episteme must be fundamental to any feminist program. On these key issues, as well as on many others, feminism has much to gain from an alliance with postmodernism. An alliance with modernism, on the other hand, can only result in a perpetuation of the Enlightenment/modernist epistemology that inevitably places women in an inferior position.

Advancing an argument for a postmodern approach to feminism is by no means simple. The modernist legacy of feminism is not a superficial aspect of contemporary feminism. Questions such as whether a postmodern feminism offers an adequate political program and whether the emancipatory impulse of both liberalism and Marxism must be abandoned are of central importance. Discussions of postmodernism and feminism are already seeking to resolve these questions. It is my intention to contribute to that resolution by constructing an argument for a postmodern approach to feminism. This argument has several aspects. First, it involves chronicling similarities between postmodernism and feminism. Second, it involves arguing that a postmodern position can resolve some of the key issues debated in contemporary feminism, issues such as the existence of woman's "nature." Third, it involves the argument that feminism can contribute to the postmodern position by adding the dimension of gender, a dimension lacking in many postmodern accounts.

In order to illustrate the importance of a postmodern approach to the issues of contemporary feminism, it is useful to examine the methodological dispute that has dominated the social sciences since at least the turn of the century. Examining this dispute is instructive for a number of reasons. First, many of the issues that have been discussed in the dispute over the methodology of the social sciences are strikingly similar to issues that are being debated in contemporary feminist theory. The specific disputes within the social sciences that set the stage for the advent of postmodernist thought parallel the disputes that feminists are engaged in today. Thus a comparison between these two disputes throws light on the nature of the relationship between the two movements. Second, issues in feminist theory frequently overlap those of the social sciences since both are concerned with the study of human beings, or, as the social sciences have characterized it for so long, with "man."

The contemporary debate over the methodology of the social sciences traces its roots to the *Methodenstreit* of Max Weber and his contemporaries. Since then the issue of the proper methodology for the social sciences and their relationship to the natural sciences has continued to be a controversial topic. Two principal positions that emerged from this debate set the stage for the discussion in the twentieth century: the argument that, epistemologically, the social sciences are no different from the natural sciences and that they should, as a consequence, mimic the methods of the natural sciences; and the argument that, although there are similarities between the social and natural sciences, they require different epistemologies and, hence, methodologies, because the goal of the social sciences – understanding – is distinct from that of the natural sciences – explanation.

Until quite recently these two positions dominated the methodological debate in the social sciences, with the positivists or empiricists (the latter-day heirs of the Enlightenment tradition) espousing the former position and humanists or interpretive social scientists espousing the latter. But in recent years postmodern thinkers have formulated a position that challenges both sides in this debate. This position is radical in the literal sense of the word because it challenges what lies at the root of both positions: Enlightenment epistemology. The position espoused by such challenges defies brief summary, but one aspect of it stands out: the rejection of the attempt to find an absolute grounding for knowledge, or what Richard Rorty calls "metanarratives" (1983: 585). One of the best summaries of this principal thesis of postmodernism is that found in Jonathan Culler's commentary:

> If "sawing off the branch on which one is sitting" seems foolhardy to men of common sense, it is not so for Nietzsche, Freud, Heidegger, and Derrida; for they suspect that if they fall there is no "ground" to hit and that the most clear-sighted act may be a certain reckless sawing, a calculated dismemberment or deconstruction of the great cathedral-like trees in which Man has taken shelter for millenia. (1982: 149)

The postmodern rejection of metanarratives has taken many different forms, but two of these forms have had a significant impact on discussions in the social sciences: the rejection of the dualisms of Enlightenment thought and the argument that the model of knowledge embodied in the scientific method of the natural sciences is not the only paradigm of knowledge. Calling into question the Enlightenment model of knowledge has enabled the postmoderns to reformulate the relationship between the natural and the social sciences and the dualisms on which it rests. Both sides in the debate between positivism and humanism defined the natural sciences as embodying the paradigm of true knowledge. Although humanists argued for a "separate but equal" status for the social sciences, their position was always constituted as a defense of social scientific knowledge *vis-à-vis* that of the natural sciences. Thus the priority of the natural scientific paradigm was not seriously questioned; both sides in the debate accepted the epistemological priority of the natural sciences. They differed only in that the humanists argued that the natural science model is not appropriate to the social sciences. The postmoderns challenge this hierarchial view of knowledge. They assert that, far from possessing the one model of true knowledge, the natural sciences embody a model of knowledge that is a "special case." Their argument focuses on the interpretive character of all human knowledge and removes the privileging of the scientific model that characterizes Enlightenment thought. A parallel revolution in the natural sciences, furthermore, has reinforced the postmoderns' case in this regard. Many contemporary philosophers of science are questioning the appropriateness of the rationalist epistemology of the Enlightenment for the natural sciences as well. Some have even come to the conclusion that knowledge in the natural sciences, despite the fact that it represents a "special case" of knowledge, does not transcend the universal, hermeneutical character of all knowledge. They conclude that the natural sciences, like the social sciences, are fundamentally hermeneutical disciplines.

The contemporary feminist critique reiterates many of the themes found in the postmodern argument about the relationship of the social and natural sciences. Feminists, like the postmoderns, attack Enlightenment epistemology, specifically its rationalism and dualism. But, unlike the postmoderns, feminists reject Enlightenment thought because of its gendered basis. They argue that the rationalism that is the source of Enlightenment epistemology has been defined as a specifically masculine mode of thought. Thus, for example, they interpret the positivists' claim that only rational, abstract, universalistic thought can lead to truth as a claim about the masculine definition of truth. Similarly feminists assert that the dualisms at the root of Enlightenment thought are a product of the fundamental dualism between male and female. In each of the dualisms on which Enlightenment thought rests, rational/irrational, subject/object, and culture/nature, the male is associated with the first element, the female with the second. And in each case the male element is privileged over the female.

From this it would seem that the relationship between feminism and postmodernism is quite simple: the feminist critique extends the postmodern critique of rationalism by revealing its gendered character. But the relationship between the two movements is by no means so simple. The first problem lies in the fact that many feminists, although they identify Enlightenment dualisms and the privileging of the male that is the consequence of these dualisms, refuse to accept the postmodern argument that these dualisms must be dissolved. They argue, instead, that the dualism should be maintained but reversed, privileging the female over the male. Against this, postmoderns assert that the attempt to privilege the other side of the dualisms will only meet with failure because it will result in perpetuating these dualisms. It is significant that the attempt to redefine rather than dissolve Enlightenment dualisms was precisely the error of the humanist/interpretive critique or positivism. Weber's position is an excellent example of this error. Without challenging the subjective/objective dichotomy of the positivists he argued that the social sciences are subjective, but that this subjectivity is their strength, not their weakness. He also tried to define a kind of subjectively rooted objectivity that characterized the social sciences. Despite his efforts, however, the objectivity of the natural sciences remained the standard by which other variants, that is, that of the social sciences, were judged. Weber's work did not alter the inferiority of the social sciences because he did not challenge the dichotomies on which that position rests.

Many contemporary feminists are making a parallel move in feminist theory. Their rejection of rationalism entails the privileging of the irrational (hence female) over the rational (male). They claim that we need a feminist epistemology to replace the masculinist one that has dominated for so long. They exalt the virtues of "female nature," nurturing, relatedness and community as opposed to the "male" values of domination, rationality, and abstraction. But, as the history of the methodological dispute in the social sciences reveals, this move is ultimately self-destructive because it reifies the Enlightenment epistemology that it seeks to overcome. Like the anti-positivists before them, the feminists will not succeed in privileging the female over the male because they have not attacked the dichotomy that constitutes the female as inferior. The rationality of male thought is still the standard by which the virtues of "female nature" are judged.

A second problem in attempting an alliance between postmodernism and feminism lies in the difficulty of applying the postmodern rejection of absolutism to the feminist movement. The charge that postmodernism, because it rejects absolute values, cannot provide a viable political program is one that feminism must take seriously. If, as the postmoderns insist, there is not one truth but many, this leaves a postmodern feminism in an awkward position because feminism, unlike postmodernism, is necessarily a political as well as a theoretical movement. The specter of relativism, even nihilism, that haunts postmodernism, poses a critical problem for feminism in both theory and practice. A related problem involves the fact that a postmodern stance in feminism entails rejecting the idea of an innate "female nature." Many contemporary feminists, particularly radical feminists, want to talk about the "essentially feminine," discussions that contradict the postmodern's anti-essentialism. Both of these problems point to the fact that, although the rejection of male-defined absolutism would seem an obvious goal of feminism, it entails consequences that are not easily reconciled to the feminist program, either politically or theoretically.

This brief sketch of the issues reveals the difficulty of even trying to define the relationship between postmodernism and feminism, much less formulating a coherent postmodern feminism. The central problem revolves around the fact that, on one hand, feminism has much in common with postmodernism's attack on Enlightenment epistemology because it is an epistemology that places women in an inferior position. On the other hand, however, feminism is also tied to that Enlightenment epistemology, both because of its modernist legacy and because even radical feminists adhere to dichotomies and absolutes. Feminists have devoted extensive discussions to these issues and have established three principal positions on the question of where feminism should stand with regard to the modernism/postmodernism dispute. The first position is that feminism should retain the "good" aspects of modernity while at the same time rejecting its problematic features. This position is analogous to that taken by Habermas on the question of modernism. Habermas argues that we should not give up modernity as a "lost cause" but, rather, "we should learn from the mistakes of those extravagant programs which have tried to negate modernity" (1981a: 11). An example of a feminist position that echoes this Habermasian view is that taken by Eisenstein (1981). She asserts that liberal feminism, despite its flaws, possesses a radical potential that feminists can build on in their effort to move beyond the liberal program. Although she acknowledges the problems of liberalism, and modernism in general, she argues that it should not be abandoned altogether. Similar feminist arguments have been made in defense of a Marxist feminism. The problem with this approach is its eclecticism. Critics of Habermas have noted that he cannot simply pick and choose among the elements of modernism, saving those he likes and discarding those he does not. The epistemology of modernism is a unitary whole, not a piecemeal collection. The same criticism applies even more forcefully to feminism. Feminists cannot simply choose the elements of modernism that they like, the emancipatory impulse of liberalism and Marxism, for example, and discard those they do not like, such as sexism. In her discussion of western philosophical theories Finn makes this point very clearly:

> You cannot "doctor" these theories with respect to women and at the same time save the theory. The philosophical system does not survive the doctoring. The exclusion or denigration of women is integral to the system and to give equal recognition to women destroys the system. (1982: 151)

A second position in this dispute is the attempt by some feminists simply to avoid the issue of where to place feminism in the modernism/postmodernism debate. One way of doing this is to reject the "feminist" label altogether. Because of feminism's identification with humanism and liberalism, socialist women in particular have difficulty accepting the feminist label (Balbus, 1982: 62). These women argue that if feminism is an offshoot of liberalism then socialist "feminists," who reject every aspect of liberalism, should have no part of it. The same conclusion has been reached by some French feminists who also object to the humanist roots of the feminist legacy, but on other than socialist grounds. Theorists such as Helene Cixous refuse the label "feminist" because of its suspect theoretical roots. Another way of avoiding the issue is to claim that feminism must be "non-aligned" (Bunch, 1981: 46). Some feminists have claimed that we cannot allow feminism to be "tainted" by the doctrines of male theorists. Rather, they argue that feminism should go its own way, formulating its own position independently of current doctrines. Radical feminists who ignore the explicit issues of the modernist/postmodernist dispute claim to be non-aligned in this sense. But by perpetuating the Enlightenment dichotomies they are in actuality taking sides in the debate. This position of avoidance has serious drawbacks. The modernism/postmodernism debate is the principal intellectual issue of our time. It is an issue that is central to feminism and one on which feminists must take a stance. Rejecting the feminist label or claiming to be non-aligned will not advance the cause of feminism in the present intellectual climate.

The third position is one that a number of feminists both in America and France are attempting to formulate: a postmodern approach to feminism. This position has several advantages over the other two. As the history of methodological disputes in the social sciences has illustrated, anything short of outright rejection of the dualism and rationalism of Enlightenment thought will not be a successful strategy. The social sciences could not eschew their inferior status until they rejected the epistemology that defined them as inferior. Similarly, feminists cannot overcome the privileging of the male and the devaluing of the female until they reject the epistemology that created these categories. The attempt to preserve the "good" aspects of modernity, or even to privilege the feminine over the masculine, cannot escape from the inherent sexism of Enlightenment epistemology.

Another advantage of this position is that postmodernism can reveal some of the errors of contemporary feminist positions. The postmodern position reveals the futility of the attempt to define an essential female nature or to replace the masculinist epistemology with a feminist epistemology. Further, post-modernism's rejection of the subject/object dichotomy, and its definition of all knowledge as interpretive adds depth and substance to the feminist critique. But if postmodernism corrects feminism it is important to note that feminism also acts as a corrective to postmodernism. The postmodern critique of Enlight-enment rationalism reveals the failure of what Foucault calls the modern episteme to describe the phenomenon of human understanding, particularly in the social sciences. It represents a radical critique of modern western thought that, as Richard Rorty (1979) argues, transforms the project of philosophy itself. The postmodern critique of Enlightenment dualism and the privileging it entails, however, is incomplete without the feminist contribution to that critique. The postmoderns see the error of Enlightenment dualism but the feminists complete this critique by defining those dualisms as gendered. The two movements, then, are complimentary and mutually corrective.[3] Feminists see the gendered basis of Enlightenment thought but postmodern thought expands and concretizes that vision.

In order to present an argument for a coherent and viable postmodern femi-nism it is necessary to criticize the other feminist positions described above. This can be accomplished by defining specific postmodern thinkers and positions that are relevant to feminist issues. Although they are certainly not the only writers whose works have feminist implications, the works of Foucault, Derrida and, to a lesser extent, Gadamer, are particularly germane to feminist issues.[4] There are significant differences between these writers, but it is nevertheless possible to define common themes among them that can be applied to the feminist critique. The first task in my attempt to define a postmodern feminism is to analyze the work of these influential postmodern thinkers and assess their relevance in feminist terms. The second task is to circumscribe this unwieldy topic and reduce it to manageable proportions. Although both feminism and postmodernism are complex movements, the focus of both positions, at least in epistemological terms, is challenging the hierarchical dualisms of Enlightenment thought. The attack on the dualisms of rational/irrational, subject/object and culture/nature is central to both the postmodern and the feminist critiques. Organizing the discussion around an examination of these dualisms reveals the relationship between postmodernism and feminism and can serve as the basis for the formulation of a postmodern feminism. The third task of this examination is to use these analyses to refute the principal criticisms of postmodernism by feminist critics. Unless these criticisms, particularly the political critique, are addressed, an argument for a postmodern feminism cannot be advanced.

An issue that is central to all these discussions is the definition of "epistemology." The Enlightenment defined "epistemology" as the study of knowledge acquisition that was accomplished through the opposition of a knowing subject and a known object. This definition is problematic for both feminists and postmoderns. Feminists reject the opposition of subject and object because inherent in this opposition is the assumption that only men can be subjects, and, hence, knowers. Postmoderns reject the opposition because it misrepresents the ways in which discourse constitutes what we call knowledge. Strictly speaking, then, when feminists and postmoderns discuss the constitution of knowledge they are not engaged in "epistemology" as the Enlightenment defined it. They reject both the notion that knowledge is the product of the opposition of subjects and objects and that there is only one way in which knowledge can be constituted. In light of this difficulty, some theorists have argued that we ought to discard the term altogether. A postmodern approach to feminist issues entails the attempt to formulate not an "epistemology" in the sense of a replacement of the Enlightenment conception, but, rather, an explanation of the discursive processes by which human beings gain understanding of their common world. A related issue is the question of whether the attempt to formulate a postmodern feminism entails the definition of a "feminist epistemology." This phrase is appealing because it seems to entail a rejection of masculinist epistemology. But it is misleading as well. If a "feminist epistemology" is an epistemology that privileges the feminine as opposed to one that privileges the masculine, then it cannot be the goal of a postmodern feminism. A postmodern feminism would reject the masculinist bias of rationalism but would not attempt to replace it with a feminist bias. Rather it would take the position that there is not one (masculine) truth but, rather, many truths, none of which is privileged along gendered lines.

The task of formulating a postmodern feminism is difficult, yet, given the contemporary intellectual climate, also compelling. Both feminism and postmodernism have had and will continue to have a profound impact on the course of intellectual inquiry. And, despite feminism's ambiguous legacy, they complement each other in important ways. Richard Rorty claims that the task of philosophy is not to discover absolutes but to continue the "conversation of mankind." Despite the gendered connotations of this phrase, it describes the spirit of this work. My intent is to foster this conversation by promoting a conversation between postmodernism and feminism, a conversation which can significantly benefit both participants.

2

Rational/Irrational

I Postmodernism and Rationality

Supposing that Truth is a woman – what then? Is there not ground for suspecting that all philosophers, in so far as they have been dogmatists, have failed to understand women – that the terrible seriousness and clumsy importunity with which they have usually paid their addresses to Truth, have been unskilled and unseemly methods for winning a woman?

(Nietzsche 1964b: 1)

In this passage Nietzsche expresses what will later become one of the central themes of postmodernism: the rejection of the dogmatism of Enlightenment thought and the formulation of a new definition of truth. This passage also presages the connection between the postmodern critique of truth and rationality and contemporary feminism. The critique of the Enlightenment concept of rationality and its unitary definition of truth forms the basis of postmodern thought. It is also central to contemporary feminism. Feminists have defined what the postmoderns call "logocentrism" as an inherently masculine mode of thought. Thus, like the postmoderns, they challenge the Enlightenment's concepts of truth and rationality. Although the other dichotomies that inform the postmodern position are important, the rational/irrational dualism is particularly fundamental to the postmodern attack on logocentrism and the connection between that attack and contemporary feminism.

One of the principal chroniclers of the postmodern movement, and certainly the most influential in America, is Richard Rorty. In his important book, *Philosophy and the Mirror of Nature* (1979) Rorty attacks what he identifies as the tradition of "foundational" thought in the history of western philosophy. Rorty argues that until the present postmodern (antifoundational) movement, philosophers were unanimous in the assertion that knowledge must be grounded in absolute truth. Although knowledge was usually defined in rational terms, this definition was not exclusive; Husserl, for example, defines truth as subjectivity. The point is that unless knowledge has an absolute ground it cannot qualify as truth. In opposition to this tradition Rorty both describes and advocates the work of what he calls "edifying philosophers" who, far from seeking absolute foundations for knowledge, aim at "continuing conversation rather than discovering truth" (1979: 373). What Rorty seeks to do in this work and other related essays is to argue that no absolute grounding in rationality or any other universal is a necessary condition of truth. Rather he argues that we have all the grounding we require in our common history, tradition and culture, a grounding that we have created ourselves. He asserts that

> there is nothing deep down inside us except what we have put there ourselves, no criterion that we have not created in the course of creating a practice, no standard of rationality that is not our appeal to such a criterion, no rigorous argumentation that is not obedience to our own conventions. (1982: xiii)

This central attack on foundational thought and the rationality that has defined it particularly since the Enlightenment takes different forms in the three theorists under discussion here. But at least two common themes derive from their shared antifoundational impulse. First, Gadamer, Foucault and Derrida all reject the abstraction that is definitive of rationalist thought. Rationalism rests on the notion that there is an Archimedean point from which knowledge is acquired. The existence of such an Archimedean point that abstracts the knower from the known is, for rationalism, definitive of truth. Postmoderns, in rejecting this Archimedean abstraction frequently describe the Enlightenment position as a form of "privileging." The postmoderns claim that the Enlightenment privileged rational discourse by identifying it as the sole avenue to truth. Postmodernism rejects this privileging of rational discourse, arguing that the Enlightenment erred in seeking to define one privileged discourse and, furthermore, in defining that discourse in terms of its abstraction from the social context.[1]

The second commonality among the three theorists is a rejection of the necessity for absolute grounding for knowledge and, hence, the unitary definition of truth. As Rorty puts it, postmodernism rejects "metanarratives" – the absolute justifying mechanisms of foundational thought (1983: 585). Gadamer, Foucault and Derrida all argue that such metanarratives are both unnecessary and undesirable. They argue for a plural definition of truth to replace the Enlightenment's unitary definition. But the different ways in which each of the three theorists reject Enlightenment metanarratives is significant, and those differences are potentially important for contemporary feminism. Gadamer, while rejecting the rationalist metanarratives, argues that our knowledge is informed by tradition and prejudice which, although not universal or abstract, provide the necessary basis for human understanding. Tradition does not figure in the accounts of Foucault and Derrida. Foucault explores the ways in which particular discourses create their own definitions of truth. Derrida engages in the task of deconstructing the definitions of truth that have structured the metanarratives of western thought. Despite these differences, however, the commonalities that unite the theorists are of more consequence than these divergences. Most interpreters of postmodern thought agree that, at root, postmodernism involves a crisis of cultural authority (Owens, 1983: 57). Gadamer, Foucault, and Derrida are all challenging the Enlightenment concepts of truth and rationality that have provided the legitimacy for knowledge in the modern era. In this sense their theories entail a radical reversal of intellectual discourse.

Gadamer

A philosopher whose roots lie in the hermeneutic tradition, an approach that emphasizes tradition, prejudice and the interpretation of classical texts, would seem an odd choice for an ally of postmodern feminism. But Gadamer's work[2] provides important support for the postmodern position, particularly its attack on the Enlightenment concept of reason. His *Truth and Method* (1975) consists of a fundamental challenge to Enlightenment rationality and, as such, is an important document for both postmodernism and feminism.

The key to understanding Gadamer's task in *Truth and Method* lies in understanding what he is *not* doing as much as what he is. Gadamer is adamant in his assertion that the philosophical hermeneutics that he espouses in this work is not designed to provide a method for the human sciences (1975: xiii). Unlike Schleiermacher and Dilthey, Gadamer, following Heidegger, defines hermeneutics as the foundation of philosophy itself, not a methodological tool for the human sciences. The principal thesis of *Truth and Method* is that all understanding is linguistic and that hermeneutic understanding is the basis for all human communication. The linguisticality and universality of understanding provide the basis for the philosophical hermeneutics that Gadamer advocates.

Central to Gadamer's attempt to explicate the nature of hermeneutic understanding is his argument that we encounter ''experiences of truth'' other than that provided by the method of the natural sciences. He turns to art to provide an example of such an experience, and a significant portion of *Truth and Method* is devoted to an explication of the experience of truth encountered in art. Ultimately, however, his aim in this is to clarify the status of the human sciences. He argues that the model provided by the natural sciences is not the only source of truth and, hence, that truth can be found in art or the human sciences as well. But his argument goes considerably beyond this. He asserts that hermeneutic understanding, an understanding which has always been defined as the basis of the human sciences, is fundamental to *all* understanding, and, thus, also forms the basis of natural scientific understanding. In a later article he states this point very succinctly:

If *Verstehen* is the basic moment of human *In-der-Welt-sein* then the human sciences are nearer to human self-understanding than the natural sciences.

The objectivity of the latter is no longer an unequivocal and obligatory ideal
of knowledge. (1979: 106)

Much of *Truth and Method* is devoted to an explication of precisely how
hermeneutic understanding is achieved. Central to that understanding is
Gadamer's concept of prejudice and the closely related concept of tradition, terms
which have been widely misunderstood by Gadamer's critics. By prejudice
Gadamer means the pre-understandings that make all human communication
possible. For Gadamer prejudice is not arbitrary, unexamined bias but, rather, is
consistent with Heidegger's notion of the "fore-structure" that makes understanding itself possible (1975: 237). Tradition, likewise, is, for Gadamer, neither
arbitrary nor, as the Enlightenment claimed, opposed to reason. For Gadamer the
basic misunderstanding of the Enlightenment was its rejection of tradition and
prejudices: "the fundamental prejudice of the enlightenment is the prejudice
against prejudice itself which deprives tradition of its power" (1975: 239–40).

Furthermore, Gadamer, following Heidegger, describes understanding in
terms of the hermeneutic circle. For both philosophers the hermeneutic circle is
not "vicious," but, rather, the positive possibility of all understanding. It
describes understanding as the interplay of the movement of tradition (1975: 261).
Gadamer's explication of the hermeneutic circle definitively lays to rest the possibility of an Archimedean point, an abstract, universal standpoint from which
"objective knowledge" can be achieved. All understanding, in art, the human
sciences, and the natural sciences, is understanding that is contextual and historical, rooted in tradition and prejudice. Understanding always involves, in
Gadamer's terms, a fusion of horizons: a meeting of the contextual understanding
of the interpreter with that of the interpreted (1975: 273–4). In describing the
hermeneutic circle Gadamer establishes what one commentator has described as
the 'triunity" of understanding, interpretation, and application (Llwelyn,
1985: 111).

Although Rorty classifies Gadamer as one of the "edifying philosophers" who
eschews foundational thought, Gadamer is not often labelled a postmodern
thinker. But even this brief overview of Gadamer's position indicates its importance for the postmodern critique. Like the postmodern movement in general,
Gadamer produces a compelling attack on the rationalism of Enlightenment
thought. He argues that the model of knowledge that the Enlightenment claimed
as the only possible path to truth is fundamentally misconceived. Its emphasis on
abstraction and its rejection of tradition and prejudice deny what Gadamer defines
as the basic insight of hermeneutics: that all understanding is contextual, rooted in
prejudice, and historically grounded (1985: 179). One of the most important
effects of his position is to displace the hierarchical relationship between the natural
and the social sciences that is characteristic of Enlightenment thought. Instead of
conceding that the human sciences are subjective (and hence irrational) he rejects
the rational/irrational dichotomy itself and argues that the human sciences are

actually closer to the basic hermeneutic understanding that is the foundation of all human meaning. His intention here is not to reverse the dichotomy between the natural and the social sciences, making the social sciences superior. Rather, he wants to alter the Enlightenment understanding of truth. He argues that there is not, as the Enlightenment claimed, one means of attaining truth but, rather, many experiences of truth all of which, including that of the natural sciences, are rooted in hermeneutic understanding. But although Gadamer rejects the absolutism of Enlightenment rationalism, it does not follow that he is asserting that any interpretation is as good as any other. Gadamer argues that tradition and prejudice provide the basis for interpretation that is necessary for the achievement of understanding but that this process allows for and even demands both criticism and critique. Gadamer explicitly appeals to the use of "critical reason" to distinguish between what he calls legitimate and illegitimate prejudices (1975: 246). Gadamer's position avoids the nihilism of an "anything goes" approach to interpretation while at the same time rejecting the abstraction of rationalist thought.[3]

If Gadamer's postmodern credentials are fairly easy to establish, however, the same is not true of his feminist credentials. Two principal problems arise in attempting to establish Gadamer's relevance for contemporary feminism. First, how can a philosopher who relies on tradition and prejudice be relevant for a movement, feminism, which is profoundly anti-traditional and whose explicit goal is to overturn the dominant prejudice of western culture? Gadamer's position allows for a number of answers to this question. Most important is the point that his arguments in favor of prejudice do not amount to an advocacy of bias. Rather, they involve the assertion that all understanding is rooted, contextual, and historical. What he is asserting is that we must and do understand through the "prejudices" of our culture, a fact that any feminist will readily acknowledge. Equally important is the fact that Gadamer's understanding of prejudice involves critique and self-understanding. Prejudice is not arbitrary understanding but, rather, a knowledge of what our prejudices are, an understanding that involves and entails critique. To understand the hermeneutic basis of all meaning entails a critical understanding of what we are as a culture. Gadamer argues in *Truth and Method* that such an understanding is fundamental to the human sciences.

Stated in this way, Gadamer's relevance to feminism is easier to articulate. Much of contemporary feminist writing is involved in the attempt to understand and explicate the "prejudices" of western culture, particularly those prejudices that relegate women to an inferior role. Gadamer's hermeneutics can be a useful tool in exploring these prejudices. The self-understanding of our culture that has been a result of such feminist analyses is compatible with Gadamer's conception of the role of hermeneutic understanding. Of course, feminists do not want merely to understand the prejudices that relegate them to inferior status. They want to go on to criticize those prejudices and argue for their elimination. Gadamer's work is also compatible with this attempt. It follows from his argument that self-understanding entails critique and that the self-understanding fostered by feminist analysis is at the same time a critique of the sexist prejudices of our society. As one commentator puts it, for Gadamer prejudices are thresholds as well as limits (Warnke 1986: 4). By attacking the dichotomies of Enlightenment thought, Gadamer is attacking an epistemology that has defined the feminine as inferior. The dichotomous, hierarchical thought of the Enlightenment necessarily disprivileged the "feminine" side of each of its dichotomies. Gadamer's radical attack on these dichotomies and the hierarchies they entail thus can and should be an important element of a postmodern feminism.

The second problem involved in arguing for the relevance of Gadamer to feminism centers around the issue of whether it is possible to distinguish a "feminist epistemology." One of Gadamer's principal arguments is that understanding is not a product of rationality and abstraction, but, rather, that of the contextuality and relatedness of prejudice. But this creates a problem for feminist theory in general and postmodern feminism in particular. Feminists have shown that Enlightenment thought has identified the values Gadamer is rejecting – rationality and abstraction – as masculine and those that he espouses – contextuality and relatedness – as feminine. Indeed, feminists have shown that this dichotomy between masculine abstraction and feminine contextuality has been the central means of excluding women from the sphere of rationality and maintaining their inferiority. Although this insight is undoubtedly accurate it raises a serious problem. It seems to follow that, in feminist terms, Gadamer's position entails substituting a "feminist epistemology" for the "masculinist epistemology" of the Enlightenment. This is further complicated by the fact that Gadamer claims that what the Enlightenment has defined as this "feminine" way of knowing is universal. Thus he seems to be substituting a universal model of truth (a "feminist epistemology") in place of the "masculinist" model that the Enlightenment proclaimed to be the unique source of truth.

Such an interpretation of Gadamer's position is misleading. It is neither an accurate reading of Gadamer's aim nor a positive goal of feminist theory. The question of a feminist epistemology, furthermore, is not one that is unique to a discussion of Gadamer's position. It is question discussed by many contemporary feminists in a range of different contexts; the question of "women's way of knowing" is a popular one. It is significant that a number of these feminists specifically advocate the adoption of a feminist epistemology, arguing that this contextual "feminine" understanding is superior to the abstract, rationalist "masculine" model. This position is anathema to a postmodern feminism for a number of reasons. Most significantly, it perpetuates the dichotomies of Enlightenment thought that establish female inferiority. The feminists who argue for a feminist epistemology are making the same move as the interpretive social scientists who accepted the "subjectivity" of the social sciences. In both cases an attempt is being made to revalorize the "disprivileged" side of the dichotomy and thus to reverse it. But this tactic is doomed to failure. In *Truth and Method* Gadamer reveals why this tactic failed for the human sciences. Those who accepted the "subjectivity" of the human sciences failed to remove the inferior status of those sciences. The same argument can be applied to the feminist case. The feminists who argue for the superiority of "feminine" values will fail to privilege these values because their argument leaves the dichotomy that defines that inferiority intact. The privileging of the masculine is integral to that dichotomy; it cannot be conveniently detached. Only a frontal assault on the dichotomy itself can remove the privileging implicit in it.

Another problem a "feminist epistemology" poses for a postmodern feminism is that it entails that feminists are attempting to substitute another absolute, a feminist epistemology, for the masculinist epistemology that they reject. This position is opposed to the postmodern emphasis on plurality and fluidity. Feminists have revealed that the contextuality and relatedness that Gadamer identifies with the universality of hermeneutic understanding have been labelled "feminine" traits by the dominant masculinist epistemology. Their analyses have also revealed that the rational, abstract model of knowledge that Gadamer attacks has been associated with the masculine. It would be false to assume, however, that a feminist reading of Gadamer entails that he is seeking to replace masculinist values with feminist values. On the contrary, the point of his work is to attack the dichotomies of Enlightenment thought. It follows that if these dichotomies are displaced their gendered connotations would also be displaced: if, as Gadamer advocates, we displace the distinction between the rational and the irrational then the gendered connotations of these terms would be obviated. The thesis of *Truth and Method* is that there are many experiences of truth, but that at the root of all human understanding is the contextuality and relatedness that constitute prejudice. The fact that contextuality and relatedness have been associated with the feminine through the misconceived dichotomies of Enlightenment thought is part of the problem that would be overcome should these dichotomies be displaced. To assume that Gadamer is attempting to substitute one orthodoxy for another is false to his whole enterprise. It is also false to the enterprise of a postmodern feminism.

Gadamer's relevance for the formulation of a postmodern feminism is not exhausted by these arguments. But at the very least they indicate that Gadamer's thought has much to contribute to the articulation of this position. Gadamerian hermeneutics entails a critique of prejudice and tradition as well as material for an attack on the gendered connotations of ways of knowing. Both of these positions must be fundamental to a postmodern feminism. And, most importantly, rather than attempting to privilege "feminine knowledge" over "masculine truth," Gadamer offers a means of displacing the gendered division of knowledge that is one of the inherent qualities of Enlightenment thought.

Foucault

Although it is much easier to make the case that Foucault[4] can be placed under the "postmodern" label, he explicitly denies that this label characterizes his work.

This in itself is not unusual. From the very beginning of his career Foucault has resisted labels. Although his critics have repeatedly categorized him, he has declared vehemently that he is neither a structuralist, a Marxist, nor a Freudian (Foucault and Raulet 1983: 198). The postmodern label, however, seems particularly apt and many of his contemporaries consider his position to be the very essence of postmodernism. This flies in the face of his statement that "I do not understand what kind of problem is common to the people we call post-modern or post-structuralist." He goes on to dismiss the label as Habermas's way of describing contemporary French thought (Foucault and Raulet, 1983: 205). Despite this disclaimer, however, to deny that Foucault is a postmodern makes no sense in the present intellectual climate. His position represents most of the key elements of postmodernism as it is commonly understood.

Attempting to summarize Foucault's complex and sometimes contradictory thought is particularly difficult because, unlike Gadamer, Foucault did not publish one definitive work that states his theoretical position clearly and succinctly. On the contrary, Foucault's work is diffuse and wide-ranging and he has repudiated his only strictly methodological work, *The Archeology of Knowledge* (1972). If there is a central focus to his work, however, it is his attention to language and his articulation of a theory of discourse. It is in the context of working out his theory of discourse, furthermore, that Foucault presents a critique of Enlightenment rationality that is particularly relevant to both postmodernism and feminism.

Two elements of Foucault's theory of discourse stand out as significant innovations. First, he argues that discourse creates subjects as well as objects. It was one of the principal theses of interpretive social science that the object of social scientific analysis differs from that of natural scientific analysis. This thesis made the social sciences aware of the relationship between discourse and objects. Foucault's insight extends this thesis by arguing that discourse creates subjects as well. His second innovation is that knowledge and power are inextricably linked in discourse. His entire corpus is informed by this insight and it is explicitly developed in *Power/Knowledge* (1980). His basic claim is that power and knowledge are fused in the practices that comprise history and that discourses partake of power, not knowledge alone. His argument about the power/knowledge nexus sets his theory apart from other twentieth-century language-based theories. It also constitutes an element of his thought that has a great deal of relevance for feminism. Foucault's theory of discourse, with its emphasis on subjects and power, unites the diverse analyses in *Madness and Civilization* (1973b), *The Birth of the Clinic* (1973a), *Discipline and Punish* (1977), and *The History of Sexuality* volumes 1 (1978a), 2 (1985), and 3 (1986). In each of these works he analyzes a specific discursive formation, the kind of subjects that it creates and the kind of power it deploys.

The work that is specifically relevant to Foucault's attitude toward Enlightenment rationality, however, is *The Order of Things* (1971). In this work Foucault, like Gadamer, presents a critique of Enlightenment thought and an explanation of why the human sciences have failed in the twentieth century. His explicit goal in this work is to analyze the transition from classical to modern thought. He does so by revealing what he labels the "*a priori* of thought," both classical and modern:

> This *a priori* is what, in a given period, delimits in the totality of experience a field of knowledge, defines the mode of being of the objects that appear in that field, provides man's everyday perception with theoretical powers, and defines the conditions in which he can sustain a discourse about things that is recognized to be true. (1971: 158)

He argues that the transition from classical to modern thought came not through a "rational" process of scientific analysis but through a shift in "what it makes sense to say."

Although Foucault's aim is to examine the full range of the modern episteme, his discussion of the human sciences is particularly relevant. He argues that the human sciences do not fit into the modern episteme because of the ambiguity surrounding the concept of "man":

> Western culture has constituted, under the name of man, a being who, by one and the same interplay of reasons, must be a positive domain of *knowledge* and cannot be an object of *science*. (1971: 366)

Foucault discusses the contradictions inherent in the concept of "man" in the context of what he refers to as man's "doubles." Much of his discussion revolves around the argument that these internal contradictions will lead to the demise of the concept itself. His larger point, however, is that Enlightenment thought (the modern episteme) provides no place for the human sciences. Its rationalism and scientism leave human beings in an untenable position: as both subject and object of knowledge. Thus, like Gadamer, he challenges the hegemony of reason that the Enlightenment claims and the ambiguous space it creates for the social sciences.

There is, however, also an important difference between the critiques of Gadamer and Foucault. Gadamer's critique is at once more circumscribed and more ambitious. It is more limited in the sense that it is only concerned with the analysis of one mode of thought, that of the Enlightenment. But it is more comprehensive in that his analysis goes beyond Foucault's to examine philosophically the nature of human understanding itself. Foucault, on the other hand, goes beyond Gadamer to argue that *all* discourses, not just that of the Enlightenment, create subjects, objects, and regimes of power and truth. He thus gives us a way to analyze any discursive formation for the kind of power/knowledge nexus that characterizes it. This analysis is particularly relevant to the concerns of contemporary feminism because of its specific connection between power and knowledge. But it raises a problem as well. Foucault's approach, many critics have claimed, is relativistic, even nihilistic. He is not concerned, as is Gadamer, to examine the nature of human understanding itself. Rather, he is concerned exclusively with the plurality of discourses, not with the underlying phenomenon of understanding that makes discourses possible. The only common-alities he discusses are the creation of both power/knowledge and subjects/objects that characterizes all discourses. The alleged relativism this implies, however, is a stumbling block for many feminists.

Even though Foucault's analysis centers around a critique of Enlightenment thought (the modern episteme), he nevertheless claims to be ambivalent about it. He asserts that he refuses to be "blackmailed" by the Enlightenment and resents the necessity today to be either for or against it. He argues:

> I think the Enlightenment, as a set of political, economic, social, institu-tional, and cultural events on which we still depend in large part, constitutes a privileged domain for analysis. (1984: 42)

Instead of condemning the Enlightenment he wants to separate it from humanism which is a "thematic" that "can be opposed by the principle of a critique and a permanent creation of ourselves in our autonomy – a principle found in the Enlightenment" (1984: 44).

In *The Order of Things* Foucault is concerned not only with the character of the different discourses he discusses but also with another issue that is relevant to the postmodern critique in general and feminism in particular: his discussion of the way in which discourses change. His analysis leads him to the conclusion that the concept that has been the focus of the social sciences in the modern episteme, the concept of "man," is about to be eclipsed. He then questions how the demise of "man" is to take place, that is, how we are to awake from this "anthropological sleep" to an 'imminent new form of thought" (1971: 342). His answer to this question is that at least three sciences today represent a move to another form of thought: psychoanalysis, ethnology, and linguistics. These "counter sciences," he asserts, although not less "rational" or less "objective," flow against the tide of the modern episteme, they "unmake man" (1971: 379–81). In other words these counter sciences challenge the dominant episteme and offer the possibility of displacing that episteme. It is interesting to note that both postmodern social science and feminism fit this description. Although Foucault does not make this point, feminism is particularly effective as a counter science because it challenges "man" as both a gendered *and* generic concept.

Foucault's critique of Enlightenment rationalism in *The Order of Things* repre-sents a compatible extension of Gadamer's critique. Gadamer shows the rational/irrational dualism of Enlightenment thought to be misconceived and thus relieves the social sciences of the stigma of irrationality and subjectivity. His approach is also relevant to the task of relieving women of this stigma because the Enlightenment thought that he attacks excludes women from the sphere of rationality. Foucault extends this Gadamerian insight by showing in more concrete terms how discourses create subjects and objects. Feminists can use his work to explicate how the Enlightenment discourse on rationality has created woman as the irrational and emotional counterpart to rational man. His thesis regarding the link between knowledge and power, furthermore, is an idea that has the potential to make an important contribution to feminist theory. The discourse on rationality has not "only" excluded women from the sphere of rationality; this is not exclusively a semantic issue. Rather, Foucault's analysis can be used to show that the designation of women as irrational is directly tied to the social institutions that define women's inferior status. Knowledge and power are two sides of the same coin. By showing that the (masculinist) rationalism of the modern episteme is not an absolute, but merely one of a plurality of discourses, Foucault's analysis also suggests the possibility of the creation of a discourse that does not constitute women as inferior. It opens up a new way of thinking about women, knowledge and power that is very productive for feminist theory.

Another way of arguing for the relevance of both Foucault and Gadamer for the feminist project is to contrast their approaches to that of Habermas. Habermas has objected to the positions of both Gadamer and Foucault on the grounds that their total rejection of Enlightenment rationalism is too extreme and leads to relativism and nihilism. Against the postmoderns Habermas argues for the rationality of western thought, or, as Giddens puts it, that "West is best" (1985: 133). But Habermas, while clinging to what he considers to be the good elements of the rationality of Enlightenment thought cannot neatly detach the sexism that is inherent to the episteme. Many of Habermas's critics argue that, by not rejecting Enlightenment rationalism Habermas fails to complete the critique of Enlightenment thought that is a necessary response to the demands of contemporary thought. Huyssen puts this critique very succinctly:

> The critical deconstruction of enlightenment rationalism and logocentrism by theoreticians of culture, the decentering of traditional notions of identity, the fight of women and gays for a legitimate social and sexual identity outside of the parameters of male, heterosexual vision, the search for alternatives in our relationship with nature, including the nature of our own bodies – all these phenomena, which are key to the culture of the 1970s, make Habermas' proposition to complete the project of modernity questionable, if not undesirable. (1981: 38)

This passage makes it clear that, particularly for feminism, a half-way critique of rationalism is not an adequate alternative to the liabilities of the modern episteme.

Derrida

If it was difficult to categorize Foucault's work or to describe his "methodology," the work of Derrida[5] presents an even greater challenge. Derrida has not
written a methodological work for the simple reason that he eschews the whole
notion of method. One of the central tenets of his work is his rejection of binary
oppositions, and he defines any methodology as caught up in what he calls the
"play of opposites." If any "style" can be assigned to Derrida it is that of
plurality. Following Nietzsche he calls for a plural style that rejects the hierarchy
of dualistic thought. While Foucault moved beyond Gadamer's attack on the
rationalism of Enlightenment thought to detail the way in which any discursive
formation deploys both knowledge and power, Derrida moved beyond even this
ambitious goal. He is concerned to show the error of western philosophy as a
whole, and, more specifically, the history of western metaphysics. Furthermore,
like Gadamer and unlike Foucault, Derrida is interested in exploring the phenomenon of discourse itself. His discussion of *différance* and trace represents an
attempt to examine the question of how meaning is deployed in discursive formations, an attempt that Foucault generally avoids.

Derrida identifies western metaphysics as a history of metaphors, a history
based on polarities in which one of the elements of the polarity is privileged. But
his central thesis with regard to this tradition is that its "matrix is the determining
of Being as presence" (1978b: 279). What Derrida identifies as the "metaphysics
of presence," a tradition he also labels "logocentrism," he equates with the
history of western thought. Derrida's point is not so much that this history must
be dismantled and replaced. On the contrary, he is vehement in his claim that he is
not errecting a new method much less proposing new concepts to replace the old
concepts he is criticizing. Rather, in an argument similar to Foucault's in *The
Order of Things*, he states that this metaphysics is coming unravelled of its own
accord. He claims that a "rupture" occurred when the "structurality of structure
began to be thought" and it became necessary to begin thinking that there was no
center. He goes on, "This was the moment when language invaded the universal
problematic, the moment when, in the absence of a center or origin, everything
became discourse" (1978b: 280). But philosophy as it has been conceived in the
west cannot deal with decentering, with multiplicities; it is always looking for *one*
truth. The rupture that has occurred, then, challenges the very root of this
tradition of thought. It demands that we move beyond the field of this dying
episteme (1976: 93).

The focal point of the metaphysics of presence is the binary opposition of
positive and negative terms. Derrida discusses many of these oppositions, but the
opposition that is integral to his argument is that between writing and speech
which, he claims, pervades the metaphysics of presence. In his discussion of
Rousseau in *Of Grammatology* he asserts that, for Rousseau in particular and the

western tradition in general, writing is the destruction of presence and the disease of speech (1976: 142). In a more playful look at the writing/speech opposition, Derrida spoofs the relationship between Plato and Socrates in *The Postcard* (1987). His aim, however, is a serious one. He wants to explore how this "odd couple" and the opposition that they have fostered has profoundly affected western thought. What Derrida has to say about writing, however, is not that we should simply reverse the priority in the polarity. He does not claim that writing is prior to speech, but rather that they are no longer opposed and are identical (Johnson 1981: xiii). In the history of the metaphysics of presence, writing was conceived as a supplement to the naturalness of language, an artificial addition. The relationship of writing to speech was seen as analogous to that of masturbation to "normal sex." Derrida counters this by asserting that writing was never a simple supplement and that we need to construct a new logic of the supplement to understand the place of writing (1976: 7).

The theme of displacing the episteme, the metaphysics of presence, informs Derrida's discussion of writing. The theory of writing, he claims, needs an intrascientific and epistemological liberation (1976: 83). We must understand that language is already a writing, but not the "linear writing" that characterized the past century. With the destruction of linear writing came the destruction of man, science, and the line and access to "pluridimensionality" and "delinearized temporality" (1976: 63, 87). Writing does not lead to a "decoding of meaning or truth" which is the essence of the metaphysics of presence (1982: 329). Rousseau saw writing as a supplement, Lévi-Strauss as the origin of violence and domination in human society (1976: 130, 144). As a counter Derrida argues that "there has never been anything but writing; there have never been anything but supplements . . ." (1976: 159).

Despite Derrida's rejection of method, however, there are two terms that Derrida himself uses to describes his position: grammatology and deconstruction. In *Of Grammatology* Derrida defines this term as the "undoing of logocentrism," the knowledge that writing is the plurivocity of this concept (1976: 74). Grammatology, he claims, must be one of the sciences of man, but it must not be one regional science among many (1976: 83). At another point, however, Derrida qualifies this by arguing that grammatology is "less another science, a new discipline charged with a new content or domain, than the vigilant practice of this textual division" (1981b: 36). He argues:

> Grammatology must deconstruct everything that ties the concept and norms of scientificity to ontological, logocentrism, phonologism. This is an immense and interminable work that must ceaselessly avoid letting the transgression of the classical project of science fall back into a prescientific empiricism. This presupposes a kind of *double register* in grammatological practice: it must simultaneously go beyond metaphysical positivism and scientism, and accentuate whatever in the effective work of science contributes to freeing it of the

metaphysical bonds that have borne on its definition and its movement since its beginnings. Grammatology must pursue and consolidate whatever, in scientific practice, has always already begun to exceed the logocentric closure. (1981b: 35–6)

This passage indicates that grammatology and deconstruction are closely related: grammatology is the "science" that deconstructs concepts. Derrida's critics have been very concerned about the alleged "negative" character of deconstruction. Deconstruction, they charge, is a method of negation, of negativity, of destruction. Derrida vehemently denies this. First, deconstruction is not a "method." Unlike methods it does not remove itself from its subject matter as a method does. Nor does it advocate a unitary position. Deconstruction is plural, open; it is not an attempt to find essences or principles (Gasche, 1986: 8, 100, 123). Second, deconstruction, according to Derrida, is positive rather than negative. Its result is not neutralization but displacement. Deconstruction involves "being alert to the implications of the historical sedimentation of language which we use – and that is not destruction" (1970: 271). One of Derrida's critics, David Allison, has described deconstruction in a way that makes it sound very similar to Foucault's uncovering of the *a priori* of thought. Allison identifies deconstruction as the project whose critical task is to locate and take apart those concepts that serve as axioms or rules for a period of thought (1973: xxxii). But in Derrida's understanding deconstruction goes beyond mere uncovering. He states:

Deconstruction cannot limit itself or proceed immediately to a neutralization; it must, by means of a double gesture, a double science, a double writing, practice an *overturning* of the classical opposition *and* a general *displacement* of the system. It is only on this condition that deconstruction will provide itself the means with which to *intervene* in the field of oppositions that it criticizes, which is also a field of non-discursive forces. (1982: 329)

Deconstruction always involves both a reversal and an intervention (1981a: 6). It does so, however, not by passing from one concept to another, but by overturning the conceptual and nonconceptual order.

Central to Derrida's project of deconstruction, and also the most difficult aspect of that project to define, are the concepts of "*différance*" and "trace." "*Différance*" combines the sense of the English verbs "to differ" and "to defer." An important aspect of this term, however, is that even in French it is impossible to distinguish between "*différance*" and "*différence*" in speech. It is only in reading and writing that the distinction can be made, emphasizing once again Derrida's campaign against the privileging of speech over writing (1981b: 8). The concept of "*différance*" is the closest that Derrida comes to a foundational concept, but he is very careful to deny it any foundational qualities. The graphics of *différance*, he claims, belong neither to science nor to philosophy (1987: 288).

He defines "*différance*" as that which permits the articulation of speech and writing, it is the foundation of form (1976: 63): " '*Différance*,' the disappearance of any ordinary presence is *at once* the condition of possibility *and* the condition of the impossibility of truth" (1981a: 168). "*différance*", he claims, is removed from all classical conceptual oppositions (1978b: 198); it is both origin and non-origin at the same time: "To say that '*différance*' is originary is simultaneously to erase the myth of a present origin . . . It is a non-origin that is originary" (1978b: 203).

One way of attempting to understand what Derrida means by this concept is to define it as that which always escapes, is deferred in the attempt to define absolute knowledge as presence. Derrida states that, despite the claims of phenomenology, the "thing itself" always escapes (1973: 104). He frequently refers to the "play of differences" within language, a play that defines the relationship between speech and language, but in a way that has nothing to do with binary oppositions (1982: 15–16). Rather, "*différance*" would allow us

> to think a writing without presence, without absence, without history, without cause, without *archia*, without *telos*, a writing that absolutely upsets all dialectics, all theology, all teleology, all ontology. (1982: 67)

Derrida defines the concept of "trace" as closely linked to that of "*différance*": "The (pure) trace is '*différance*' " (1976: 62); trace is the radically other within the structure of "*différance*." Derrida's critics are divided on whether his concept of trace amounts to the establishment of a new foundational system. Gasche claims that Derrida's concept is "quasi-transcendental" (1986: 317) while Spivak claims that, because the trace breaks up causes or origins it cannot be labelled transcendental (1987b: 46). Taking a somewhat different line Handelman claims that the absence that is the result of both *différance* and trace is Derrida's defining mark: "he is the new high priest of the religion of absence" (1982: 172). Derrida confounds all of these interpretations by, on one hand, denying that the trace has any metaphysical connotations, yet at the same time claiming that it is the "absolute origin of sense in general," which, he adds, is the same thing as saying that there is no absolute origin of sense in general (1976: 65). Although Derrida's concept of "trace" has some affinity to Heidegger's concept of Being, Derrida is not looking for a "lost presence," a privileged signifier (Spivak, 1976: xvi, 1). Rather, for Derrida, "the thought of the trace" always escapes the binarism that is the hallmark of the Being of presence (1978b: 230).

There is no doubt that Derrida's thought occupies one of the most radical positions in the critique of modernity among postmodern thinkers. He attacks not only the rationalism at the heart of Enlightenment thought, but the binary oppositions that have structured western thought since its inception. It is this radical character of Derrida's thought that makes it particularly relevant to the concerns of contemporary feminism. Derrida reveals more clearly than any other postmodern figure that at the root of logocentrism is a set of inflexible binary oppositions. Informing all of these binary oppositions is the masculine/feminine opposition. Each of these oppositions is constituted by a hierarchy in which the privileged side is associated with the masculine, the disprivileged with the feminine. Thus, as Derrida himself argues, logocentrism is phallocentrism. From a feminist perspective, Derrida's attack on these oppositions is thus a feminist gesture. If feminism is to be successful, it must begin by attacking and displacing the masculine/feminine hierarchy at the root of the western episteme. Derrida's project of deconstruction is an invaluable tool in this task. Many feminists reject deconstruction as a destructive tactic, arguing that what is needed is a positive restructuring of the category "woman." The point of Derridean deconstruction, however, is not to erase categories, but to displace the oppositions that have structured the dichotomies of western thought. So conceived, deconstruction is not a negative project; it is not an effort to reverse binary oppositions or to replace them with a new orthodoxy. Rather, it involves the displacing of the play of oppositions that has informed not only western thought but also the inferior status of women.

Despite these arguments, however, there are strong objections to Derrida's position among feminists. At the root of these objections is the claim that in his critique of modernism Derrida, like Foucault, denies the emancipatory impulse that many feminists define as the cornerstone of feminism. This denial, they claim, leads to relativism and nihilism. They argue that such a position is anathema to a feminism that must be politically active and seeks the removal of the oppression of women. One of the principal tasks of the following discussion is to construct an argument that refutes these objections and articulates a postmodern feminism that utilizes a Derridian perspective.

Nietzsche: Truth is a Woman

Many commentators on postmodernism see Nietzsche as the founding father of the movement and, significantly, both Foucault and Derrida look to him as a kind of fore-runner of their attack on western rationalism. In his book on the postmodern era, Allan Megill even argues that Nietzsche sets the agenda for modernity as well as postmodernity (1985: 1) For these reasons alone he is important to a discussion of postmodernity and feminism. But there is another reason to look at Nietzsche's work: he explicitly discusses the relationship between women and truth and thus provides a bridge to the discussion of a postmodern feminism. Despite his obvious misogynism and his attack on the feminist movement of his day, his position introduces important elements of the feminist critique of rationality.

Nietzsche's attitude toward truth and rationality in general presages the basic postmodern position. He argues that all knowledge is relational and that all existence is interpretive, perspectival, and, hence, incomplete (Granier, 1977: 192–4). He asks:

> What therefore is truth? A mobile army of metaphors, metonymies, anthropomorthisms: in short a sum of human relations which become poetically and rhetorically intensified, metamorphosed, adorned, and after long usage seem to a nation fixed, canonic and binding; truths are illusions of which one has forgotten that they *are* illusions, worn-out metaphors which have become powerless to affect the senses; coins which have their obverse effaced and now are no longer of account as coins but merely as metal. (1964a: 180)

Man arrives at a "sense for truth" only because he is unconscious of the origins of truth, that is, that man himself is the creator of truth. If he could ever "get out of the prison walls of this faith" his self-consciousness would be destroyed at once (1964a: 104). Most critics agree that his view of truth leads Nietzsche to a kind of nihilism, but exactly what kind of nihilism he espouses is not clear. Nietzsche's nihilism appears to exhibit both positive and negative aspects. On one hand he advocates "dancing on the void," that is, rejoicing in the absence of meaning and truth, but, on the other hand, he seems at times to draw back from the void with a shudder (Megill, 1985: 33–4).

In *Beyond Good and Evil* Nietzsche extends his discussion of truth to include women. In the passage quoted at the beginning of this chapter Nietzsche suggests that "truth is a woman." He claims that philosophers, in so far as they have been dogmatists, have tried to understand truth with their "terrible seriousness." But, because truth is a woman they have failed because they employed inappropriate methods for winning a woman. He concludes by arguing that there are good grounds for supposing that all dogmatism in philosophy is "noble puerilism." After this enigmatic beginning Nietzsche frequently returns to the subject of women in the course of the book. These references, however, are disappointing; they echo the stereotypes about women that were commonplaces of his day. Women, he claims, are motivated by personal vanity and scorn even other women (1964b: 88). Their play is "mediocre" because they neither love nor hate the game (1964b: 92). Women, furthermore, are opposed to both science and all scholarly activity. They are hostile to science because they see it as devoid of shame (1964b: 94). This is just as well, he concludes, because scholarly inclinations on the part of a woman are an indication of something wrong with her sexual nature (1964b: 96).

In the latter part of the book Nietzsche's discussion of women revolves around the theme of woman's "nature" and her attempt to escape from that nature and achieve independence, a discussion that leads him to a critique of the feminist movement of his day. His first comment on woman's nature is that she has a "genius for adornment" (1964b: 96). Women who seek equality with men will, he claims, necessarily lose this quality in their effort to become equal, that is, they will lose both modesty and taste (1964b: 187). It follows from this that woman's wish to be independent can only cause "the general *uglifying* of Europe." Woman's drive for equality in the scientific realm, he claims, will have equally disastrous results. Woman's "clumsy attempts at feminine scientificality" reveal only that she has cause for shame (1964b: 182). Nietzsche asks:

> Is it not in the very worst taste that woman thus sets herself up to be scientific? . . . But she does not *want* truth – what does woman care for truth? From the very first nothing is more foreign, more repugnant, or more hostile to woman than truth – her great art is falsehood, her chief concern is appearance and beauty. (1964b: 183)

At the end of this diatribe he concludes that woman's independence involves merely her learning to imitate all the stupidities of man in western culture. The result is that she is less capable of fulfilling her most important function: bearing children (1964b: 189).

In the effort to make sense of these scattered, even contradictory remarks most commentators have argued that Nietzsche is ambivalent toward the subject of woman. Some have even argued that he is both a feminist and an anti-feminist (Allen, 1979: 118; Derrida, 1977: 180). This is correct in a limited sense. Nietzsche is against the kind of feminism that tries to cast women in the mold created by western conceptions of rationality and truth. In this he presages the argument of twentieth-century feminists that feminism must not entail women aping the patterns of masculine thought. In contemporary terms Nietzsche is opposing feminists who adopt a modernist epistemology, and, thus, attempt to define truth in dogmatic, absolutist terms. Since Nietzsche opposes this dogmatism, he is opposed to it in women as well as in men. In the case of women, however, it is even more onerous because it entails a contradiction of their nature. Nietzsche's greatest contribution, however, lies in his insight that truth and rationality as they have been conceived in the west are specifically masculine modes of thought. Woman is always the "other" that is opposed to the pursuit of truth, a pursuit that is exclusively masculine. Nietzsche is one of the first critics of modernism to reveal that the "deconstruction" of western rationality necessarily entails the rejection of the masculine definition of "truth." It is this connection between truth and masculinity that explains his ridicule of what he calls "feminism" and his impatience with women who try to copy the masculine definition of truth. Derrida articulates Nietzsche's condemnation of feminism very succinctly in his commentary on Nietzsche's theory:

> Feminism, indeed, is the operation by which woman wants to come to resemble man, the philosophical dogmatist who insists on truth, science,

objectivity – together with the whole virile illusion, the whole castration effect that goes with it. (1977: 182)

Nietzsche's connection between truth and the masculine, however, creates a serious problem for him. Although he wants to reject the dogmatic absolutism that is identified with the masculine, his only alternative is the feminine, a mode of thought that he finds equally abhorent. For Nietzsche, women represent a slave morality (Parsons, 1979: 244). Women are irrational and fickle, they are hostile to science. Nietzsche's problem here, however, is easy to diagnose from a postmodern perspective: he fails to reject the binarism implicit in the epistemology that he is attacking. Although he appears to be challenging the very root of western thought and, specifically, its conception of rationality, he nevertheless embraces the basic dualism on which that rationality rests: the assumption of a fixed nature for men and women. Despite his identification of the dogmatic conception of truth as masculine and his facetious suggestion that "truth is a woman" he has no intention of "feminizing" truth. He despises what he defines as woman's nature as much as he despises the masculine definition of truth.

But this is not the end of the story. There is also an ambivalence in Nietzsche's attitude, an ambivalence that creates an opening for the postmodern perspective. Although Nietzsche accepts the masculine/feminine dualism and the stereotypes implied by it, he holds out the possibility that the feminine, because it is the "other" that challenges the dominant mode of thought, may contain the seeds of change. He suggests that the feminine may be the means by which the masculine regime of truth will be brought down and a new regime ushered in. In this sense Nietzsche is speaking as a woman when he criticizes western rationalism. Finally, his suggestion that woman is truth may not be entirely facetious. Woman may, indeed, be truth in the sense that truth, like woman, is elusive. Philosophers have hitherto failed to capture truth because they have used the wrong tactics. This implies that other tactics, those more suitable to women, should be employed.[6]

These ambivalences, however, ultimately lead Nietzsche into confusion because they do not represent a clear break with the masculine/feminine stereotypes of western rationalism. Far from attempting to feminize truth, it makes more sense to interpret Nietzsche's ultimate aim as an attempt to make truth more fully masculine. In *Thus Spoke Zarathustra* Nietzsche appears to be looking for a more truly masculine conception of truth, a conception which rejects the weaknesses embodied both in Christianity and in the female. Similarly, in *Human, All Too Human*, he refers to truths that are "*hard* won, certain, enduring" as "manly" and identifies this "manliness" as the proper goal of all mankind (1984: 15).

Nietzsche's thoughts on women and feminism offer an excellent introduction to the themes of postmodern feminism. More than any of the other critics of rationalism he makes it clear why a displacement of the dualisms of modernist thought is necessary if the critique of rationalism, particularly the feminist critique, is to be successful. Nietzsche embodies many of the elements of the postmodernist critique of rationalism. He attacks its dogmatism and its absolutism and, most importantly for feminism, he identifies that rationalism as a masculine mode of thought. But Nietzsche's critique fails because he cannot reject the basic dualism that informs rationalism: the masculine/feminine dualism. Because he accepts the stereotypes of the masculine and the feminine his critique of rationalism reaches a dead end. Although he rejects masculinist rationalism he cannot unambiguously argue for a feminine version of truth because, for him, the feminine represents the irrational, even the slavish. Finding both the masculine and the feminine alternatives to be equally unacceptable, Nietzsche turns to a re-evaluation of the feminine and a search for the "truly masculine" – moves that lead him to ambiguity if not contradiction. It is Nietzsche's failure, then, that is the most important element of his critique. That failure reveals why the feminist critique of rationalism informed by a postmodern perspective is necessary if the critique of rationalism that he began can be completed.

II The Feminist Critique of Rationality

Language and Reality

The feminist critique of rationality is a wide-ranging and by no means monolithic exposition of the "maleness" of reason in western thought. Linguists, anthropologists, rhetoricians as well as philosophers have contributed to this critique. Many of the themes that dominate this critique are similar to those of postmodernism. Some, particularly those of the radical feminists, are contradictory. It is possible, however, to define one theme that unites all of these critiques: an emphasis on language and discourse. This emphasis on language represents a significant connection between postmodernism and feminism (Scott, 1988: 34). The attack on rationality by both feminists and postmoderns is an attack on a particular discourse and the power deployed by that discourse. The contemporary crisis in modernity that has fostered the postmodern critique is an epistemological crisis rooted in an attack on Enlightenment rationalism. Feminists have contributed to his critique by pointing out that it is a crisis in a set of discourses created by men (McDermott 1985: 24). Even though some feminists reject the postmodern diagnosis of this crisis and many postmoderns ignore its gendered connotations, they are linked by a common opponent – rationalism – and a common emphasis – language/discourse.

Postmodern reflections on language and discourse led to Foucault's connection between language and power, Derrida's attack on dualism, and even his insight that logocentrism is phallocentrism. The postmodern critique attacks the hierarchical nature of Enlightenment thought and its privileging of an abstract rationality. Feminists concur in many of these arguments. But their attack on rationality is more radical than the postmodern critique: it defines causes whereas the postmoderns are only dealing with symptoms. The fact that women are identi-fied with the irrational and men with the rational is a symptom of the underlying problem that all the dualisms of Enlightenment thought are defined by the basic masculine/feminine dualism. Even more significantly, feminists have pointed out that this dualism is not symmetrical (Marks and de Courtivron, 1980: 4). Woman is always defined as that which is *not* man (McDermott, 1985: 15); she is a "minus male" who is identified by the qualities that she lacks (Spender, 1980: 23). Lan-guage establishes and maintains the basic gender identity that creates female inferiority. It effectively erases the distinction between female and feminine that is central to an understanding of the nature of the oppression of women. The language that we speak creates a situation in which the qualities that women possess as a result of their biological sex become indistinguishable from those that they are told they *should* possess in order to be "feminine;" sex and gender, in other words, become intertwined. Much of the work of contemporary feminists has been aimed at separating biological sex from imposed gender roles in linguistic practice.

Many feminist analyses of language focus on the way in which linguistic practice forges a connection between personal identity and gender identity. In an insightful article on language, sex and gender, Barbara Fried argues that language and gender identity appear at the same time in children's lives, a fact that is far from coincidental: "Language does not simply communicate the link between one's sex and one's gender identity; it constitutes that link" (1982: 49). Children who grow up hearing English spoken, furthermore, never learn a sense of "per-sonhood," only female personhood and male personhood (Beardsley, 1976: 287). It is not the case, however, that personhood is merely tied to biological sex. It is linked, rather, to a specific gender identity, an identity which embodies the society's understanding of what is "feminine." This feminine gender identity covers a broad range of qualities, but central to that identity is irrationality. One feminist linguist has demonstrated that by age five, both boys and girls have learned separate languages that relegate women to the sphere of irrationality. Men, who are identified as the "natural" occupants of the sphere of rationality, are contrasted to women whose sphere is that of emotion and feeling, the irrational. This dichotomy leaves women two unacceptable options: either they can talk like women and be "feminine" but irrational or they can talk like men and be rational but "unfeminine" (Lakoff, 1975: 6).

The fact that, through their control of language, men have dominated not only women but every aspect of the world in which we live is obvious. The conse-quences of linguistic domination have been extensively documented in the feminist literature. Two aspects of that literature are particularly relevant here because they structure the way in which knowledge has been produced and deployed in academic institutions. The first is a discussion of how linguistic practices in the knowledge-creating institutions have been structured along gendered lines since their inception with the Greeks. Walter Ong (1977: 1981) has been the pioneer in these studies. Ong argues that the roots of western academicism are both oral and agonistic. The Socratic emphasis on speech and Plato's reservations about writing established an oral tradition at the root of western academic life. The adversarial, agonistic element was central to the Greek's use of logic, and this element was intensified in the Middle Ages when learning became a process of disputation; knowledge was defined through verbal contests that were similar to the medieval jousts. The learning of Latin, the language of knowledge, was seen as a kind of male puberty rite. It was a process that was oral, agonistic and exclusively male. Until very recently the process of knowledge acquisition was one in which men disputed with each other in their exclusive tongue, Latin.

Ong argues that the recent entry of women into universities has coincided with the demise of Latin and, with it, the oral, agonistic culture that it defined (1981: 135). This conclusion, however, is not the only significance of his work for the feminist critique of rationality. Ong's analysis explains one of the mechanisms by which the creation of knowledge has been preserved as a male domain. Latin, which was taught only to men, constituted the world of knowledge as an exclusively male world. Its contrast was the vernacular, the "mother tongue," that is taught by mothers to both sons and daughters. Another important element of Ong's work is that it appears to raise questions about Derrida's thesis regarding the privileging of speech over writing. As Ong himself points out, Latin is exclusively male and exclusively written (1977: 29). This would seem to contradict Derrida's assertion that speech is privileged over writing in the west. But this contradiction is only apparent. In the academic world Latin was a spoken as well as a written language. And it was the specifically oral use of Latin that defined the agonistic culture that constituted the world of knowledge. The advent of women in academic life coincide with the demise of that orality – the introduction of written examinations – as well as the reduction of adversativeness – less combative teaching methods. Thus Derrida's thesis holds: women, who are associated with the disprivileged side of the dichotomy between speech and writing, represent a challenge to the domain of knowledge as it has been constituted in the west.

Another interesting corollary of Ong's research concerns the subject of rhetoric. Ong, who classifies himself as a rhetorician, notes that since the Greeks rhetoric has been opposed to the institutions that create "true" knowledge; the relativity and sophistry of rhetoricians was opposed to the absolute foundations for knowledge espoused by the academicians. It is thus interesting that the current revival of rhetoric, the "new rhetoric," is often seen in postmodern terms (Nelson et al., 1987). Some of the contemporary practitioners of the "new rhetoric" define it as a means of combating the "decaying empire of foundational thought" (Leff, 1987: 19). Rhetoricians have always argued that reason is a socio-linguistic practice; they have always been opposed to the effort to define reason in absolutist, foundationalist terms. The contemporary "new rhetoricians" have emphasized this antifoundational tendency. But what is particularly significant about the "new rhetoric" of Ong and others is that it joins the postmodern and feminist critiques of rationality. It both criticizes the foundationalism of the modern episteme and details how that episteme has been defined in exclusively male terms.

A second aspect of the literature that concerns academic knowledge creation and deployment deals with the connection between the real and the rational. Concepts formed from the male point of view create a male reality; both the real and the rational are defined in exclusively male terms. One consequence of the male definition of reality is that women's experiences become invisible, particularly to male academics (Spender, 1980: 75). It also follows that women are inarticulate because the language they use is derivative of male definitions of reality (Kramarae, 1981: 2). Although men would have us believe that the term "man" is generic, that is, that it includes the experience of both men and women, a simple example proves this false: the statement "man has difficulty in childbirth" is nonsense (Spender, 1980: 156). This male definition of reality has been particularly problematic in history and the social sciences whose task it is to analyze and make sense of the experience of "mankind." Recent feminist critics of the discipline of history have argued that history has excluded women because "history" has been defined in terms of the public realm occupied exclusively by men. The same phenomenon has occurred in sociology. Dorothy Smith argues that we know the world sociologically through male categories. The categories of sociology are conceived in terms of man's experiences and leave women's reality "outside the frame" (1979: 148). The sociology of Max Weber is a good example of this phenomenon. Weber's system is built on the foundation of the rational, hence, male actor. Although Weber is blind to the gendered connotations of his system, it follows that since only men are rational and only men can be subjects, that only men are actors and hence the subjects of his sociology of action. Although the postmodern critique is sensitive to this connection between language and reality, feminist criticisms of the specifically masculine creation of language and reality such as these have significantly expanded that critique.

Although the theorists discussed above have very different solutions to the problems that they have outlined, their diagnosis of the problem is remarkably similar. All agree that the oppression of women is rooted in male-dominated language and a male definition of reality. What is significant about this agreement in the present context is that it is an extension of the point that the postmoderns argue in their connection between language and reality. The postmoderns assert that the discourses that create knowledge create reality as well. The feminists expand this by arguing that that definition and that reality are exclusively masculine. The two critiques reinforce and strengthen each other.

The "Man of Reason": The Diagnosis

The discussion of the masculine domination of language sets the stage for the examination of a more specific discussion of one aspects of that domination: the association of the masculine with the rational, the feminine with the irrational.

Most contemporary feminists agree on the diagnosis of this problem: since Plato, and most particularly since the Enlightenment, reason and rationality have been defined in exclusively masculine terms; the "Man of Reason" is gendered, not generic. But although there is agreement on this diagnosis, the discussion of masculine definitions of rationality and a possible feminist alternative have been the source of a great deal of dissension among feminist theorists. Those who analyze the "Man of Reason" draw very different conclusions from their analyses and these differences have created what, for some feminists, constitutes a crisis in feminist theory (Riemer, 1986: 1). The modernism/postmodernism dispute generated by the crisis in western epistemology has its parallel in feminist theory. The issues that divide feminist theorists on the issue of rationality reflect the modernist/postmodernist dispute in epistemology.

Most feminists who discuss the maleness of the "Man of Reason" focus on Enlightenment thought and its consequences for contemporary discussions. But several writers have traced the maleness of rational thought back to the Greeks and, consequently, claim that western thought as a whole and not just the Enlightenment is the cause of this particular aspect of female oppression. In a brilliant analysis of Plato's allegory of the cave, Luce Irigaray shows that the masculine definitions of concepts of truth and rationality are central to Plato's concept of knowledge. In her analysis she carefully dissects the elements of the allegory and draws out their significance. She begins by observing that the prisoner is brought out of the cave as a child is brought out of the womb in a difficult delivery (1985a: 279). This statement sets up the basic interpretive elements she employs in her analysis. The feminine imagery is negative: the cave represents woman's womb; breaking out of the womb means breaking into truth and knowledge. Masculine images, on the contrary, are positive: throughout the allegory light and knowledge are associated with the masculine, earth and non-knowledge with the feminine. This dichotomy is clarified in Irigaray's statement that the earth is defined as "dark holes in which lucid reason risks drowning" (1985a: 302). This connection between light and knowledge, furthermore, establishes an association that will come to dominate western thought: vision is a "masculine" sense, while touch, on the other hand, is a feminine one. The certainty of knowledge is always associated with "seeing," a masculine way of knowing from which the feminine is excluded (Keller and Grontkowski, 1983: 213).

The association of the masculine with rationality, the feminine with irrationality in the history of western thought has been extensively documented in contemporary feminist scholarship. That women should be excluded from the realm of knowledge scarcely needs documentation. The exclusion of women from the political sphere, although closely related, is less obvious. Okin's *Women in Western Political Thought* (1979) and Elshtain's *Public Man, Private Woman* (1981) argue that the exclusion of women from the sphere of rationality is the cause of their exclusion from the political sphere. Since women are not rational they cannot be allowed to participate in the realm that is the highest expression of man's rationality: politics.[7] The charge that women have been excluded from both politics and rationality since the inception of western thought has become a commonplace that is rarely challenged. It is interesting to note that even those scholars who attempt to argue that women were not completely devalued in this tradition do not challenge this exclusion of women from the sphere of rationality. Both Saxonhouse (1985) and Slater (1968), for example, argue that women figured prominently in Greek political life but agree that they were excluded from action in the political realm. Saxonhouse in particular notes that Greek women were a respected, even integral part of Greek life, but that they were not treated as men's equals in the political sphere.

In the course of her discussion, Saxonhouse also makes another point that has become a central theme of feminist scholarship in this area. She argues that it is only with the advent of liberalism that woman's inferior position became fixed through a strict division between the public and private realms (1985: 15). It seems to be the consensus of most feminist writers that the dominance of the "Man of Reason" is most pronounced in the Enlightenment era and, particularly, under the aegis of liberalism. Feminist discussions of the implications of the masculinity of reason as it was defined by the Enlightenment in general and liberalism in particular are varied. It is possible, however, to summarize the principal arguments presented in these discussions by looking at three representative works: Lloyd's *The Man of Reason* (1984), Harding's "Is gender a variable in conceptions of rationality?" (1984), and McMillan's *Women, Reason, and Nature* (1982). Although each of these works discusses the implications of the masculine definition of reason in Enlightenment thought, each comes to a very different conclusion as to the significance of this fact for feminism. An examination of these works thus indicates the nature of the "crisis" that this issue has caused for feminist scholarship.

The central theme of Lloyd's account is her assertion that more is at stake in assessing our ideals of reason than "just" questions of truth. She argues that our conception of reason also informs our conception of personhood and what we identify as a good person (1984: ix). Her argument in this respect reinforces the linguistic argument noted above. Concepts of gender and personhood are inextricably linked in the language that we employ. This language, first, links rationality with what it means to be a good, fully human person and, second, excludes women from that sphere because they are excluded from the realm of rationality. It follows that women can be neither fully rational nor fully human in a moral sense. This is a theme that figures prominently in the feminist indictment of liberalism. Another theme of Lloyd's discussion is the change that occurred in conceptions of reason at the time of the Enlightenment. Focusing on Descartes, Lloyd argues that the legacy of his thought is an association of women with the sensuous realm of the body, men with the non-sensuous realm of reason (1983: 508). The association between women and the realm of the senses is closely related to an issue that has generated an extensive literature among feminists: the association between women and nature.[8] In her discussion Lloyd attributes much of woman's exclusion from the sphere of rationality to this association. Not only are women deemed irrational and hence not fully human, but, because of their association with nature, they are also associated with unknown, dark and mysterious forces.

Lloyd's discussion is insightful and provocative. It convincingly documents how and why women have been excluded from the sphere of rationality and, hence, morality. But it is a curious argument in one sense: it is wholly descriptive. Lloyd does little more than catalogue the exclusion of women from rationality in western thought. She does not present an argument as to the significance of her revelations, merely noting that the idea that women have their own mode of thought has surfaced in contemporary thought (1984: 75). In a sense Harding's work picks up where Lloyd leaves off by arguing that we must move beyond the errors of masculine thought to a "feminine perspective." Harding wants to identify the errors of the mode of thought that produced the exclusion that Lloyd merely describes. In the history of western thought, she argues, sex has been considered a variable in the distribution of rationality whereas, in fact, it is gender that is involved (1984: 43–4). In this she is following what has become one of the central themes of feminist scholarship: the distinction between sex and gender.

Harding moves from this point to argue that the conception of rationality behind the "Man of Reason" is essentially flawed: it is both one-sided and perverse. She thus asserts that there would be little point to an effort to incorporate women into the masculine conception of reason. Harding's argument here is both important and one that has become increasingly common in feminist circles. She is attacking a notion that has been prominent among liberal feminists in both the nineteenth and twentieth centuries: that the liberal/Enlightenment conception of reason could simply be "opened up" to include women. Although liberal feminists do not deny that liberals, along with other Enlightenment thinkers, exclude women from the realm of reason, they do argue that that definition of reason can and should be changed so as to include women. Harding is arguing that such a move is both futile and self-defeating because the liberal-Enlightenment conception of reason is distorted. Thus it cannot and should not be a conception that we, as feminists, seek to emulate.

In an argument that sounds very Gadamerian, Harding contends that while the masculine mode of knowing – rationality and abstraction – involved distortion, the feminine conception of epistemology involves a hermeneutic mode that does not (1984: 57). This argument is not without its problems. Most importantly it, raises questions regarding the validity of a feminist epistemology discussed above. But it is important for two reasons. First, Harding makes it clear that feminists must reject the rationalist epistemology that created the dilemma of the "Man of Reason" in the first place. Second, it is important because the argument has a great deal of affinity with the postmodern critique of rationality. Both identify the problem as Enlightenment rationality itself and reject the possibility of redefining that conception.

By far the most controversial approach to the question of women and "The Man of Reason," however, is that offered by McMillan. Like Harding, McMillan's argument has an affinity with the postmodern critique because she attacks the masculine conception of reason itself and offers an alternative to that conception. Unlike Harding, however, McMillan's argument focuses specifically on the moral connotations of the "Man of Reason." She asserts that the exclusion of feeling, emotion and intuition from the sphere of rationality is at the root of the Enlightenment's misconception of reason. The Enlightenment dichotomy between reason on one hand, feeling and emotion on the other, she claims, involves a fundamental misunderstanding of both reason and morality (1982: 21). Like Gadamer she states that knowledge in general and morality in particular are contextual and relational. Armed with these insights she then goes on to argue that those who assert that women are not rational, which, she notes, even includes some feminists, are wrong because they misunderstand the nature of rationality. Those who exclude women from the realm of rationality are accepting the Enlightenment definition that associates rationality with scientific abstraction and irrationality with feeling and emotion. In a passage that could have been written by Gadamer she states: "It is more to the point, therefore, to show not that women too can excel in scientific activities but that science is not an absolute gauge of what counts as knowledge" (1982: 42).

It is at this point in her argument, however, that McMillan's discussion takes a startling turn. She asserts that feminists are alienating women from their "true nature" because they subscribe to the rationalist view that she is rejecting (1982: 153). Because it enjoins women to adopt the masculine definition of reality, McMillan identifies and condemns the women's liberation movement as a rebellion against "nature" (1982: 118). She claims that women's realm, the private sphere of the home and childrearing, is just as human and therefore "rational" as the public sphere of men. She concludes that women need not and should not renounce this realm in favor of the male realm of rationality and abstraction. Although she does not go as far as Nietzsche in his assertion that women who engage in science are denying their nature, the implication of her argument is much the same. Like Nietzsche's work, furthermore, McMillan's argument is a curious amalgam of modernist and postmodernist themes that ultimately leads her to a contradiction. Like the postmoderns, McMillan rejects the Enlightenment conception of reason and, specifically, the dichotomy between reason and emotion. But, unlike the postmoderns, she then goes on to accept, even reify, that dichotomy in her attempt to define women's "true nature." Unfortunately for the logic of her argument, she cannot have it both ways. Either the dichotomy itself is flawed and thus cannot be an accurate description of either the masculine or the feminine (the postmodernist move) or it is accurate and describes essential masculine and feminine nature (the modernist move).

McMillan's argument fails because she wants to adopt both arguments at once.

Despite its reactionary conclusions, however, McMillan's work illustrates very clearly the difficulties that the critique of the masculine definition of rationality poses for feminist thinking. Lloyd, who limits her critique to a description of women's exclusion from rationality, leaves open the question of the implications of this critique for feminist theory. Harding and McMillan move beyond this analysis to challenge the epistemological basis of the "Man of Reason" but come to radically different conclusions regarding what this critique entails for feminism. What is significant about both of their approaches, however, is the fact that they both assert the existence of a feminine "nature," perspective, or way of knowing. Although the appeal to the essentially feminine is muted in Harding and McMillan's anti-feminist use of the concept is one that most feminists would not find difficult to reject, this commonality between the two accounts is nevertheless noteworthy. It is representative of a strong tendency in contemporary feminist theory to appeal to a universal feminine nature, a feminist epistemology, a distinctive feminine way of knowing, or "maternal thinking." Postmodernism offers a number of convincing arguments as to why such a move in feminist theory is self-defeating. Before moving to a discussion of those arguments, however, it is useful to look again at the history of the methodological debate in the social sciences. The masculine definition of rationality has created problems in the social sciences that offer an instructive parallel to those encountered in feminist theory.

Since the Enlightenment the social sciences have taken great pains to prove their "scientific" status. In terms of the Enlightenment definition of science this means that they must show themselves to be rational, capable of abstract analysis, and able to generate universal laws. Each of these criteria have proved difficult for the social sciences to meet. Social scientific positivists or empiricists, accepting this definition of the scientific, have exerted great effort in the attempt to force the social sciences into this mold. Interpretive or humanist social scientists have taken a different tack. They argue that the social sciences cannot and should not attempt to meet these criteria. The result of their position, however, is that the social sciences must be excluded from the realm of scientificity. Since the scientific, rational realm is also the realm of the masculine, this entails that the social sciences, if they are excluded from this realm, must be declared "feminine."

The dilemma created by this dichotomy and its gendered connotations is particularly evident in the work of one social scientist, Freud, who was especially concerned with a specific aspect of scientific knowledge, its completeness. Freud, who was very anxious to create a *science* of psychoanalysis, was galled by the incompleteness of the knowledge that he acquired in his psychoanalytic studies. In a perceptive feminist examination of Freud's analysis in the Dora case, Toril Moi argues that Freud can define knowledge only as something that is "finished, closed, whole" and, as such, also the basis for the exercise of power (1985a: 194). Yet Freud also admits that psychoanalytic technique does not lend itself to complete knowledge; it can only produce knowledge that is fragmentary and incomplete. In a revealing passage he even admits that his knowledge of femininity in particularly is "certainly incomplete and fragmentary." Moi puts Freud's dilemma this way: "To admit that there are holes in one's knowledge is tantamount to transforming the penis to a hole, that is to say, to transforming the man into a woman" (1985a: 197). The conclusion that follows from this is that the social sciences are "feminine" sciences, or, as one commentator put it, psychoanalysis is doing "women's work" (Miller, 1976: 26). This conclusion, unacceptable as it was to Freud, is nevertheless inevitable if we accept the masculine conception of rationality as definitive.

Freud's dilemma, and the dilemma of the social sciences that his work illustrates, is instructive for feminist theory. If the dichotomy between the rational and the irrational is accepted in the social sciences, then these sciences will remain inferior to the natural sciences and excluded from the realm of the scientific and the rational. The same is true for feminist theory. As long as the association between the rational and the masculine, the irrational and the feminine is maintained, the feminine "way of knowing" will be conceptualized as inferior to that of the masculine. Efforts to revalorize this realm are futile unless the dichotomy itself is displaced. It is this conclusion that points to the necessity for the postmodern critique in both the social sciences and feminist theory.

The "Man of Reason": The Alternatives

That rationality has been defined in masculine terms in the history of western thought is a fact about which most feminists can agree. What they cannot agree on, however, is the proper feminist response to this fact. It is possible to identify three principal positions that contemporary feminists have argued with regard to the question posed by the "Man of Reason." First, some have argued that we should accept the masculine definition of rationality, attempting to redefine it only in the sense of opening it up so that it includes women. A second position is that we should accept the rational/irrational dichotomy as the Enlightenment defined it because it accurately portrays the true nature of both men and women but revalorize the feminine side of that dichotomy. Third, some feminists, following the postmoderns, have argued that we should abandon epistemology in its traditional sense and thereby displace the rational/irrational dichotomy of modernist/ Enlightenment thought. As a result we would lose not only the gendered connotations of certain ways of knowing (the rational male, the irrational female) but also the search for the one, correct path to truth.[9]

Although, in a logical sense, these categories encompass the only possible alternatives to the problem posed by the masculine definition of rationality, they create strange alliances among feminist groups that would seem to have nothing in common or are even opposed to each other. The first category, for example, encompasses both liberal and socialist/Marxist feminism. Although liberal and socialist feminists have been strongly opposed to each other politically, epistemologically they share the same ground. Both are rooted in a modernist epistemology that, among other things, accepts the "Man of Reason." Both socialist and liberal feminists argue that the modernist conception of rationality is flawed only by its sexism, a flaw, they argue, that can be corrected. Their adherence to this modernist epistemology, furthermore, has structured the political and theoretical practice of both liberal and socialist/Marxist feminism. The principal goal of liberal feminism as a political and theoretical movement has been to allow women into the sphere of rationality as it has been defined by men. What Betty Friedan and others have labelled the "First Wave" of feminism in America is characterized by the effort to allow women into a world previously occupied exclusively by men. The case of socialist/Marxist feminism, however, is less obvious. Socialist/Marxist feminists strongly repudiate liberal feminism's political program. Establishing the modernist credentials of Marxism, however, is not difficult. It might even be possible to argue that Marxists are the quintessential modernists because Marx's project is an attempt to complete the Enlightenment project of liberation that liberalism failed to achieve. Socialist/Marxist feminists have inherited the modernist epistemology of Marx. They accept not only the rational/irrational dichotomy so central to that epistemology but also the modernist search for truth and liberation. Although both liberal and socialist/Marxist feminists object to the sexism of modernist epistemology, far from wanting to repudiate that epistemology they want only to bring women into the male categories.

Feminist Marxists have argued against the Enlightenment/modernist label in a number of ways. The most persuasive of these arguments involves the claim that Marx's dialectical thought is a clear alternative to the dualism that characterizes Enlightenment thought (Ring, 1986; Hartmann, 1981; Jaggar, 1983: 358). There are two problems with this argument. First, it does not negate the points made above. Despite its dialectical method Marxism remains a product of modernist thought in its search for truth and liberation. Second, although dialectical thought claims to transcend dualisms, it does so by positing a third term, a term that will necessarily create a new set of hierarchies and privileging. Dialectical thought does not displace the search for unitary truth, it merely moves that search to a different plane. A good illustration of this is the hostility with which socialist/Marxist feminists have greeted the work of Foucault. Foucault's "relativism" and his denial of the emancipatory impulse are anathema to the Marxist feminist camp. Their insistence that we must cling to "truth" and emancipation reveals their ultimate adherence to the modernist epistemology.[10]

The second category defined above creates an even stranger alliance than that between liberal and socialist/Marxist feminism: it unites antifeminist conservatives such as McMillan and radical feminists such as Daly (1978, 1984) and Griffin (1978, 1981). Both antifeminists who advocate traditional "feminine" values and radical feminists who exalt feminine as opposed to masculine qualities accept the basic rational/irrational dualism and its portrayal of male and female "nature."

Further, the radical feminists along with McMillan and other antifeminists, particularly antifeminist political activists such as Schlafly, argue that woman's "nature" is different from that of men and that both men and women should accept that fact. There is, of course, a significant difference between the two positions with regard to what each sees to be the implications of the fact that men and women have different natures. The antifeminists claim that women are less rational that men, that they excel in nurturing values, and that they should put the care of their men and children above all other concerns. Although McMillan would like to claim "separate but equal" status for the feminine sphere; antifeminists such as Schlafly claim that women should accept men's leadership as well. It is easy to dismiss this position on the grounds that it perpetuates the status quo that it is the purpose of feminism to alter. Radical feminism, however, poses a more difficult problem. The radical feminists, following the Enlightenment dichotomy, define women as less "rational" than men, but see this as an asset rather than a liability. Feminist theorists such as Daly and Griffin argue that if the "Man of Reason" is associated not only with rationality but also with domination, the rape of nature, and all the attendant evils of the modern world, then women are fortunate not to be a part of it. They argue that the "feminine" values of caring, nurturing, relatedness, and even, in the case of Daly, mystery and spirituality (i.e., irrationality) should be privileged above that of the male. In short, they accept the dichotomy and go on to argue that we should reverse it by privileging what has hitherto been disprivileged: the feminine.

The privileging of feminine irrationality by radical feminists has disturbed many feminists who are not unsympathetic to some of the goals of the radical movement (Eisenstein 1983; Cocks 1984). The problems posed by the privileging of the values traditionally associated with the feminine have become central issues in contemporary feminist literature. The question of whether feminists should espouse "maternal thinking" (Ruddick, 1980; 1984) as the basis for a new female ethic is one that has sharply divided contemporary feminist thinkers (Grimshaw, 1986: 221ff). The problems with this approach are numerous. First, it has conservative implications not only because of its affinity with the antifeminists but also because it exalts traditional "feminine" values (Stacey, 1983). Second, it entails a false universalism and essentialism (Grimshaw, 1986: 17). It posits an a-historical "feminine nature" that does not allow for historical, social and cultural definitions of the feminine. But the most significant argument against the radical feminists is an epistemological one. By accepting the rational/irrational distinction that privileges the masculine, radical feminists perpetuate the dichotomy that constitutes feminine inferiority. Much as we might laud the "feminine" values the radicals proclaim, these values will continue to be viewed as inferior until the dichotomy itself is displaced. The hierarchy implicit in the rational/irrational dichotomy is not external to it; it cannot simply be reversed, leaving the dichotomy itself intact. The experience of the social sciences discussed above illustrates this point. Their attempt to define a "separate but equal" status for the social sciences ended in failure. The radical feminist attempt to make the same move is also doomed. Only a move that dissolves the dichotomy can successfully remove that prescribed inferiority.

The third alternative argued by feminists involved in the critique of the masculine definition of rationality is one that has an affinity to the postmodern alternative. Although this alternative is by no means a popular one among feminists, nevertheless an increasing number of feminist theorists are attempting to chart "the treacherous course between postmodernism and feminism" (Owens, 1983: 59). It is impossible to look to one theorist or group of theorists for a definitive statement of the postmodern feminist critique of rationality. The work of contemporary French feminists, particularly that of Irigaray, Cixous, and Kristeva have been important in formulating the postmodern feminist position. In addition, a number of American theorists, particularly those who have been influenced by these French writers, have been significant. But no clear statement of the position has as yet emerged; its theoretical dimensions remain ill-defined. This is partly due to the fact that the writers in both of these groups are frequently more interested in issues of literary criticism than theoretical development. Despite this, however, it is possible to outline the main elements of a postmodern feminist critique of rationality.

The central theme of the French feminist' attack on western rationality and its phallocratic assumptions is that woman's oppression is rooted in language. Phallocratic language offers women only two options: either they can speak as women, and, hence, speak irrationally, or they can enter the masculine sphere of rationality and speak not as women but as men. Much of the effort of the French feminists has been to avoid either of those mutually unacceptable alternatives, that is, to carve out a space for women in a phallocratic linguistic universe. Such an effort, however, is by definition radical and revolutionary. The development of a woman's language, a "feminine writing" (*ecriture feminine*) is a subversive activity, an activity that deconstructs and destabilizes phallocratic language (Culler, 1982: 61). The French feminists are well aware of this, defining their activity as simultaneously deconstructive and revolutionary.

Luce Irigaray's attack on phallocratic language is a good example of this movement. Her discussions in *This Sex Which Is Not One* (1985b) and *Speculum of the Other Woman* (1985a) represent attempts to formulate a woman's language that invades and displaces the masculine sphere. Two aspects of Irigaray's work in particular indicate that she is not formulating a woman's language along masculinist, that is, rationalist, lines. First, she refuses to develop a "theory" *per se*. Irigaray, and the French feminists in general, are anti-theoretical. They see the "will to theory" as masculine and antithetical to their project (Marks and de Courtivron, 1980: xi). Their task is not to develop another "theory" but that of "jamming the theoretical machinery" (Irigaray, 1985b: 78). Second, Irigaray is not attempting to set up a feminine truth in opposition to masculine truth. The thesis of *This Sex Which Is Not One* is that women's language, like women's sexuality, is plural, not unitary. The search for a unitary truth is a masculine effort; her effort is to espouse a plural, fluid, diffuse woman's language that does not so much oppose masculine language as subvert it (Burke, 1981: 289; Sayers, 1982: 132; Faure, 1981: 85). In a revealing passage from *Speculum* Irigaray describes how this subversion of phallocratic language takes place:

> Turn everything upside down, inside out, back to front. *Rack it with radical convulsions*, carry back, reimport, those crises that her "body" suffers in her impotence to say what disturbs her. Insist also and deliberately upon those *blanks* in discourse which recall the places of her exclusion and which, by their silent plasticity, ensure the cohesion, the articulation, and the coherent expansion of established forms. Reinscribe them, hither and thither as *divergences*, otherwise and elsewhere than they are expected, in *ellipses* and *eclipses* that deconstruct the logical grid of the reader–writer, drive him out of his mind, trouble his vision to the point of incurable diplopia at least. *Overthrow syntax* by suspending its eternally teleological order, by snipping the wires, cutting the current, breaking the circuit, switching the connections, by modifying continuity, alternation, frequency, intensity. (1985a: 142)

The fact that Irigaray places "body" in quotes indicates her refusal to appeal to the essentially female. Unlike the radical feminists, Irigaray identifies the female body as a social construct, not a biological given. Her conception of "feminine writing" thus does not appeal to a definition of essentially feminine qualities.

The theme of feminine writing and its effects is developed most extensively in the work of Helene Cixous. Cixous' connection to postmodernism in general and Derrida in particular is more pronounced than is that of any of the other writers in this group. The central theme of Cixous' work is her attack on the dualisms that structure western thought, dualisms that seem to proliferate endlessly (1981: 44; 1980: 90–1). Her point in discussing these dualisms is two-fold. First, she argues that dualisms are always both oppositional and hierarchical, never neutral (Cixous and Clement 1986: 63–4). Second, they all stem from the opposition to woman, the man/woman opposition:

> Man/woman automatically means great/small, superior/inferior . . . means high or low, means Nature/History, means transformation/inertia. In fact, every theory of culture, every theory of society, the whole conglomoration of symbolic systems – everything that is, that's spoken, everything that's organized as discourse, art, religion, the family, language, everything that seizes us, everything that acts on us – it is all ordered around hierarchical oppositions that come back to the man/woman opposition . . . (1981: 44)

In a very Derridian fashion, Cixous argues that her task is to "work on the couple," to deconstruct and transform this dualistic language in which woman is

the basic opposition that informs all the others (1981: 44). Also following Derrida
she makes the link between logocentrism and phallocentrism: "Organization by
hierarchy makes all conceptual organization subject to man" (Cixous and
Clement, 1986: 64–5). Just as Derrida eschews theory formation and the creation
of a new orthodoxy to oppose phallocentrism, so Cixous argues that we should
avoid the masculine tendency to find "the truth" through interrogation (1981: 45).
In her commentary on Cixous, Conley argues that what this comes to is that
Cixous is formulating a kind of sexual "différance" that extends Derrida's
concept (Conley, 1984: 13). Rejecting the masculine/feminine opposition in
which woman is always the other, Cixous is trying to formulate a concept of
woman that is not opposition, not the other. Derrida's concept of différance is
useful to her in this attempt.

Cixous' principal strategy is a direct attack on the masculine/feminine
dichotomy. Her clearest statement of this attack is in The Newly Born Woman:

> But we must make no mistake: men and women are caught up in a web of
> age-old cultural determinations that are almost unanalyzable in their com-
> plexity. One can no more speak of "woman" than of "man" without
> being trapped within an ideological theater where the proliferation of repre-
> sentations, images, reflections, myths, identifications, transform, deform,
> constantly change everyone's Imaginary and invalidate in advance any con-
> ceptualization. (Cixous and Clement, 1986: 83)

Although Cixous continues to use the words "man" and "woman," "masculine" and "feminine," she makes it clear that these words do not refer exclusively
to one gender; she does not equate the feminine with woman, the masculine with
man (Cixous in Conley, 1984: 154). She even states that the use of the word
"feminine" is "one of the curses of our time" (Cixous in Conley, 1984: 129). She
is evidently not attempting to replace an essentially masculine writing with an
essentially feminine writing. Nor is she attempting to define the essentially
feminine; she rejects all such essentialist moves. Rather, she is trying to displace
the opposition and, thus, bring about a new inscription of the feminine.

Her means of accomplishing this new inscription is "feminine writing." What
she and the other French feminists mean by this term is not easy to define. That
Cixous is not developing a "theory" of feminine writing, however, is one of the
aspects of her approach that is clear. She states:

> It is impossible to define a feminine practice of writing, and this is an
> impossibility that will remain, for this practice will never be thought,
> enclosed, encoded – which doesn't mean that it doesn't exist. (1976: 883)

Despite this qualifier, however, Cixous discusses aspects of feminine writing
in her work. Since, in the masculine linguistic economy, woman is reduced

to silence, she must break out of that silence, but not in a masculine mode:

> It is in writing, from woman toward woman, and in accepting the challenge
> of the discourse controlled by the phallus, that woman will affirm woman
> somewhere other than in silence, the place reserved for her in and through
> the symbolic. (Cixous and Clement, 1986: 93)

Feminine texts, are different from masculine texts. They do not "rush into" meaning. They remain at the threshold of feeling; they are tactile. Writing the feminine is writing what has been cut off by the (masculine) symbolic (1981: 54). The point of feminine writing is not the creation of a new theory but a displacement of the old oppositions, particularly that of the masculine/feminine. It will thus have a formlessness that is antithetical to dualistic thought.

Thus far Cixous' approach, and even her advocacy of feminine writing, seems compatible with the postmodern position. It is pluralistic, anti-theoretical, anti-essentialist, and aimed at the displacement of dualisms. A difficulty with Cixous' position arises, however, when she begins to discuss the connection between feminine writing and the body. Women, she claims, must bring themselves into the text (1976: 875); there is a connection between writing and the libido (Cixous and Clement, 1986: 92). Women, in short, must "write the body," and since "woman is body more than man is . . . more body, hence more writing" (Cixous and Clement, 1986: 94–5). The problem with these formulations is that they seen to entail an essentialism that the rest of Cixous' work eschews. Moi makes this point when she argues that Cixous' vision is that feminine writing will establish a spontaneous relationship to the physical, the *jouissance* of the female body. It follows, Moi claims, that Cixous departs from Derrida's anti-essentialism by proclaiming a feminine and masculine libidinal economy (1985b: 110–21).

There is no easy answer to this charge of essentialism. It is a problem that exists for Cixous as well as Irigarary and Kristeva. As soon as these theorists begin to discuss the "feminine" and the feminine body the danger of essentialism exists. Cixous' work provides several defenses against this charge, however. First, she claims that "feminine writing" does not represent the feminine in any essentialist sense. Rather, it is writing *said to be* feminine (Cixous in Conley, 1984: 147). Feminine writing is a style, not a signature; it can be written by a man or a woman. The point of encouraging feminine writing is that it subverts masculine writing: "A feminine text cannot fail to be more than subversive" (1976: 888); it is a means of overcoming cultural repression (Cixous and Clement, 1986: 168). Cixous sees linguistic revolution as social revolution; displacement equals resistance to oppression (Conley, 1984: 125). A second and more compelling reply to this charge is that Cixous does not see "the body" as a biological given; it, too, is a social construct. She rejects an "anatomical determination" of sexual difference (Cixous and Clement, 1986: 81). The body that we, as women, write from is a body that has been culturally, not only biologically defined. Most importantly, it has been defined by masculine language.[11] Writing from that body is thus not a return to our "true nature" but an effort to transform masculine language by subverting it from within (Gilbert, 1986: xvi).

The point of this excursion into feminine writing and writing the body is to illustrate the way in which the French feminists and Cixous in particular have developed a feminist critique of the masculine language of rationality that is consistent with the postmodern position. It avoids dualities, essences, and the temptation to valorize the feminine over the masculine. It displaces the dualisms of masculine thought and suggests a pluralism and fluidity that transforms those dualisms. As such it offers a more radical and complete critique of rationality than the other two alternatives.

The effort to transform and replace phallocratic language that defines the French feminists' writings also characterizes the work of some radical feminists, particularly that of Mary Daly. Daly develops what she calls "gynocentric" writing in her redefinitions of words and her attempt to escape from the masculine domination of language (1978, 1984). Susan Griffin's startling prose is another example of an attempt to accomplish the reformation of language in a feminist direction. But although there are similarities between the efforts of these radical feminists and those of the French feminists, equating the two is misleading. Although Cixous may sometimes incur the danger of essentialism while at the same time rejecting it, these radical feminists are explicitly attempting to define the "feminine" as an essential quality that must be developed in opposition to the masculine. They thus perpetuate the oppositional, hierarchical epistemology of phallocratic thought while the aim of the French feminists is to transform that epistemology.

The argument that feminist language and feminine writing should serve as the basis for a universal critique of epistemology is not entirely limited to the French feminists (Marcil-Lacoste, 1983: 127). American feminist theorists have become increasingly interested in this aspect of the work of the French feminists and discussions of their work are becoming common in American publications.[12] Yet despite this interest, American feminists are far from embracing the cause of the French feminists or, more broadly, the postmodern approach. Two good examples of this reluctance are the works of Iris Young and Sandra Harding. Young divides contemporary feminist thought into humanist (modernist) feminism on one hand and "gynocentric" (feminine essentialist) feminism on the other. Although she defines problems with both approaches, she does not see the French feminist view as a solution to these problems (1985). Harding is likewise interested but hesitant about the postmodern option. Like the postmoderns, Harding argues both against the rationalist epistemology of Enlightenment thought and for the use of feminist thought as a way of transforming that epistemology. In her critique of scientific knowledge, however, Harding is reluctant to embrace the postmodernist position. One of the themes of her work is the caution that there are serious problems with what she identifies as "relativist epistemologies" (1983: 319). In a later discussion of the coincidence between African and feminine views of self Harding once more espouses themes that are consistent with postmodernism (1987). She calls into question the neat dichotomies of masculine/feminine and European/African and advocates a theory that can explain historical and cultural differences. But she stops short of an advocacy of postmodernism despite its similarities to her position.

This reluctance is unwarranted. The foregoing explication of the postmodern feminist approach to the critique of the "Man of Reason" reveals its advantages *vis-à-vis* the other two options espoused by feminist theorists. Along with the other feminist critics, the postmodern feminists argue that, since the Greeks, rationality has been defined as a masculine mode of thought exclusive of women, that logocentrism is phallocentrism. What is unique about the postmodern feminist position, however, is that it avoids the modernist move of trying to incorporate women into the masculine definition of rationality and the radical move of attempting to reverse the privileging of the rational/irrational dichotomy. Instead the postmodern feminists argue that we should deconstruct and transform the rationalist epistemology in which the dualism is rooted. This involves, as the French feminists have argued, rejecting phallocentric unitary language for a plurality of languages that does not strive for the creation of a new orthodoxy, a unitary "truth.'

III Liberalism and Feminism

The feminist critique of rationality and the role of postmodern thought in that critique is not limited to epistemological issues. In order to illustrate the dimensions of this critique and the modernist/postmodernist debate in which it is rooted it is useful to look closely at the relationship between feminism and the school of modernist thought that has influenced it most profoundly – liberalism. The problems created by the conflict between the modernist roots of feminism and the postmodernist implications of feminism's critique of rationality are most evident in the ongoing dispute over liberal feminism, particularly on the American scene. An examination of this debate reveals not only the seriousness of this dispute but also why the postmodernist move in feminist theory is so compelling.

The question of the relationship between feminism and liberalism has received considerable attention in contemporary feminist theory. Although there is no unanimity of opinion among feminist theorists as to the nature of this relationship there is, nevertheless, agreement on the importance of defining that relationship; feminists agree that how the relationship between liberalism and feminism is defined will have profound implications for both the theory and practice of feminism. One definition of this relationship is that proposed by liberal feminists: feminism originates in liberalism. The liberal feminist argues that feminism is an offshoot of the emancipatory impulse of liberalism. Liberalism, as a product of the rationalism of Enlightenment thought, defines man (*sic*) as rational, autonomous, equal, and free of the bias of subjectivity. It is the equality men share in rationality that, in the liberal creed, entitles them to equal participation in the political sphere. Liberalism's progression has been synonomous with bringing formerly disenfranchized groups into the political sphere. The admission of these groups into politics is always justified in terms of their right to an equal share of political power, a right grounded in their equal share of rationality. On the face of it, it would seen that women are one of these groups. Although the founding fathers of liberalism, among them John Locke, excluded women from the spheres of rationality and politics, liberal feminists argue that the logic of liberalism dictates that women, like the other disenfranchized groups that have benefited from liberalism, should be free to enter those spheres and assume their rightful position as free, autonomous, rational, equal individuals.

Both socialist and radical feminists object to this definition of the relationship between liberalism and feminism on the grounds that the political categories of liberalism are inadequate to the feminist cause. They argue not only that liberalism initially excluded women from the realm of politics but also that liberalism, because of its individualistic grounding, cannot provide the basis for a viable political program. But the socialist/radical critique of liberal feminism does not repudiate the dichotomy that lies at the heart of liberal feminism: rational/irrational. The socialist feminist, like the liberal feminist, wants to bring women into the sphere of rationality. The radical feminist wants to revalorize the irrational, private sphere defined as feminine by liberal epistemology. Neither, however, breaks out of that epistemology and the inferior status it defines for women.

In opposition to these critiques the postmodern critique of liberal feminism focuses on the modernist/Enlightenment epistemology of liberalism. Liberalism derives its definition of self from the Enlightenment dualism between the rational and the irrational. In its original formulation liberalism explicitly excluded women from the sphere of rationality and politics. This exclusion was effected by relying on the dualism between the public and the private, placing men in the former category and relegating women to the latter (Elshtain, 1981; O'Brien, 1982)[13] The postmodern feminist critique argues that liberalism, despite its emancipatory emphasis, is rooted in an epistemology that effectively bars women from the liberating realm of politics by defining them as irrational. They argue, furthermore, that the rational/irrational, public/private dichotomies are fundamental to liberalism's epistemology; they cannot be "opened up," eliminated or reversed without altering that epistemology beyond recognition. Their argument differs from that of the radical feminists, however, in that they want to displace rather than reverse these dichotomies.[14] They conclude that liberal feminism is an epistemological impossibility.

In order to assess the principal elements of this debate it is necessary to begin with an examination of liberal feminism itself. Although Locke excluded women from the sphere of rationality and politics by arguing that they "cannot know and therefore must believe," liberal feminists have attempted to alter Locke's verdict on women. In *A Vindication of the Rights of Woman* (1967) Mary Wollstonecraft attempts to open up the sphere of rationality to women. Her argument appeals directly to the Enlightenment concept of reason in order to assert woman's status as a "rational creature" (1967: 150; Donovan, 1986: 9). She argues that if men and women were educated similarly all but the physical differences between them would disappear. The clearest statement of the liberal position on feminism, however, is that found in John Stuart Mill's *The Subjection of Women*.[15] What Mill accomplishes in this work and related essays on women is a straightforward application of the principles of liberalism to the position of women in society. A second aspect of Mill's discussion, furthermore, is particularly relevant to the contemporary debate: his discussion of the "natural" as opposed to the environmentally produced qualities of women. This discussion involves Mill in a series of contradictions that reveal precisely the liabilities of liberal feminism that contemporary feminists emphasize.

One of the foundations of Mill's argument for the emancipation of women is a principle dear to his heart: the utilitarian principle. He argues that the present system in which the skill of women is lost is wasteful, particularly in light of the fact that there are too few qualified men (1971: 487; Okin, 1979: 208). Mill then goes on to a discussion of the status of women in which he supplements the utilitarian principle with the fundamental tenets of the liberal creed. First, he argues that the central problem encountered by women is that they are denied a free and rational choice as to how they are to lead their lives. Instead of a life of "rational freedom" that is the cornerstone of the liberal identity, they can only "choose" the life of servitude in marriage (1971: 465; Okin, 1979: 211). Second, Mill argues that women are denied the autonomy of the individual. A woman is only free if she can be independent, and to achieve independence she must earn her own subsistence (Mill and Mill, 1970: 74). In the married state she is denied this independence. She is also denied another essential element: equality. The liberal code demands that only when relations between men and women are based on complete equality will women really be free (1971: 427).

Having established that women have been denied the freedom, autonomy and equality that is their due, Mill goes on to ask why, despite the advances of civilization, this is the case. He argues that the position of women rests not on a reasoned analysis of their situation, but, rather, on tradition and the use of force. The subjection of women exists because "no other way has been tried." Their domination, furthermore, has no other source in law than in the law of the strongest (1971: 431-3). Even though women's subjection appears natural, Mill notes that all dominations have appeared natural to those who wield them (1971: 440). Mill's argument here rests on three additional aspects of the liberal creed. First, it illustrates the liberal animus against power and Mill's life-long campaign against abuses of power (Fawcett, 1971: xvii). Second, it is an example of the opposition of Reason on one hand and Tradition and force on the other that is one of the central aspects of liberalism and Enlightenment rationalism. Third, it indicates the progressive assumptions inherent in the liberal creed. "Modern" life demands that women be accorded the equality, autonomy and freedom that men were beginning to achieve (1971: 445). The continued subjection of women reveals that the "law of the strongest" has not yet been conquered by the rational principles of modern life (1971: 433).

Mill's argument thus far remains within the parameters of liberalism and utilitarianism. He has simply applied the liberal principles of rationality, autonomy and egalitarianism to the position of women. If this were the extent of Mill's argument its conclusion would be obvious: theoretically, there is no difference between men and women as far as liberalism is concerned. This conclusion is born out in a statement found in an essay attributed to Harriet Taylor Mill: "In the present closeness of association between the sexes, men cannot retain manliness unless women acquire it" (Mill and Mill, 1970: 110). As far as liberalism is concerned, women must and can acquire man's rational nature in order to secure the benefits of the liberal creed for both women *and* men.

There are other passages in *The Subjection of Women*, however, that suggest a different conclusion and reveal the confusions implicit in Mill's attempt to define a liberal feminism. In the course of his analysis Mill takes up the difficult question of the relationship between woman's "nature" and her environmentally determined character. He wants to explore the question of how this relationship affects woman's social and political status. There are a number of important and, ultimately, contradictory strains to his argument on this issue. At the outset, Mill boldly states that the supposed "natural" differences between men and women are a result of their different education and circumstances (1971: 489). As proof of this thesis he points to the fact that in different cultures women are attributed different "natural" qualities (1971: 505). This explicit statement of environmental determinism, Okin points out, was an unpopular stance in the England of Mill's day. English intellectuals were reacting against the environmental theories of Helvetius and Holbach and were therefore not receptive to Mill's espousal of the same theory (Okin, 1979: 216). Nevertheless, Mill is adamant on this issue and much of his essay is an attempt to catalogue these environmental influences on women and their effect on women's character.

To present Mill as an environmental determinist, however, would be a serious distortion of his thought. Although Mill is aware of the environmental influences on women, he is not only interested in discussing, as Simone de Beauvoir put it, how women are made, not born; rather, he is interested in identifying the environmental influences that shape woman's character so that they can be eliminated and he can get to the core of the issue: women's true nature. This interest derives from a concern that forms one of the unifying themes of his work: the creation of a science of "ethology," the scientific study of the laws of character formation. In volume 6 of the *Logic* Mill elaborates his understanding of ethology and what he identifies as its paramount importance for the creation of the scientific study of human beings. His interest in this context in the ethology of women is merely part of this larger concern. In *Subjection* he states:

> Of all the difficulties which impede the progress of thought, and the formation of well-grounded opinions on life and social arrangements, the greatest is now the unspeakable ignorance and inattention to the influences which form human character. (1971: 452)

What is important to note in this context, however, is that central to Mill's science of ethology is the assumption that human beings' "character" is ultimately grounded in a basic "nature." He is thus not content, as are many twentieth-century feminists, to attribute the differences between men and women to environmental influences alone. He presupposes that women have a "nature" different from that of men and sets out to answer the question of how the environmental influences that form woman's character relate to that basic nature (1971: 452).

His answer to this question is that we cannot tell. In the present state of society, he states, it is impossible to ascertain the natural differences between the sexes because of the deplorable state of the study of ethology (1971: 453, 507). Mill's scientific interest in ethology and his acknowledgement that it is impossible at this point to tell which of women's characteristics are "natural" and which acquired combine to create confusion in this discussion. It is far from clear whether Mill sees the characteristics he discusses as primarily environmentally produced or as indications of women's "true" nature.

It is precisely because of this ambiguity that Mill's discussion of woman's character/nature is instructive. His first claim is that women are more practical than men, a quality he identifies as a product of women's intuition. Women's intuitive perception is

> a rapid and correct insight into present fact. It has nothing to do with general principles. Nobody ever perceived a scientific law of nature by intuition nor arrived at a general rule of duty or prudence by it. (1971: 494)

He goes on to assert that even women who receive a masculine education are more practical than men, thus implying that this particular characteristic of women is innate rather than acquired (1971: 495). Second, Mill discusses women's inability to pursue abstract thought. This quality is related to her practical nature, but, Mill argues, her deficient feminine education plays the key role here. The kind of education women receive at present makes them "incapable of persisting long in the same continuous effort" but, he suggests, they may be capable of doing so with proper education. With regard to woman's "fickleness" in this respect Mill states, "They perhaps have it from nature, but they certainly have it from training and education'' (1971: 502). Third, Mill's discussion of women's moral character also relies heavily on environmental rather than natural causes. He denies that women are more susceptible to moral bias than men, arguing that if women, like men, were educated for public duty, they, too, would perceive their duty to more than their immediate families (1971: 519–32). In the same context he calls into question the sincerity of men who claim the moral superiority of women, commenting acidly:

> They are declared better than men: an empty compliment, which must provoke a bitter smile from every woman of spirit, since there is no other situation in life in which it is the established order and considered quite natural and suitable that the better should obey the worse. (1971: 518)

At least two different conclusions follow from Mill's analysis of the relationship between woman's character and her underlying nature, but neither is a conclusion that feminists would find acceptable. First, Mill may be assuming that women's nature is inherently different from men's but that these differences are unnecessarily intensified by the faulty education that women receive. It would follow from this that women can become more like men if their education is improved but that the basic differences, and, hence, inequality, between the sexes must necessarily persist. The problem with this conclusion is that it entails that women never really acquire the equality that is the avowed goal of liberal feminism. A second conclusion, however, is also possible. Mill could be arguing that women do not differ from men in their essential nature and that with improved education they could become precisely like men. The problem with this conclusion is that it privileges the ''masculine'' values of rationality, abstraction and universality and permanently disprivileges the intuitive, relational and contextual style of women. Even with the assumption that these ''feminine'' characteristics are merely a product of faulty education, the disprivileging of these values is not an acceptable conclusion for feminists.

Significantly, it is also not an acceptable conclusion for Mill himself. One of the themes of Mill's discussion of woman's nature and character is the contrast between the practical, intuitive style of women and men's capacity for rational abstraction. A superficial reading of these passages would lead to the conclusion that Mill sees the masculine pattern as innately superior and faults women for their failure to achieve it. But a more careful reading leads to another conclusion. At a significant point in his argument Mill suggests that man's capacity for rational abstraction, a central tenet of the liberal creed he espouses, may not be as advantageous as it has been assumed. He states that

> it remains to be shown whether this exclusive working of a part of the mind, this absorption of the whole thinking faculty on a single subject and

concentration of it on a single work is the normal and healthful condition of the human faculties, even for speculative uses. (1971: 502)

Mill suggests that this masculine capacity for sustained abstract thought must be complemented by woman's more practical and intuitive style. It follows from this that Mill is not ready to eliminate these values altogether. Although this complementarity thesis still places women in an inferior role, Mill's admiration for woman's mental style and his questioning of abstract rationality is nevertheless noteworthy.[16] His critique presages the critique of Enlightenment rationalism that occupies the attention of so much of twentieth-century philosophy and, significantly, is also central to contemporary feminism. What is relevant here is that Mill identifies this rationalism as a masculine trait and at least suggests that woman's lack of this trait may be part of her nature.

Mill's dilemma here is a serious one. Neither of the possible conclusions that follow from his analysis of women are acceptable to feminists or consistent with his own position. This problem is reflected in the strategies he recommends to improve the status of women. On the face of it Mill appears to be arguing for a strict equality between the sexes. He argues that women and men should have equal educations (1971: 532), that women should share equal rulership in marriage (1971: 473), and that women, like men, should be free to choose their careers because "The proper sphere for all human beings is the largest and highest which they are able to attain" (Mill and Mill, 1970: 100). But Mill also introduces a number of limitations on woman's supposed "equality" that amounts to a significant reduction of her freedom, even as he defines it. The most significant of these is that, should a woman "choose" marriage as a career, he asserts that no other career should be open to her. Although he qualifies this by asserting that in particular cases married women with "faculties exceptionally adapted to any other pursuit" might combine marriage with another career, he obviously assumes that in most cases women's career choice will be marriage (1971: 484). This essentially limits women's equality to single women, since, as he himself has argued, only women who can earn their own subsistence can be truly independent. Even within marriage Mill places limits on the supposed equality between the sexes. He asserts that the married woman's role is to "adorn and beautify" her husband's life since the "great occupation of woman should be to beautify life". A further restriction is found in his assertion that both women and men should abide by the division of labor in which men take on tasks that require muscular exertion and women concern themselves with the fine arts. He asserts that this traditional division of labor is "natural" and "healthy" (Mill and Mill, 1970: 77).[17] Brennan and Pateman conclude from this that married women are a permanent embarrassment for liberal theory. Why should a free and equal individual place herself under the control of another free and equal individual as she must in the marriage role (1979: 183)?

Not only do these proposals for bettering the position of women reveal the contradictions inherent in Mill's theory, they also reveal the impossibility of a liberal feminism. Liberal feminism offers two options to women: either they can model themselves on the rational ideal of men and, hence, deny what the rationalist epistemology defines as their "feminine nature;" or they can accept their different status with regard to rationality and hence be allowed into the sphere of rationality as second-class citizens. It is significant that in Mill's own account it is not clear which of these alternatives he adopts. It is also clear that neither is desirable or coherent.

This analysis of Mill's liberal feminism illustrates one of the principal feminist criticisms of the liberal creed: its reliance on the rational/irrational dualism. Mill's attempt to admit women into the sphere of rationality is, ultimately, a failure because of his confusion concerning the connection between rationality and the masculine. Although Mill wants to admit women to the public sphere as free, equal, and, hence, fully rational individuals, the liberal epistemology that he espouses prevents him from achieving this goal. A further analysis of the liberal ideology, however, leads to the conclusion that liberal epistemology entails another exclusion as well: women, who are not fully rational, cannot be fully moral. For liberal epistemology equal participation in the political realm is contingent on the achievement of full rationality. But the criterion of rationality is also constitutive of the moral sphere. For the liberal morality is rooted in rationality: it is man's rationality that allows him to distinguish the moral from the immoral. Contemporary feminist critics have explored this connection between the rational and the moral and its implications for the status of women.

In a Different Voice (1982), Carol Gilligan's widely acclaimed study of men and women's moral development, argues that men's moral development differs significantly from that of women. Following the pathbreaking work of Nancy Chodorow, Gilligan notes that in order to achieve adulthood, men must separate themselves from the mother and attain an autonomous, individual existence. Women, on the other hand, do not need to make this break with the mother. Thus while for males the values of autonomy and individualism are central to their moral development, for women the values of attachment and connection are paramount. Gilligan puts her point this way:

> The elusive mystery of women's development lies in its recognition of the continuing importance of attachment in the human life cycle. Woman's place in man's life cycle is to protect this recognition, while the developmental litany intones the celebration of separation, autonomy, individuation and natural rights. (1982: 23)

Gilligan relates her findings with regard to the differing moral development of men and women to the established tradition of moral development theory. Focusing on the influential work of Kohlberg, she analyzes the different stages of moral development that he outlines in his theory. She finds that what Kohlberg identifies as the highest level of moral development, and hence what he defines as the fully moral human being, is based on the male rather than the female model of moral development. Kohlberg's highest stage of moral development is defined as that which is characterized by the highest degree of abstraction, generalization and rationality. The individual, or, better, man, who achieves this highest level is remarkably similar to the idealized man of Mill's account. He is a separate, autonomous being who is able rationally to abstract from a situation and render a moral judgment according to universal principles. Thus fully moral individuals are ones who are, as Benhabib puts it, "disembedded and disembodied" (1986b: 406). An important consequence follows from the establishment of the male experience as the model of moral maturity: women, who view moral problems in contextual, relational terms, are defined as inferior moral beings, as deformed males (Scheman, 1983: 239). Their pattern of moral reasoning, because it differs significantly from the male's, is defined as a lower stage of moral development. Because they remain mired in relationships and fail to achieve the separation that males define as complete moral development, they are excluded from the highest sphere of morality (Gilligan, 1982: 156).

There are two other connections between Gilligan's research and the foregoing discussion of Mill. First, the moral pattern of women that Gilligan identifies is identical to that noted by Mill. But there is a significant difference in how Mill and Gilligan treat this pattern. Mill dismisses the relational quality of women's moral reasoning as a temporary phenomenon that can be eliminated with proper education. Gilligan, on the other hand, defines it as a much more fundamental product of female-identified child-rearing practices. This, in itself, has important implications for the relationship between liberalism and morality. If Gilligan is right then the moral equality between men and women that Mill forsees is an impossibility as long as women retain the primary role in child-rearing. A second connection between Gilligan and Mill also has important implications for Mill's attempt to formulate a liberal feminism. As both Flax (1980) and Benhabib (1986b) point out, the liberal definition of self is rooted in rationality, autonomy, individuation, perhaps even solipsism. For Mill as well as Hobbes and Locke the fully moral, rational being must eschew the relatedness and connectedness that characterizes not only women's moral development but their identity as well. Women do not fit the liberal definition of rationality and morality because the liberal definition of self is based on masculine values of separation and autonomy. This means that, according to the liberal ideology, women are not only barred from the spheres of rationality and morality, but their very identity is questioned as well.[18]

The reaction to Gilligan's thesis in the feminist community has been overwhelming. Although Gilligan is not without her detractors, her thesis has been widely acknowledged as an important contribution to feminist theory. A number of studies have operationalized and extended Gilligan's perspective on women's moral development (Lyons, 1983; Belenky et al., 1986). These studies establish a clear distinction between the "justice" or "rights" perspective idealized by Kohlberg and the "care" perspective that characterizes women's pattern of moral reasoning. Although these studies stress that the distinction between these two categories is not based solely on gender, there is nevertheless a call for a "feminist moral theory" that reflects women's moral experiences (Held, 1987: 114). Many of the authors in the collection, *Women and Moral Theory* (Kittay and Meyers, 1987), argue that the care perspective does not preclude but rather supports many of the values embodied in the justice/rights perspective, particularly moral autonomy. Although this literature is by no means monolithic, its theme is clear: the pattern of women's moral reasoning is different from that of men and to account for that difference, as Kohlberg has, by categorizing it as a lower stage of development, is unacceptable.[19]

The foregoing shows that Gilligan offers a means of calling into question the possibility of a liberal feminism. But the usefulness of Gilligan's theory in developing this critique is limited by an ambiguity in her position. In developing her critique Gilligan is not always as careful as she should be to avoid the essentialism and gender stereotyping that characterizes both liberal and modernist epistemology. The most serious question raised by Gilligan's approach concerns the issue of whether her statements regarding moral development are meant to be universal. Is she saying that all women and men must necessarily develop along the lines she has outlined or only that this had been the case in our society? This is a problem that originates in the work of the theorist that Gilligan uses as the basis of her research: Nancy Chodorow. In her *The Reproduction of Mothering* (1978) Chodorow fails to specify whether her statements about the effect of mother-dominated child-rearing are universal or societally specific. This failure constitutes a fundamental problem with both accounts. As many of Gilligan's critics have noted, her presentation is a-historical and ignores structural as opposed to individual influences on psychological development (Nicholson, 1983: 530; 1986: 205; Gottlieb, 1984; Harding, 1981: 64). If what Gilligan is saying is that women's moral nature is essentially different from that of men's then this does not constitute an advance over the characterization of women as irrational. Although Gilligan, unlike Enlightenment/modernist thinkers is trying to revalorize the feminine moral pattern, if her aim is to describe the essential, universal morality of women then she is merely reinforcing the gender stereotypes of the modernist epistemology.

Such an interpretation, however, is unfair to Gilligan. Gilligan is not making the radical feminist move of attempting to substitute the feminine model of moral reasoning for the masculine. A better interpretation of her project is that she is making the postmodern move of arguing that there are different patterns of moral reasoning.[20] On this interpretation what Gilligan has achieved is a critique of yet another aspect of Enlightenment thought: moral theory (Flanagan and Adler, 1983: 576). What she shows is that the rationalist, abstract, universalizing pattern of moral reasoning is one way of moral reasoning, but neither the only nor the superior way. She shows that the contextual, relational model that characterizes women's moral reasoning is just as valid as the rationalist model. She argues, furthermore, that it represents a model of reasoning that has a long history in moral philosophy (1987: 83). Stating Gilligan's project in these terms reveals the connection between her position and that of Gadamer. Gilligan has accomplished in moral theory what Gadamer accomplished in epistemology. While Gadamer argued that the Enlightenment's way of knowing is neither exclusive nor superior to other ways of knowing, Gilligan argues that the same is true for the Enlightenment's moral theory. Gilligan's theory also has an affinity with another postmodernist – Derrida. Gilligan is making a Derridian move in that she is deconstructing the rationalist model of morality, questioning its privileged status, and arguing for the validity of the disprivileged side of the dichotomy between the abstract masculinist model and the contextual feminine model. Interestingly, Gilligan, like the postmoderns, has been accused of relativism for questioning the rationalist model. In Kohlberg's defense of his position against Gilligan's attack, he claims that "truly moral reasoning involves features such as impartiality, universalizability, reversability and prescriptivity" (1982: 524). Gilligan's position, in contrast, is defined as entailing the abandoning of objectivity that leads to moral relativism (Broughton, 1983).

Gilligan's analysis, along with the postmodern critique of Enlightenment rationalism, strengthens the argument that a liberal feminism is both an epistemological impossibility and an undesirable goal for feminist theory. But rejecting the liberal heritage altogether is not as simple as revealing its epistemological and moral limitations. It is undeniable that the emancipatory impulse of liberalism is directly responsible for the rise of feminism in western democracies. Thus, for many feminists, discarding liberalism entails discarding feminism's historic roots, not a task to be undertaken lightly. As a consequence, many feminists have argued that we should stop short of an outright rejection of liberalism. One solution to the problem of how feminists should regard their liberal heritage is that suggested by Zillah Eisenstein (1981). Eisenstein argues that a radical potential exists in mainstream liberal feminism and, specifically, in the writings of Wollstonecraft, John Stuart Mill, Harriet Taylor and Elizabeth Cady Stanton. Although Eisenstein's sympathies for the liberal program are circumscribed by her Marxist perspective, she nevertheless offers a spirited defense of the *possibilities* of liberal feminism. Her argument rests on the identification of internal contradictions in the liberal program. Specifically she identifies a contradiction between the feminism of these works, their sexual egalitarian and collectivist themes, and the dominant themes of liberalism, patriarchy and individualism (1981: 3). These internal contradictions, she argues, contain the seeds of the liberation of liberal feminism (1981: 9). The key to these contradictions is something Eisenstein labels "sex class." She claims that implicit in the works of Wollstonecraft, Mill, Taylor and Stanton is a recognition of the fact that women are oppressed as a class and that the collective nature of their oppression puts them outside of the liberal categories of individual power (1981: 6). In the case of Wollstonecraft, Mill and Taylor she argues, however, that although they recognize the sex class of women they cannot express it because of their adherence to the liberal ideology (1981: 104, 117). As the book progresses it becomes clear that Eisenstein's underlying purposee is to berate contemporary feminist leaders (particularly Betty Friedan) for forsaking this radical potential in liberal feminism (1981: 178ff).

This is a curious argument. What Eisenstein is asserting is that we should emphasize and preserve precisely those elements of liberal feminism that contradict and transcend the liberal ideology; in other words, it is the illiberal elements of liberal feminism that we must stress. Although this argument is understandable in light of her Marxist perspective, it nevertheless entails an odd assessment of liberal feminism. It would not be difficult to argue that this argument, like that of the liberal feminists Eisenstein attacks, is internally contradictory. But there is another element to Eisenstein's argument that throws light on this apparent contradiction. A careful reading of her argument reveals that she wants to retain at least one element of liberal ideology in her conception of feminism. Near the end of the book she asserts that even though liberal feminism is inadequate "we can recognize the necessity of a theory of individuality within Western feminism" (1981: 191). Feminist theory must recognize the individualist nature of western liberal societies before it can transcend it. She concludes: "This theory of individualism must recognize the individual character of our social nature and the social nature of our individuality" (1981: 191).

Although as it stands this statement makes very little sense, it does begin to explain Eistenstein's tentative espousal of the liberal ideology she claims to reject. In her own words she want to retain its "individuality" while rejecting its "individualism" although she offers no clues as to how this feat is to be accomplished. Given the force of her preceding condemnation of liberal ideology it seems fair to remain skeptical as to the feasibility and wisdom of the course that she advocates. Perhaps more than anything it indicates a tacit recognition of the fact that, for now at least, liberal feminism and, specifically, individualism, is an almost necessary political idiom for feminism. Claims about the political aims of feminism are cast in terms of this idiom even by those who insist that they reject its principal tenets.

The contradictions inherent in liberal feminism have been noted by other feminists as well. Cott (1986) and Elshtain (1986a) talk about the "paradoxes" and contradictions in the feminist tradition and Rhode (1986) discusses the "tensions" between feminism and the liberal ideology. She concludes:

> As contemporary theorists have increasingly recognized, if feminism is to achieve its objectives of full equality between the sexes, it must transcend the focus on individual rights that remains at the core of liberal ideology. (1986: 151)

But liberal ideology, particularly as a basis for a program of political reform, remains strong despite these criticisms. In a recent article Susan Wendell (1987) presents what she identifies as a "qualified" defense of liberal feminism. Like Eisenstein, Wendell identifies herself as a socialist and thus someone who is critical of liberalism's basic tenets. But, also like Eisenstein, Wendell defends what amounts to the illiberal aspects of liberal feminism, claiming that "liberal feminism is a philosophically better kind of liberalism" (1987: 66). Her article advances two principal arguments. First, she claims that Mill and other advocates of liberal feminism do not adhere to the abstract individualism that is the hallmark of liberalism. Rather, she claims, liberal feminists emphasize relationships and stress community. Second, she argues that liberal feminism's political program offers both the best political strategy for feminists and the best chance for radical social change. As such she defends it as a viable option for feminist politics. Wendell's defense of liberal feminism, however, falls prey to the same problems that are found in Eisenstein's assessment. Both theorists emphasize the elements of liberal feminism that contradict or transcend the liberal ideology, an ideology that both claim, as socialists, to reject. Like Habermas, they want to select elements of the liberal/modernist epistemology while rejecting others. Such an eclectic approach to epistemology does not work any better for Wendell and Eisenstein than it does for Habermas.

This analysis of the connection between liberalism and Enlightenment rationalism as well as the link between rationality and concepts of morality strongly supports the argument advanced at the outset: the necessity of displacing that epistemology in feminist theory. The Enlightenment/modernist epistemology that informs both liberalism and the individualistic moral code to which it is linked is inherently sexist; the gendered connotations of the rational/irrational dichotomy are not optional. Rather, they inform that epistemology in all of its dimensions. It is an epistemology that not only defines women as incapable of reason and morality, but it also questions their very identity. The liberal feminists who want to retain the "good" elements of this epistemology while rejecting its sexism misunderstand the deep-rootedness of that sexism. An epistemology that defines women as not fully rational, moral or even human cannot be simply repaired to allow women a new status. It must be rejected outright.

Unfortunately it is easier to call for a rejection of the liberal/rationalist epistemology than to achieve it. Feminism's ties to both liberalism and the rationalism of the Enlightenment are deep. There is a fear, particularly among some contemporary French writers, that feminism may be unavoidably trapped within Enlightenment epistemology. Julia Kristeva expresses this fear most clearly when she asks whether "feminism is simply a moment in the anthropomorphic era which blocks the horizon of the discursive and scientific adventure of our species" (1981: 35). Although there are good reasons for Kristeva's doubts regarding the future of feminism, from the fact of feminism's modernist roots it does not necessarily follow that feminism must suffer the same fate as the modernist epistemology that has been so widely attacked. The effort to formulate a postmodern feminism offers a means of escape from the modernist roots of feminism. It is an effort that has important implications for the future direction of the feminist project.

Notes

1 Hindess and Hirst argue that rejecting the dogmatism of a certain form of discourse also entails rejecting epistemology (1977: 21), an argument that was discussed in chapter 1. On this point see Thompson (1984: 96-7).

2 For a fuller position of Gadamer's thought see my *Hermeneutics and the Sociology of knowledge* (1986: 91-117).

3 Gadamer's discussion of truth in this context has been the subject of many criticisms. See Hekman (1986: 112ff) and Warnke (1986: 168) for a discussion of this controversy.

4 See Hekman (1986: 171-87).

5 See Hekman (1986: 187-96).

6 See De Lauretis for an elaboration of this interpretation of Nietzsche (1987: 31-2).

7 For a discussion of the history of female inferiority see Hillman (1972).

8 See chapter 4 for a discussion of this literature.

9 I am indebted to Christine Di Stefano's "Dilemmas of difference" (1988) for a clear statement of these categories.

10 One school of feminist thought that does not fit neatly into any of these categories is "dual systems theory" which embodies the claim that women's oppression arises from two systems: patriarchy and capitalism. This theory unites radical and Marxist feminism (Young 1980: 169-70).

11 Gross argues that Kristeva and Irigaray likewise avoid essentialism by appealing to a socially constructed body (1986b: 140).

12 In addition to those noted above, discussions of postmodernism and feminism include: Fraser and Nicholson (1988); Flax (1986a, 1986b, 1987a, 1987b); Diamond and Quinby (1988a); Jardine (1985); the articles in *Feminist Studies* 14 (1988); Ferguson (1984); Gallop (1982); Holland (1986); Jones (1981); Plaza (1978); Stanton (1980); Duchen (1986); Alcoff (1988); Balbus (1985); DeLauretis (1987); McDermott (1987); Moi (1987); Weedon (1987).

13 An interesting corollary of this theory is that advanced by Illich in *Gender* (1982). Like contemporary feminists, Illich argues that it is impossible for women to attain equality under the modern liberal episteme of rationality and autonomy. But he argues that equality can only be found in the separate but equal status women enjoyed in the pre-modern era, a period he identifies as that of "vernacular gender." Contemporary feminists have advanced strong arguments against his views (Bowles et al., 1983).

14 For a scathing indictment of all social contract theories from a feminist perspective see Pateman (1988).

15 I will not discuss here the controversy surrounding Mill's authorship of these and related works on women and the influence of Harriet Taylor on Mill's thought. For a discussion of these issues see Fawcett (1971) and Rossi (1970).

16 Mill's discussion of Bentham and Coleridge also reveals an ambiguity concerning abstract rationality (1963: 27–123).

17 Harriet Taylor Mill's views on these issues are somewhat more radical. She argues, for instance, that married women can and should work. For a discussion of their differences see Rossi (1970).

18 For a critique of the association between maleness and liberal individualism see Grimshaw (1986: 149ff).

19 Advocacy of a "care" perspective has reached beyond moral theory. Martin (1985) uses it to formulate a new approach to education, Jones (1988) to develop a different model of authority. Finally, Sagan (1988), although he is not following Gilligan, wants to define women as the originators of morality, not, as Freud defined them, incompletely moral.

20 Gilligan defends her position as anti-essentialist in Kerber et al (1986).

3

Subject/Object

I Postmodern Philosophy and the "Death of Man"

Introduction

That the dichotomy between rationality and irrationality is one of the definitive characteristics of the modern episteme is widely acknowledged. That this dichotomy is centrally important for feminist thought is equally obvious. There is a second dichotomy, however, that is just as fundamental to the project of modernity: the subject/object dichotomy. The rationalism at the root of the epistemology of modernity is a rationalism of the subject. As many critics of modernity have noted, the modern episteme is defined by the Cartesian dichotomy between subject and object. The driving force of the modern age is the search for certainty, the effort to use reason to establish absolute and universal truth. Since Descartes that search for certainty has been firmly grounded in the rationality of the knowing subject. Descartes' *ego cogita ergo sum* placed the certainty that is the goal of the modern episteme firmly within man himself. Descartes' subject, which serves as the focal point for the beginning of the modern age, is a departure from the Aristotelian concept of the subject that dominated ancient and medieval thought (Ong, 1967: 225–6). For Descartes and, hence, for modernity, the subject is the self-conscious guarantor of all knowledge (Lovitt, 1977: xxv–xxvi). As one commentator puts it, "When the subject totally comprehends the object and the object is perfectly reflected in the subject, the doubt and uncertainty with which modern philosophy begins are finally overcome" (Taylor, 1987: 3).

The subject-centeredness of the modern episteme has been one of the principal themes of the attack on modernism by postmodern philosophers. As with many aspects of the postmodern critique, the beginnings of the attack on the subject are found in the work of Nietzsche. In a move that presages the work of Heidegger, Foucault and Derrida, Nietzsche undermined the subject/object dualism by claiming that the subject alone is demonstrable; an object is only a kind of effect produced by a subject on a subject (Megill, 1985: 11, 86). Nietzsche's attack on the subject/object dualism has taken different forms in the postmodern era but in its broadest sense it has resulted in a rejection of the whole notion of epistemology. The replacement of the transcendental subject of Enlightenment thought with a subject that is historically situated and not, as Descartes presupposed, the sole guarantor of truth, undermines the modernist conception of epistemology itself (Shapiro, 1984: 216). The postmodern challenge to epistemology involves two arguments. First, postmoderns argue that knowledge is not acquired through the abstraction of an autonomous subject from a separate object, but, rather, that knowledge, along with subjects and objects, is constituted collectively through forms of discourse. Second, they challenge the notion that there is only one, true method by which knowledge is acquired. Instead they define knowledge as plural and heterogenous; there are "truths," not "Truth." The related concepts of objectivity and subjectivity, furthermore, are also called into question by this critique. The goal of acquiring objective knowledge that is the result of the subject's acquisition of the object no longer makes sense if modernist epistemology is rejected.[1]

The debate over the status of the subject in the postmodern era is inseparable from another dispute that has received much attention in recent philosophical literature: the attack on the humanist tradition. Humanism, which, by definition, is subject-centered, has been singled out for particular censure by postmodern thinkers. This attack has generated a great deal of acrimony on both sides of the debate. Humanism's defenders have argued that the attack on humanism creates serious political and epistemological problems which the postmoderns ignore. Their argument regarding the political liabilities of the postmodern position revolves around the claim that the humanist tradition is a valuable one that has established and preserved the most precious rights and freedoms of the modern world. The attack on humanism, they claim, is tantamount to "Leninism" and the demise of all the values of human dignity and autonomy (Smith, 1985: 653). Furthermore they claim that the postmoderns' rejection of the subject precludes the possibility of resistance and revolt that is to central to the humanist tradition (Thompson, 1984: 252). The epistemological argument of the humanists is closely related. While they argue that, politically, anti-humanism precludes action they assert that, epistemologically, it precludes knowledge. They claim that the postmoderns, by rejecting a subject-centered, unitary knowledge and replacing it with a plurality of "truths" are incurring epistemological chaos.

This debate over humanism and the role of the subject has had a profound influence on contemporary thought, but its implications for the social sciences and contemporary feminism are particularly significant. In the social sciences the debate over humanism has revealed the sterility of the positivist/humanist dispute that was the focal point of the philosophy of the social sciences for decades. Since the turn of the century humanists in the social sciences have opposed their positivist counterparts by arguing that the *object* of social scientific investigation differs from that of the natural sciences and thus that the social sciences are necessarily "subjective" disciplines. Until well into the twentieth century this humanist argument seemed to offer a clear alternative to positivist social science. The postmodern attack on humanism in recent decades, however, has revealed the shallowness of the humanists' claim. The essence of the humanist argument was to assert the subjectivity of the social sciences as opposed to the objectivity of the natural sciences. In doing so, however, they were in effect reifying the Enlightenment epistemology they claimed to oppose. While acknowledging the subject/object, subjectivity/objectivity split central to Enlightenment thought, they attempted only to revalorize the "disprivileged" side of these dichotomies. Thus instead of escaping the epistemology that defined the social sciences as inferior they were effectively embracing it.

The postmodern attack on humanism has revealed that this dispute between positivism and humanism is futile because, epistemologically, positivism and humanism are two sides of the same coin. The humanists did succeed in attacking the absoluteness of the object of knowledge posited by Enlightenment thought through their attack on objectivity. What they failed to do was to attack the subject side of the dichtomy as well and thus the basis of the dualism itself. The humanists' attempt to oppose Enlightenment epistemology made two errors. First, it accepted the Enlightenment dualisms, and, second, it attempted to replace the absoluteness of objectivity with the absoluteness of subjectivity. In contrast the postmoderns' critique of the absoluteness of the subject and their argument that discourse creates subjects as well as objects does more than merely complete the critique begun by the humanists. Rather, the postmoderns succeed in displacing the Enlightenment dichotomies altogether. They reject both subjects *and* objects as essential entities and, with them, the goal of absolute knowledge. Their approach has altered the foundation of epistemological debates in the late twentieth century, but the social sciences have been particularly affected by this critique. Most importantly, the postmodern revolution has meant that the social sciences are no longer forced into the inferior status that was decreed by Enlightenment epistemology.

If the postmodern attack on the subject and the tradition of humanism has created a revolution in the social sciences, it has had an equally profound effect on feminism. Both historically and theoretically humanism and liberalism have been closely connected. The emancipatory impulse that informs liberalism originates in the humanist tradition. Thus the connection between liberalism and feminism that has been so central to the development of feminist politics and theory extends to humanism as well. The alleged "anti-humanism" of postmodern thought, thus, poses a problem for feminist thinkers. On one hand the implications of the postmodern critique of humanism suggest that the humanist tradition offers a poor foundation for feminism. Feminists have identified the "homocentrism" of humanist thought (Lemert, 1979) as referring to gendered rather than generic man; the man-centeredness of humanism entails an epistemology that is exclusive of women. On the other hand, however, feminists have frequently appealed to the values of humanism – dignity, autonomy and rights – as the basis for their arguments against the oppression of women. Furthermore, the charge that the demise of the subject obviates agency is a particularly relevant one for feminism. This ambiguity in feminism's relationship to the humanist tradition structures both the feminist critique of humanism and its response to the postmodern critique of the subject. The alternatives for feminism are similar to those created by the feminist critique of liberalism. Some feminists have argued that we should retain humanism but purge it of its sexism. Others have argued that we should restructure the subject of the modernist/humanist tradition by defining a new sense of subjectivity, that is, that we should both problematize the subject and embrace a new subjectivity for women (Ferguson, 1988: 8). Finally, some feminists have argued that the Cartesian subject cannot be reconstituted but, rather, must be rejected outright. How this debate is resolved will have profound implications for the future of feminist theory.

The Postmodern Critique of the Subject: Gadamer, Derrida, and Foucault

Many critics have pointed out that the attack on the subject and the resulting decentering of man that is characteristic of postmodern thought originates in the work of Heidegger (Megill, 1985: 138; Hoy, 1985: 47; Shapiro, 1984: 217; Ricoeur, 1983: 191). Heidegger was the first clearly to identify the Cartesian subject as the central presupposition of modern thought. His "Letter on Humanism" is one of the basic documents in the movement that would later be labelled the "death of man." Furthermore in *The Question Concerning Technology* he argues that the key to understanding the modern age is the fact that man becomes a subject (1977: 128). Man is the source of all truth; he sets himself up as one who constitutes himself. Heidegger rejects what he identifies as the man-centeredness of the modern world in a number of ways. First, he rejects the transcendental, privileged status of the Cartesian subject. Man, he claims, is always historical, rooted, and a product of a particular manifestation of Being. Second, Heidegger rejects the definition of truth as the agreement between known object and knowing subject; he defines truth instead as "uncoveredness" or "unhiddenness." Third, he attacks the Cartesian subject because it gives metaphysical priority to man the subject. It thus provides man with a privileged standpoint, an Archimedean point, that violates the historicity of Being. This aspect of Heidegger's critique of the subject represents an important element of the contemporary attack on the subject: the connection between the metaphysics of the subject/object dichotomy and Cartesian epistemology. The Cartesian subject's search for truth entails both an ontology and a metaphysics: an ontology of truth and a metaphysics of subjects and objects. Thus, as both Heidegger and Derrida make clear, the critique of the subject is not only epistemological but is also a critique of metaphysics.

Gadamer's analysis begins from this Heideggerian perspective. Although his

attack on the subject is not as explicit as that of Derrida and Foucault, his approach
to hermeneutics presents a contrast to the subject-centeredness of phenomenology.
Most importantly it is a sharp departure from the hermeneutic tradition out of
which he writes. The task of traditional hermeneutics was to uncover the meaning
of the text, a meaning synonomous with the author's intention. Gadamer rejects
this approach in favor of his definition of understanding as the fusing of horizons.
The aim of his hermeneutics is not to uncover the intention of the author, but to
reveal the horizon of meaning projected by the text.[2] His rejection of authorial
intention as the locus of meaning stems from his assertion that language is
"I-less." Gadamer asserts that it is more correct to say that language speaks us
rather than we speak it:

> Strictly speaking, it is not a matter of our making use of words when we
> speak. Though we "use" words, it is not in the sense that we put a given
> tool to use as we please. Words themselves prescribe the only ways in which
> we can put them to use. One refers to that as proper "usage" – something
> which does not depend on us, but rather we on it, since we are not allowed
> to violate it. (1976: 93)

The time that a text is written provides that Gadamer calls its horizon of meaning.
He claims that this horizon is more important in determining its meaning than the
subjective intention of the author (1975: 421). His central argument is that understanding is not a mysterious communion of souls in which the interpreter grasps
the subjective meaning of the text. Rather, it is a fusion of horizons: the interpreter's horizon is fused with the horizon of the author.

Gadamer's decentering of man and his rejection of the epistemological
dichotomy between subject and object form a bridge between his work and the
more explicit critiques of the subject advanced by Derrida and Foucault. Although
Gadamer does not go as far as these theorists in his critique of the subject, his
position is consistent with the decenteredness of postmodern thought (Giddens
1979: 40; Jay 1982: 96). Apel puts this point very succinctly in his analysis of
modern hermeneutics:

> Modern hermeneutics, following Heidegger and Gadamer and drawing on
> certain affinities with French Structuralism has almost dismissed (dropped)
> the problematic of understanding *subjective intentions*, e.g., of the authors of
> texts, in favor of explicating the language of texts as an autonomous
> medium and even origin of meaning. (1981: 246)

Like the postmodern thinkers Gadamer shuns the essentialism represented by the
subject-centered epistemology of the Enlightenment. His assertion of the linguisticality of meaning decenters the subject and places the locus of meaning in
language and the text.

The principal source of the attack on the subject in postmodern thought comes from the work of a group of theorists writing in post-Second World War France. The focus of this movement, that both critics and supporters have labelled the "death of man," is an attack on the humanist tradition. One of the principal documents in the movement is Derrida's essay "The ends of man" (1969). In this article Derrida traces the demise of French humanism, a movement that he defines as including Existentialism, and the rise of what would today be identified as poststructuralism. He argues that Heidegger's destruction of metaphysics is simultaneously an attack on humanism. The problem with Heidegger's analysis, however, is that the name of "man" is not displaced. Heidegger's tactic, rather, is to re-evaluate the essence and dignity of man. The implication of Derrida's argument is that Heidegger's attack on metaphysics had already effected the death of man even though Heidegger did not explicitly acknowledge that fact. Derrida concludes that the death of man did not originate with his contemporaries but that they were merely following in Heidegger's footsteps.

Aside from this essay, Derrida, unlike Foucault, does not elaborate on the "death of man" in an explicit theoretical statement. In fact he insists at one point that his intention is not to destroy the subject but merely to situate it. He claims that the subject is "absolutely indispensable," that we cannot get along without the notion of a subject (1970: 271). It is most accurate to characterize Derrida's attack on the subject, then, as an attack on the way in which the subject has been constituted in western thought and particularly since Descartes. He is challenging the autonomous, abstract subject that is constituted through its opposition to a separate object. This challenge is central to his attack on western metaphysics and the dualisms on which it is founded.

Derrida's radical approach to text interpretation is the strongest evidence for the importance of the decentering of the subject in his thought. The goal of text interpretation in the classical hermeneutic tradition was to uncover the subjective meaning of the author of the text. The thrust of the deconstructionist program that defines Derrida's approach is to challenge the assumption that the goal of textual interpretation is to uncover the subjective meaning of the author of the text. The deconstructionist rejects the notion that the task of interpretation is to find the "true" meaning of the text or to identify the author's intention. Rather the deconstructionist defines interpretation as creating a literary product in its own right. Thus for the deconstructionist different readings are not illegitimate distortions of the text, but merely a different species of production (Culler, 1982: 38). The phrase, "every interpretation is a misinterpretation," has become the rallying cry of the deconstructionist program. Deconstructionists have called their position the "birth of the reader" because it shifts the focus of attention from the author to the reader. But, as many critics have noted, this birth necessarily results in the death of the author, the subject. For Derrida, the meaning of the text is the product of the creative experience of the reader and is produced through a process he calls "grafting." The meaning bestowed by the reader is "grafted" onto that of the text, producing a creation unique to that particular reading. The effect of Derrida's approach to interpretation, thus, definitively rejects the cult of the subject that he identifies as central to the metaphysics of presence.

Derrida's attack on the subject, furthermore, has important implications for feminism. Derrida has made it clear that his attack on logocentrism is equivalent to an attack on phallocentrism because of the gendered basis of the dualisms that constitute western thought. He explicitly argues that this applies to the subject/object dualism as well, that is, that the "I" has always had a phallic character in western thought (1984: 60). Although Derrida, unlike feminist critics such as de Beauvoir, does not elaborate on the way in which men have been constituted as subjects, women as objects, he does discuss an issue that is at the center of the feminist critique of the subject: whether women should attempt to constitute themselves as subjects. His argument in this regard is a direct consequence of his thesis of the link between logocentrism and phallocentrism:

> This is the risk. The effect of the Law is to build the structure of the subject, and as soon as you say, "well, the woman is a subject and this subject deserves equal rights," and so on – then you are caught in the logic of phallogocentrism and you have rebuilt the empire of the Law. So it seems that women's studies can't go very far if it does not deconstruct the philosophical framework of this situation, starting with the notion of subject, of ego, of consciousness, soul and body, and so on. (1987: 193)

In this passage Derrida explicitly rejects a possibility that is very attractive to many contemporary feminists: reconceptualizing the subject in neutral terms. In another passage he offers a further argument against the neutralization of the subject. The neutralization of sexual marks, he claims, has the effect of giving power to man. He identifies the turn to neutralization as the "classical ruse of man" (1987: 194). Although Derrida's radical rejection of the subject is a position that many feminists question, it is nevertheless entailed by the critique of the subject in which both he and feminist critics are engaged. The subject, the phallic "I," is central to the philosophical system that constitutes women as inferior. Constituting women as subjects entails making them a part of that system, neutralizing them, and, Derrida claims, giving power to men. The only alternative, he claims, is to deconstruct the philosophical system that gave men that power in the first place.

The most sustained critique of the notion of the subject, the opposition of subject and object, and the "death of man" is found in the work of Foucault. One of Foucault's greatest contributions to social theory is his insight that discourses create subjects as well as objects. Although the interpretive/humanist critics of positivist social science had deconstructed the object side of the subject/object dualism, it was Foucault's innovation to deconstruct the subject side as well. Although he credits Nietzsche with the first attempt to abolish the founding act of the subject, Foucault sees his own work as bringing this attempt to completion (Foucault and Raulet 1983: 199). The theme of Foucault's analyses in his extentive corpus is the insight that there are no essential subjects or objects, but only individuals caught in a network of historical power relationships. In his analyses of the clinic, madness, prisons, and sexuality his focus is to reveal how discourses about knowledge create subjects and deploy power. Thus although Foucault is involved in a frontal attack on the notion of the subject as it has been conceived in western thought, his work is far from "subjectless" as some of his critics have claimed. Foucault has rejected what he calls the "philosophy of the subject," the transcendental, constituting Cartesian subject of modernist thought. The "subjects" that are central to his work, in contrast, are concrete, historical and cultural beings that are constituted by the discourses that create subjectivity (Foucault and Sennett, 1982: 9). Foucault's analysis does not abandon the subject, but reconsiders subjectivity; his analysis is neither abstract nor subjectless, but, rather, an exploration of concrete bodies and their situations (1980: 138).

In *The Order of Things* Foucault advances a theoretical argument against the concept of the subject through his attack on the concept of "man." "Man," he asserts, is a concept unique to the modern episteme and one that creates unique problems for that episteme. Because "man" is both subject and object in the discourse of modernity, the epistemological space created for the human sciences is at the vary least ambiguous: the "man" of the human sciences is on one hand the object of those sciences, the entity that is studied in these disciplines just as the natural sciences study the physical world. But "man" is also the subject that constitutes knowledge, the being that makes knowledge, even knowledge of himself, possible. This confusion at the root of the human sciences has meant that neither "man" nor the human sciences themselves have been fully integrated into the modern episteme. A common way of interpreting Foucault's argument in *The Order of Things* is to assert that he is identifying the epistemological problem caused by the concept of "man" and outlining a solution to that problem by advocating a new epistemology. If the problem is how the modern era can awake from its "anthropological sleep" then Foucault's answer seems to be that an "imminent new form of thought" is on the horizon (1971: 342). Foucault identifies psychoanalysis, ethnology, and linguistics as counter sciences that, as he puts it, "unmake man" (1971: 379–81). They offer the possibility of removing the modern episteme from the problematic epistemology of "man" and replacing it with a more viable epistemology. He ends the book with a rhetorical question: "Since man was constituted at a time when language was doomed to dispersion, will he not be dispersed when language regains its unity?" (1971: 386).

The interpretation of Foucault as both prophet and proponent of a new epistemology, however, is misleading. Foucault is not advocating the replacement of one episteme by another or the establishment of another truth to replace a discredited one. In discussing the counter sciences of psychoanalysis, ethnology, and linguistics Foucault asserts that they are not any more "objective" or "rational" than the sciences they are replacing (1971: 379). The point of moving from one episteme to another is not to discover that the previous way of thought was in error and now "Truth" is at hand. On the contrary, Foucault's criticism of the modern episteme is its claim to have an exclusive hold on truth and rationality. He objects to the exclusivity of the modern episteme by asserting that there is no one, universal truth (Rajchman, 1985: 120-1). As he sees it, in moving from one episteme to another we are simply moving from one definition of truth to another. Although the rejection of the modern episteme entails occupying a linguistic space in which subjects and objects are displaced, it does not follow that this space is any more true or rational than the one we are abandoning (Megill, 1985: 204). These objections to the epistemological presuppositions of modernity coupled with Foucault's equally important contention that the modern episteme is necessarily connected to disciplinary matrices of power offers a uniquely powerful critique of modern thought and practice.

Foucault's rejection of the subject has earned him the label "anti-humanist." Although Foucault rejects most labels that have been applied to him he does not deny this one. Rather, he has attempted to clarify what it is in humanism that he finds unacceptable. He tries to make a distinction between humanism and the Enlightenment, arguing that "We must try to proceed with the analysis of ourselves as beings who are historically determined, to a certain extent, by the Enlightenment" (1984: 43). Humanism, he claims, is another matter. It is a series of themes that has appeared in many guises, including Marxism and existentialism, and, he argues, can (and should) "be opposed by the principle of a critique and a permanent creation of ourselves in our autonomy – a principle found in the Enlightenment" (1984: 44). What this comes to is that Foucault wants to preserve what he defines as the "liberating plentitude" of the Enlightenment while at the same time rejecting humanism. For him, humanism is characterized by the endless back and forth of the doublets that define "man" and the manifestations of bio-power in the modern world (Hiley, 1985: 72-3). His point is that the subjectification of "man" that is the essence of humanism is, in reality, his subjection (Fraser, 1985a: 178).

Foucault's intent to link subjectification and subjection is most evident in his analysis in the three volumes of *The History of Sexuality*. His argument in these works is that the essence of man the subject is to be found in sexuality because, in the west, subjects fine their "truth" in their sexuality (1984: 140). The overriding theme of Foucault's work on sexuality is his attempt to remove the question of sexuality from the paradigm of repression (Poster, 1984: 127). In the first volume of *The History of Sexuality* (1978a) Foucault attacks the common interpretations of both the Victorian era and the "sexual revolution" of the 1960s. The problem with these interpretations, he claims, is that they presuppose that "sexuality" is an a-historical constant. If there is an essence to sexuality then it makes sense to say that that essence was repressed by the Victorians and liberated by the sexual revolution of the 1960s. Against this Foucault argues that "sexuality" has no essence, but, rather, is a historical construct that did not appear until the beginning of the nineteenth century. It follows that we cannot talk about the essence of "sexuality," its repression *or* its liberation. Instead Foucault is interested in exploring the different discursive constructions of sexuality and how these discourses have been deployed at different historical periods. We cannot categorize these discourses as liberating or repressive. Rather, each represents a different deployment of knowledge and power.

In the second volume of *The History of Sexuality, The Use of Pleasure* (1985), Foucault attempts to trace the origins of our notions of the subject and sexuality. He argues that the set of ideas that allow an individual to fashion himself into a subject of ethical conduct began with the Greeks, not the Enlightenment or humanism (1985: 251.) In the course of his analysis of the Greeks he discusses a number of issues that are significant not only for his attack on the subject but also for feminist thought. One of his central points is one that is the cornerstone of the feminist critique of the subject/object dualism: only men can be subjects. He argues that men but not women could be subjected to the moral code governing sexuality that was evolving in Greek society. Women were not governed by this code because it was defined as an ethics of men; women figured only as objects (1985: 22). In his analysis Foucault shows how women were systematically excluded from the moral realm. First, morality required active participants and women, along with boys and slaves, were classified as passive rather than active (1985: 47). This created a problem for the Greeks because boys, who were, as youths, passive in sexual relations, had to assume the active role as adult men if they were to be citizens (Poster, 1986: 211). It was not, however, a problem for women who were condemned to passivity throughout their lives. Second, one of the central aspects of the Greek moral code was the ideal of moderation, the suppression of sexual desire. But the concept of moderation was, for the Greeks, tied to the concept of virility. It followed that women, lacking virility, could not be moderate. This effectively excluded them from the realm of morality because the relationship of superiority and dominance over oneself that was defined as the essence of virtue was a relationship of virility. For the Greeks a self-indulgent man, one who lacked self-mastery, was called feminine (1985: 83–5).

Finally, in *The Care of the Self* (1986) Foucault chronicles the rise of the subject that is to play such an important part in the modern episteme. The attention on the self, the rule of the individual over himself and the linking of truth to self-knowledge in the Roman and early Christian eras all presage the themes of the Enlightenment and the homocentrism that characterizes it. It was in this period that the cultivation of the self became a social practice that also gave rise to modes of knowledge and science (1986: 45). What is central in this work as well as the two volumes that precede it is the link between the rise of the subject and the concern with sexuality. What Foucault is emphasizing is that it is impossible to separate the two in the history of western epistemology.

Foucault's attack on the subject is a significant contribution to contemporary social theory that is directly relevant to contemporary feminism. His discussion of how subjects are constituted by forms of discourse has not only redefined the dimensions of social theory, it has also added a new perspective to contemporary feminist research. As many feminists have shown, Foucault's perspective is a particularly fruitful one for examining the ways in which femininity is constituted by patriarchal discourse (Diamond and Quinby, 1988a). Although Foucault does not discuss specifically how femininity is constituted in our society, his perspective has nevertheless been a useful one for feminists who have attempted to explore this issue (Bartky 1988: 64).

Another aspect of Foucault's theory that is significant for contemporary feminism is his rejection of the paradigm of repression in the study of sexuality. Postmoderns in general and Foucault in particular reject the essentialism that is characteristic of modernist/Enlightenment thought. Their anti-essentialism serves as an important corrective to the tendency among some feminist theorists to define the essentially female. In their attempt to combat patriarchal definitions of the female, some feminists have sought to define not only the essential woman but, specifically, essential female sexuality. Arguing that patriarchal discourse has distorted the meaning of feminine sexuality, these feminists have sought to reconstitute feminine sexuality along lines defined by women, not men. Foucault would not deny that patriarchal discourse rather than a discourse controlled by women has constituted feminine sexuality and that that constitution forces women into sexual relations that they find abhorent. In fact, his perspective has been useful to feminists who have sought to define precisely how feminine sexuality has been constituted in our society. But to move from an objection to the patriarchal domination of definitions of feminine sexuality to the attempt to define essential feminine sexuality is self-defeating. The feminists who argue that we should define feminine sexuality apart from the distortions of patriarchal thought are mimicking the Enlightenment epistemology that is cast in terms of universals and a-historical constructs. Against this Foucault's position that ''sexuality'' is a function of history and a particular discursive formation that constitutes sexual relationships in a specific way represents an approach that succeeds in displacing Enlightenment epistemology, an epistemology that excludes women from the realm of subjectivity. Feminists can and should oppose the discourse on sexuality that characterizes the modern episteme because it is a discourse that defines women as passive objects. It does not follow from this, however, that we must presuppose an essential feminine sexuality. To do so is to remain trapped in the Enlightenment epistemology that is defined in terms of essences and absolutes.

It is important to note, furthermore, that Foucault's position on the subject does not entail that subjects are passive dupes of the discursive formations that define their subjectivity. Modernist thought has established a dichotomy between the constituting Cartesian subject who possesses agency and autonomy and the constituted subject that is wholly determined by social forces. Foucault's approach to the subject displaces this dichotomy. The subject that he describes is constituted, but is also an "agonism," a "permanent provocation" to the knowledge/power nexus that defines subjectivity (1982: 222). The constituted subject is only passively determined in the modernist conception; in Foucault's conception the constituted subject is the subject that resists. This has important consequences for feminist thought. The subject that has been defined as feminine is a subject that is passive, irrational, emotional and more "natural" than the masculine subject. Women's resistance to that constitution of their subjectivity is the essence of the feminist movement. That resistance, however, has always been cast in terms, first, of the rejection of the feminine subject as it has been characterized in the dominant discourse and, second, an appeal to other discourses that are available in particular historical, cultural situations. For western feminists this has meant primarily the discourses of liberalism and Marxism. For third world women and women of color other discourses have been more appropriate. What is significant, however, is that the result of this resistance is the creation of a new discourse, that of feminism, that, although indebted to the discourses that shaped it, is a distinctive discursive form. It is a discourse that need not rely on a transcendental, constituting subject or an essentially female but, rather, is born out of resistance to the modes of discourse that, historically, have constituted the feminine subject. Foucault's perspective on the subject provides a useful way of conceptualizing the emergence of this feminist discourse.

II The Feminist Critique of Subjects and Objects

The basic insight that animates the feminist critique of the subject/object dualism is simple and relatively uncontroversial: throughout the history of western thought men have been defined as subjects, women as objects. Although, as Foucault has shown, this basic dualism can be traced to the Greeks, it is most fully realized in Enlightenment thought and its offshoot, humanism. Like the rational/irrational dualism, the dichotomy between subject and object is central to Enlightenment epistemology which defines knowledge in terms of absolute truths that are acquired by individual autonomous subjects. The two dualisms are related not only because the privileged element is associated with the male, the disprivileged with the female. They are also linked because the definition of rationality posited by the Enlightenment is dependent on the acquisition of knowledge by an abstract subject of a distinct and separate object.

The feminist critique of subjects and objects is wide-ranging but, despite its diversity, there is agreement that the discovery of the centrality of the subject/object dualism for contemporary epistemology and the identification of subjects as men, objects as women, is significant for contemporary feminist thought. The first clear statement of the implications of this dualism for the status of women is that presented by Simone de Beauvoir in *The Second Sex* (1972). Although this

account is now dated in many ways and is flawed by its adherence to an
existentialist–humanist epistemology, it still retains much of its force today.
In *The Second Sex* de Beauvoir is attempting to accomplish a goal that has
seemed to many feminists both then and now as the obvious solution to the
problem of the exclusion of women from the realm of the subject: bringing
women into the realm of the subject. Examining the structure of de Beauvoir's
argument about the subject is thus relevant to an analysis of the current
debate.

De Beauvoir divides her analysis in *The Second Sex* into two sections. In the first
she presents an epistemological examination of women's role in history, philosophy, and myth. In the second part she presents a kind of sociology of the feminine
in which she examines how female human beings are turned into "women." The
first section of the book stands as the classic statement of how woman is constituted as object. De Beauvoir begins her analysis with what will become the central
thesis of the book: woman is always the "Other" to man's "Absolute." Her first
point is that this fundamental distinction between Self and Other is not symmetrical. The absolute human type is man; he is both positive and neutral. Thus woman
is always defined as a peculiarity; she is "not man." De Beauvoir then goes on to
assert the two central themes of the book: first, that "The category of the *Other* is
primordial of consciousness itself" (1972: 16), that "Otherness is a fundamental
category of human thought" (1972: 17); and, second, that woman is compelled to
assume the status of Other in man's world (1972: 29). For de Beauvoir the
fundamental condition of woman is that she is locked into an Otherness that is
central to human life.

What de Beauvoir defines as the Otherness of woman takes a number of
different forms which she describes in the course of her analysis. She asserts that
women are incapable of action and are thus condemned to passivity. What are
commonly defined as the primary "activities" of women, giving birth and suck-
ling, are not, according to de Beauvoir, activities at all but merely natural functions (1972: 94). Woman's incapacity to act and her inherent passivity are rooted
in what de Beauvoir sees to be the fundamental difference between men and
women: men are capable of transcendence while women are mired in immanence.
Following the existentialist creed de Beauvoir defines transcendence as the mark of
true humanity. It is the ability to move beyond the limits of nature, to transcend
the species itself. She states that "man attains an authentically moral attitude when
he renounces *mere being* to assume his position as an existent" (1972: 172).
Immanence, on the other hand, is the incapacity to rise above nature. Women,
who, according to de Beauvoir, are more prey to the species because of their
connection to reproduction, are more limited by nature that are men. Women,
who have always been more closely associated with nature, lack man's capacity to
rise above it.

As evidence of the inability of women to achieve transcendence, de Beauvoir
points to the fact that there are no myths in which woman is the subject. Women,

who cannot be subjects, cannot create myths and are thus denied the transcendence which myths provide for men:

> A myth always implies a subject who projects his hopes and his fears toward a sky of transcendence. Women do not set themselves up as Subject and hence have erected no virile myths in which their projects are reflected . . . they dream the dreams of men. (1972: 174)

Man, who creates the myths, puts women into them as nature, as Mother, as the good earth, or as wife. Although woman's fecundity, a passive quality, is important to myths because it represents the immanence that contrasts with man's "sky of transcendence," this is woman's only function. De Beauvoir concludes, "Man seeks in woman the Other as nature and as his fellow being" (1972: 175).

De Beauvoir's account of immanence and transcendence, however, is not as simple as these passages seem to indicate. In addition to claiming that woman is, in contemporary parlance, the disprivileged element of the dichotomy between immanence and transcendence she also wants to claim that woman is necessary to man the subject and his movement toward transcendence. She argues for a kind of dialectical relationship between Self and Other in a number of contexts. First, she claims, woman is cast as evil, man as good, "and yet Evil is necessary to Good, matter to idea and darkness to light" (1972: 112). Second, she asserts that man is unable to fulfill himself in solitude; he needs woman to mediate between himself and nature (1972: 172). Woman condemns man to finitude, but she also enables him to exceed his own limits (1972: 180). "Eve is given to Adam so that through her he may accomplish his transcendence, and she draws him into the night of immanence" (1972: 196). This relationship between men and women, de Beauvoir argues, can be explained by the basic ambiguity in the concept of the Other. Of woman she says:

> And her ambiguity is just that of the concept of the Other: it is that of the human situation in so far as it is defined in its relation with the Other . . . the Other is Evil; but being necessary to the Good it turns into the Good; through it I attain to the Whole, but it also separates me therefrom; it is the gateway to the infinite and the measure of my finite nature. (1972: 175)

In these passages de Beauvoir complicates her original presentation of woman as the inevitable Other, the negative side of man the subject. Here woman retains her status as the Other, but she has now become a necessary element of man's achievement of transcendence. But there is a final step in de Beauvoir's discussion of woman's status, a step that involves her in a contradiction. Woman, she claims, may not always have to accept her status as "Other." At the outset of her analysis she claims that the task of woman is to reject flights from reality and seek self-fulfillment in transcendence (1972: 63). The implications of this statement are clear: de Beauvoir is arguing that women can only achieve fulfillment as human beings by following in the footsteps of men, that is, by seeking transcendence from nature. In the second part of the book she makes it clear that the transcendence that woman must seek cannot be found in the traditional female activities of sexual love and pregnancy. On the contrary, she asserts that "If the flesh is purely passive and inert it cannot embody transcendence" and, consequently, that the mother's sense of transcendence is an illusion (1972: 513). In this discussion of how women are "made" in our society she emphasizes that women must transcend their otherness in order to become fully human. Her discussion of myths summarizes both this hope and its chances for fulfillment:

> Perhaps the myth of woman will some day be extinguished; the more women assert themselves as human beings, the more the marvelous quality of the Other will die out in them. But today it still exists in the heart of every man. (1972: 174)

This final step in de Beauvoir's discussion of the status of women is highly problematic. The source of her problem is that there is a contradiction between the first and the second parts of her book. In the first part she defines woman the other as primordial and necessary. She is an epistemological and moral necessity if man is to achieve his transcendence. In the second part of the book, however, she takes an entirely different tack. In her analysis of how woman is made, woman becomes a socially constituted being that can, by implication, be constituted differently if different social practices were instituted. Her claim at the end of her analysis that women can transcend her status as Other thus contradicts the epistemology of the first part of the book that asserts that self and Other are epistemologically necessary categories. Another way of putting this point is that de Beauvoir the philosopher comes into conflict with de Beauvoir the sociologist to create two different definitions of woman. In an insightful analysis of *The Second Sex* Sonia Kruks (1988) suggests that this contradiction stems from the fact that de Beauvoir is departing from Sartre's autonomous subject and developing a new concept of the subject that is both constituted and constituting. In *The Second Sex*, however, she does not repudiate the autonomous subject and, hence, her "new subject" contradicts elements of the Sartrian subject that she retains.

One way out of the dilemma that de Beauvoir has created is to argue that some group other than women can become this epistemologically necessary "Other." This solution will not work for two reasons. First, it would result in condemning another disprivileged group to the inferior role now occupied by women. As an existentialist – humanist, de Beauvoir could not be satisfied with this conclusion. Second, although she does not explicitly state it, de Beauvoir implies that the primordial character of the Self – Other distinction is reflected in the equally primordial character of the male – female distinction. If this is the case then another group could not fill the role of Other because any such group would lack the fundamentally oppositional role that women occupy in relationship to men.[3]

This contradiction in de Beauvoir's work is an indication of the fundamental flaw that mars her analysis. Although her examination of the role of subject and object in gender relations is pathbreaking it is in the end insufficient because it remains rooted in an Enlightenment epistemology that casts women in an inferior role (Hartsock 1983a: 286; Young 1985: 173). That de Beauvoir subscribes to a Cartesian concept of the subject is evident from her analysis in *The Second Sex*. She articulates her views on the subject more explicitly, however, in *The Ethics of Ambiguity* (1948). She states:

> It is rather well known that the fact of being a subject is a universal fact and that the Cartesian *cogito* expresses the most individual experience and the most objective truth. (1948: 17)

She asserts, furthermore, that it is the subject, through the exercise of his will, that constitutes social reality. For her, the subject is autonomous, separate and, most significantly, alone responsible for his actions and even his existence:

> only the subject can justify his own existence; no external subject, no object, can bring him salvation from the outside. He cannot be regarded as nothing because the consciousness of all things is within him. (1948: 106)

De Beauvoir's adherence to this unreconstructed Cartesian subject informs her particular variant of Enlightenment thought, existential humanism. It also exemplifies the errors of that epistemology in two fundamental ways. First, like the Enlightenment thinkers, she sees knowledge in the individualistic terms of the opposition of subject and object. At the root of her assertion that Self and Other are primordial categories is her belief that knowledge can only be acquired through the opposition of these two elements. Second, her acceptance of the Enlightenment dualism between subject and object means that she perpetuates the superiority of what the Enlightenment has defined as "masculine" values. She makes this very clear when she argues that woman's task is to achieve the transcendence that has been the sole province of men. What this comes to is that if women want to be fully human they must become men. It is significant that de Beauvoir's argument here parallels that of Mill on rationality. Both she and Mill accept the masculine definition of the privileged side of the dichotomy that they are examining and attempt to fit women into that definition. De Beauvoir would defend this move by claiming that the subject is human, rather than male. The problem with this assertion is that the qualities she associates with the subject are those that, since the Enlightenment, have been defined as masculine: autonomy, independence and rationality (Nye, 1986: 112). It also follows that she devalues what the Enlightenment has defined as specifically "feminine" traits and feminine activities by placing them in the realm of passivity and refusing to label them activities at all. The transcendence she calls for is a transcendence of the feminine realm of passivity (Lloyd, 1984: 102–4). De Beauvoir's analysis, like that of Mill, indicates with striking clarity the impossibility of constructing a viable feminist theory without explicitly challenging the Enlightenment's fundamental dichotomies. The existentialist understanding of the subject that she adopts, although it departs in some ways from the Enlightenment concept, still retains the crucial dichotomy that relegates women and the qualities that have been labelled feminine to an inferior role.

Despite its flaws, de Beauvoir's analysis of the subject/object dualism is significant as the first comprehensive statement of the problem for feminist theory. Her analysis has had far-reaching influence and it structures the subsequent debates about women and subjectivity. Contemporary feminist critiques of the subject/object dualism fall into one of two general categories. The writers in the first category follow de Beauvoir's lead in leaving the dichotomy intact and attempting to turn women into subjects along with men. Although the feminists in this group concede along with the more radical critics that Enlightenment epistemology in general and humanism in particular are thoroughly sexist, they attempt to reform rather than reconceptualize this epistemology. A good example of the attitude that dominates these critiques is Margrit Eichler's remark that feminism is a form of humanism, but a sexist humanism is no humanism at all (1980: 144). Eichler, like de Beauvoir, has no quarrel with the epistemology of humanism *per se*. On the contrary, she regards humanism as embodying ideals that both men and women should strive to achieve. Although she believes that humanism must be purged of its sexism, she maintains that the ideals of humanism can nevertheless be preserved. Eichler's position is not unique. Following the discovery of the sexist basis of humanism the first inclination of feminists has been to attempt to redefine humanism. Rather than abandoning the tradition these feminists attempt to create a non-sexist humanism in the same way that de Beauvoir tried to create a non-sexist existentialism.

In *The Second Sex* de Beauvoir moves from the analysis of woman as object to the assertion that women must be admitted into the realm of the subject. She wants women, along with men, to be subjects and thereby to partake of the transcendence that has been the province only of men. The feminists in this first category follow de Beauvoir's lead. Barbara Sichtermann, a prominent German feminist, articulates this attitude very clearly when she argues that women must have confidence in themselves as subjects, particularly in the realm of sexual relations; they must be able to see men as desirable objects. She argues

> As a sex we have become weak at forming objects but that is the legacy of history. It will not be much longer: we will bring about a new form of objectivization, by creating a new order of things. (1986: 72)

The "new order of things" that these feminists are calling for, however, is not new at all. Rather, it is a variant of the old order in which to be a full human being is to be a subject in the Cartesian sense. Monique Wittig articulates this position in her argument that, ontologically, anyone who speaks must speak as a full subject. Gender, she claims, works to annul this ontological fact. It attempts to strip women of "the most precious thing for a human being – subjectivity" (1986: 66). Her conclusion is that gender must be destroyed in order to allow women full subjectivity.

The second category of critiques is much less monolithic. The feminists in this category agree on a number of points: beginning with the ascendency of the Cartesian subject women have been systematically excluded from the realm of subjectivity; this exclusion cannot be remedied by converting women into Cartesian subjects, but, rather, this definition of the subject must be rejected. The writers in this category thus turn to the task of radically reconceptualizing the Cartesian subject. The attempts to reconceptualize the subject, however, vary widely. Kruks (1988) argues that de Beauvoir herself is the pioneer in this endeavor because she attempts to articulate a subject that occupies a middle ground between the constituting Cartesian subject and the constituted postmodern subject. A number of American feminists have followed her lead in this effort. They have argued that feminism must radically reconstitute the subject, and, specifically, that we must produce a subject that empowers women to act as agents yet does not embody the masculinist qualities of autonomy, separation and abstraction. A number of French feminists have also attempted to reconceptualize the subject, but their reconceptualization is much more radical. Kristeva, in particular, rejects the constituting Cartesian subject and replaces him with a constituted subject that owes much to the postmodern position on the subject.

One of the themes that unites the writers who engage in the critique of the Cartesian subject is cataloging the effect of the concept on the status of women. Silverman, for example, argues that the double application of the concept 'man,' both gendered and neutral, has permitted the phallocentricity of our philosophical heritage to go unquestioned (1983: 131). Iris Young also emphasizes the inherent phallocentricity of the subject. In an insightful article that presents a kind of intellectual history of contemporary feminism she asserts that we are moving from a "humanist feminism" to a "gynocentric feminism." Her point is that we must question the epistemology of humanism and, particularly, its reliance on the subject. The link between humanism and phallocratic thought stems from the assertion that humanism is a variant of Enlightenment epistemology that intensifies the Enlightenment focus on the (male) subject. What Young defines as "humanist feminism" simply dreams the dreams of men. It has no option but to transform women into men in order to admit them into the realm of the subject. What she defines as "gynocentric feminism," however, seeks to transform the epistemology that created the phallocentricity (1985: 173–4).

Feminist critiques of the Cartesian subject, however, diverge sharply once they move beyond this basic analysis. Among American feminists in particular the debate has revolved around the issues of the modernist/postmodernist dispute. A strong tendency among feminist theorists who challenge the subject is the attempt to reconstitute the subject along anti-Enlightenment lines while at the same time repudiating the postmodern alternative of decentering the subject; they want to carve out a space between the Cartesian subject and the postmodernist "death of man." Braidotti expresses this position most clearly in her statement that one cannot deconstruct a subjectivity that one never had: "In order to announce the death of the subject one must first have gained the right to speak as one" (1987: 237). Flax (1987b) echoes this sentiment in her claim that the postmodern critiques of subjectivity are incomplete and simplistic. Arguing that the postmodern option of foreswearing subjectivity is a poor one for women, she asserts that we must develop a sense of our "core self." She concludes that we should not abandon subjectivity just as we are beginning to define ourselves as agents.[4]

The issue of agency and its relationship to the postmodern critique of the subject has become an important topic in these discussions. Several feminist critiques of the subject focus on the question of agency and argue that feminism must reject the postmodern critique of the subject because it obviates the possibility of agency. De Lauretis is one of the first feminists to attempt to retain agency by grafting elements of the Cartesian constituting subject onto a constituted subject. She argues that although individuals are constructed by what she calls "codes" and social formations, they are able to rework these influences in their own particular ways and thus avoid complete determination by them. It is her position that each individual retains the capacity to constitute a particular subjective construction from the various ideological formations to which she is subject (1984: 14). De Lauretis wants to join the notion of an inner self, the basis of the Cartesian concept, with the notion of external determination, the constituted subject. She argues that the subject is formed through the interaction and intersection of these inner and outer worlds (1984: 182). Subjectivity, she claims, is an on-going construction, not a fixed entity:

> it is produced not by external ideas, values, or material causes, but by one's personal, subjective engagement in the practices, discourses and institutions that lend significance (value, meaning, affect) to the events of the world. (1984: 159)

Alcoff (1988) follows de Lauretis' lead by attacking the postmodern approach to the subject as nominalistic and claiming that it presents woman as over-determined, as purely a social construct. Alcoff also rejects what she calls "cultural feminists" who attempt to define the essential woman. Like the other feminists in this group, Alcoff tries to find an in-between position. To do so she focuses on the concept of agency. What we need to develop, she asserts, is a concept of a subject who has agency yet is part of a discursive practice, a gendered subjectively related to concrete habits, practices and discourses (1988: 425–31). Like de Lauretis she wants to retain elements of the Cartesian subject, agency and constitution, while acknowledging the determining role of social forces. Smith (1988) develops a similar concept with his notion of the "discerned" subject. Like Alcoff and de Lauretis he rejects the postmodern conception of the subject because it disallows agency and the possibility of resistance. He turns to contemporary feminism for a solution to the problem of how to unite the socially constructed subject with agency. Feminists, he claims, have fused the socially constructed subject and political agency in contemporary discourse (1988: 134). Using the term "individual" to describe his new concept, Smith argues that it is an entity that is both active and passive, one that is both formed by historical discourses and practices and a true agent that can oppose those determining forces.

The arguments of Alcoff and Smith are a variant of what is now a familiar argument: the constituted postmodern subject entails political inaction and, hence, nihilism. Even if this argument is wrong-headed, there is another problem with these accounts that is rooted in epistemology rather than politics. The attempt on the part of these writers to fuse elements of the Cartesian subject to the constituted subject results in an unworkable epistemological eclecticism. The feminists who challenge the Cartesian subject claim that they want radically to reconstitute it because it is inherently, not just superficially, phallocratic. Yet in their attempt to do so they retain some of the principle elements of the Cartesian subject: a partially autonomous constituting role and agency. De Lauretis wants to preserve the notion of a "personal subjective constitution" (1984: 14); Alcoff and Smith want to preserve agency. But the subject who has agency, who constitutes a personal subjectivity, is precisely the autonomous, abstract, individualized subject that is the basis of the Cartesian subject itself. It is impossible to retain the concepts of an "inner world" and autonomous agency and reject the other qualities to which these concepts are so intimately tied. Like the critics of Foucault's concept of subjectivity, these theorists assume a dichotomy between the constituting Cartesian subject and the constituted, wholly determined subject. In order to preserve the "good" qualities of the Cartesian subject they want to graft those qualities onto its opposite, the constituted subject. Foucault, in contrast, conceptualizes a subject that displaces the dichotomy that relegates the constituted subject to passivity. His conception avoids the eclecticism of these theorists' approach by describing a subject that is capable of resistance and political action without reference to elements of a Cartesian subjectivity.

There are a few feminists who have identified the problems involved in the effort to reconceptualize the Cartesian subject and argue that this tactic will not work. Several of the arguments they employ are rooted in the work of Foucault. Foucault argued that we must reject the philosophy of the subject because subjectivity entails subjectivation. A number of feminists have applied this argument specifically to the case of women, arguing that the philosophy of the subject has been one of the chief instruments of women's oppression. Thus Gallop asks whether one of the goals of women's studies should not be to "call into question the oppressive effects of an epistemology based on the principle of a clear and unambiguous distinction of subject and object of knowledge" (1985: 15–16). She argues that we should examine women as knowers apart from that epistemology. Similarly, Lydon argues that we should resist the temptation to define women as subjects. Also refering to Foucault, she notes the ambiguity of the concept of the subject: it entails empowerment, but also being subjected *to* (1988: 140). Another argument employed by these critics focuses on the possibility of resistance apart from a philosophy of the subject. The radical, even revolutionary, implications of decentering the subject have been a central concern of the French feminists' approach to discussions of the subject. Before turning to that discussion, however, it is significant to note that a writer who has been closely identified with critical theory has also commented on the philosophy of the subject and, specifically, on the possibilities of political action if that philosophy is abandoned. In an article criticizing Habermas' continued adherence to the philosophy of the subject Seyla Benhabib notes: "Beyond the philosophy of the subject lies a politics of empowerment that extends both rights and entitlements while creating friendship and solidarity" (1986a: 352). The criticisms of these writers, however, are relatively muted. None have resulted in an attempt fully to explore the postmodern subject in feminist theory.

The exploration of what lies beyond a philosophy of the subject has been one of the major concerns of the work of a number of French feminists in the last several decades. It is difficult to classify this work both because it is diverse and also because its intent is to redefine the category of the subject more radically than the reconstitution proposed by the theorists discussed above. Luce Irigaray's *Speculum of the Other Woman* is one of the most important attempts to accomplish this redefinition. One of the central theses of this work is that any epistemology that is rooted in the subject is inherently phallocratic. Irigaray makes it clear that her intent is to move beyond de Beauvoir's analysis of the woman as other. Although she begins with de Beauvoir's analysis of woman, she explicitly condemns the epistemology that informs de Beauvoir's analysis: the humanistic heritage that is rooted in the subject.

> We can assume that any theory of the subject has always been appropriated by the "masculine." When she submits to (such a) theory, woman fails to realize that she is renouncing the specificity of her own relationship to the imaginary. (1985a: 133)

Although this passage is not specifically directed at de Beauvoir, it represents an attack on the position she takes in *The Second Sex*. Irigaray argues that we cannot simply appropriate the myths of men because in doing so we fail to transform the phallocratic epistemology that oppresses us. This perspective is consistent with a point that has frequently been made by feminist literary critics. Irigaray argues that women writers cannot break through the theory of the subject that defines male language. Her analysis of woman's status as passive object also provides an explanation for why women have not been a presence in history. Since women cannot be subjects, they cannot be the active, autonomous agents that, men have claimed, make history. Woman does not take an active part in history, she claims, because she is "never anything but the still undifferentiated opaqueness of sensible matter, the store (of) substance for the sublation of self, or being as what is, or what is (or was), here and now" (1985a: 224).

Although Irigaray's position, as she would herself admit, is indebted to de Beauvoir's analysis, it transcends that analysis in significant ways. De Beauvoir recognized the inferior status that women were forced to assume as man's Other, but she was unwilling to reject the Enlightenment epistemology of subjects and objects that relegates women to this position. Irigaray moves beyond de Beauvoir's analysis, first, by asserting that all theories of the subject are phallocratic and that in these theories women are denied all but a "quasi-subjectivity." Second, she challenges de Beauvoir's position by arguing that the subject/object dualism itself must be rejected. Her reason is that all dichotomies always entail hierarchies:

> For Being's domination requires that whatever has been defined – *within the domain of sameness* – as "more" (true, right, clear, reasonable, intelligible, paternal, masculine . . .) should progressively win out over *its* "other," its "different" – its differing – and when it comes right down to it, over its negative, its "less" (fantastic, harmful, obscure, "mad," sensible, maternal, feminine . . .). (1985a: 275)

Following the postmodern lead Irigaray is here rejecting the Enlightenment dualism, subject/object, in favor of an epistemology that is pluralistic rather than hierarchical. De Beauvoir saw that the subject/object dualism defined woman as inferior. Irigaray goes beyond this to see that all dichotomies are both hierarchical and gendered and on these grounds rejects the epistemology that produces them.

What Irigaray is trying to accomplish in her work with regard to the subject is an aspect of her attempt to define a feminine writing. For her feminine writing disrupts the phallocratic order by rejecting its unitary character, its emphasis on oneness. This is an aim that extends to the question of the subject as well: "what a feminine syntax might be is not simple or easy to state, because in that 'syntax' there would no longer be either subject or object, 'oneness' would no longer be privileged . . ."(1985b: 134). Irigaray is attempting not to reverse phallocratic discourse, but to open it up, to get inside the figures of discourse (1985b: 75). Central to this effort is the attempt to see woman as neither subject nor object. Having defined woman as a being that defies dichotomies (*This Sex Which Is Not One*), she must reject one of the principal dichotomies by which woman has been defined: subject/object.

Cixous' discussion of the creation of a feminine writing is also concerned with the question of the subject. She defines *The Newly Born Woman* as the "birth of the feminine subject" (Cixous and Clement, 1986: 166). Like Irigaray, however, Cixous rejects the masculinist definition of the subject that is unitary and rooted in a hierarchical dichotomy. For Cixous woman's subjectivity is self-constituting, it is a "subjectivity that splits apart without regret . . . without the ceaseless summary of the authority called Ego." Central to Cixous' task of defining a feminine writing, a "feminine Imaginary," is her conviction that it cannot include a transcendental subject (Cixous and Clement, 1986: 90; Spivak 1981: 172).

The contemporary French writer who has most extensively explored the constitution of a non-Cartesian subject is Julia Kristeva. Kristeva's approach to the subject is controversial and has generated a great deal of criticism among feminists, but it occupies a central position in the debate over the fate of the subject in contemporary feminism. It represents an attempt to deconstruct and decenter the Cartesian subject, to construct an anti-Cartesian subject which, she claims, transforms phallocentric discourse from within.

The starting point of Kristeva's approach to the subject is the psychoanalytic theory of Lacan. Lacan's theories have been sharply attacked by feminists and, indeed, it is largely because of Kristeva's reliance on Lacan that her own theories have been criticized. Several feminists have argued that Lacan represents the most extreme statement of phallogocentrism. Lacan's central thesis is that the phallus is *the* signifier in our symbolic universe; it is the source of the symbolic itself and hence the root of all meaning in language. But while the phallus provides all possible meaning, woman, in contrast, is always the "Other" in the symbolic universe. She has no meaning in and of herself because the phallus is the source of all meaning. She is, quite literally, a lack, something that is not there:

> There is no such thing as *The* woman, where the definite article stands for the universal. There is no such thing as *The* woman since of her essence – having already risked the term, why think twice about it? of her essence, she is not all. (Lacan et al., 1985: 144)

Given the Lacanian theory of the phallus it is not difficult to see why many feminists define Lacan as the very epitome of the phallogocentrism that they are pitted against. Clement has even suggested the Derrida initially defined the link between the phallus and the Logos as a result of Lacan's work (1983: 188). But to see Lacan as simply a purveyor of phallogocentrism is a superficial reading of his theory. Lacan introduces two themes in his psychoanalytic work that are not only crucial to an understanding of Kristeva's work but are also significant for the development of a feminist theory of the subject. The first of these is his thesis that the subject is not a "given," natural, or instinctual entity but, rather, is constructed through language. Lacan developed his theory of the constructed subject as a product of his revolutionary attack against Freudian psychoanalysis. Lacan argues that Freud erred in locating sexuality in the realm of instinctual drives, that is, in the realm of biology. Against Freud Lacan asserts that sexuality is socially, not biologically constituted and, specifically, that it is constituted linguistically through the symbolic ordering of the phallus (Lacan et al., 1985: 74–85). For Lacan, meaning lies not in biology or instinctual drives, but in the realm of language, the realm of the symbolic. He uses his thesis to attack Freud's concepts of a biologically rooted sexuality and a subject, the Ego, that is a universal of human existence. For Lacan there is no fixed point, no knowing subject (Clement, 1983: 48). Lacan's subject is, instead, a constructed subject; he states that "the phenomenology of the the subject dictates that the subject constitutes himself in the quest for Truth" (1968: 73). The subject is constituted through discourse, and the "Truth" that he seeks is "the name of that ideal movement that discourse introduces into reality" (1968: 63). In advancing the concept of the constructed subject Lacan rejects what is the basic premise of Freudian psychoanalysis: the pre-existent human subject (Mitchell, 1985: 4).

The second aspect of Lacan's work that is significant in this context is his definition of woman. Although Lacan initially defines woman as a lack, a void, other aspects of his analysis of women reveal a less negative side to his theory. Most importantly, he rejects the notion of biologically rooted, fixed essences for men *or* women. Since both sexes are constructed through discourse, neither has a prior essence; both masculinity and feminity are linguistic constructs (Lacan et al., 1985: 106). It follows from this that the phallic signifier is not *essentially* masculine but is simply the linguistic construct that has been associated with the masculine (Gallop, 1985: 134). Lacan's assertion of the constructed rather than essential basis of masculinity and feminity is consistent with one of the central tenets of contemporary feminism: woman is made, not born. It also represents a radical departure from Freudian psychology that imparts to woman an essential sexuality.

Another aspect of Lacan's treatment of women is also relevant. Like de Beauvoir, Lacan identifies woman as the Other. He avoids de Beauvoir's confusion regarding the Other, however, by asserting unambiguously that both the Self and the Other are linguistically constructed rather than essential or primordial categories. In his discussion of the otherness of women, furthermore, Lacan uses a term that has become a controversial topic in French feminist discussions: *jouissance*. For Lacan, *jouissance* is something that woman possesses as a consequence of her role as Other, and, most importantly, it is something that exists outside of the phallic signifier. Lacan admits to being puzzled by *jouissance*, however. Because it lies beyond the phallic signifier it cannot, in the sense of his theory, exist; that is, it can signify nothing. Yet Lacan claims to 'believe' in the *jouissance* of the woman while admitting that he cannot properly explain it (Lacan et al., 1985: 144–53). Lacan's concept of *jouissance*, woman's position outside of the phallic signifier, is appropriated by Kristeva and a number of French feminists. One of Kristeva's central theses is that it is woman's position as Other and, specifically, her *jouissance*, that contains a radical potential. Because woman does not exist inside the symbolic she possesses the capacity to disrupt and transform the symbolic. Kristeva argues that it is the *jouissance* of woman that allows them to reorder and reconstruct themselves as subjects.

It is Lacan's linguistically constructed subject that forms the basis for Kristeva's discussion of the subject and the feminine. The fundamental presupposition of her analysis is a radically anti-Cartesian definition of the subject as a process rather than a pre-existent entity. She states:

> The subject never *is*. The *subject* is only the *signifying process* and he appears only as a *signifying practice*, that is, only when he is absent *within the position* out of which social, historical and signifying activity unfolds. There is no science of the subject. Any thought mastering the subject is mystical: all that exists is the field of practice where, through his expenditure, the subject can be anticipated in an always anterior future. (1984: 215)

Kristeva focuses her attention on explicating the different kinds of subjects that have been constituted by different forms of discourse. In *In the Beginning Was Love* (1987) she analyzes the psychoanalytic subject, showing that the ''knowing subject'' of psychoanalysis is a product of Freud's attempt to make a science out of psychoanalysis. In *Revolution in Poetic Language* she analyzes the Cartesian subject itself from this perspective, arguing that the constitution of this particular subject relies on a metalanguage that makes positivistic science and philosophy possible (1984: 94–5). In the course of her discussion she also examines the poetic subject and the subject of the Marxist dialectic. Her point is to contrast the revolutionary character of poetic language that seeks to transform language with the ''new subject'' of dialectical materialism that seeks to transform the real world (1984: 178). Her point in discussing these different subjects is that each is revolutionary in its own sense because each transforms the signifying process of the subject that preceded it.

What Kristeva accomplishes in these discussions of the subject is the creation of a radically different conception. The Cartesian subject is a master who discovers truth through abstract rationality. Kristeva explicitly attacks the conception of the subject as a master, arguing that this conception is a product of a particular culture, a particular linguistic constellation, and that the ''posture of this mastery'' cannot be maintained (1980b: 165). For Kristeva subjects are products of discourse, they do not exist in a pre-given sense, and they are not producers, but produced. There is a close parallel between Kristeva's discussion and that of Foucault. Both deny the knowing, pre-existent Cartesian subject, but, rather than ignoring subjects, both are intensely interested in how subjects are constituted. Kristeva's exploration of the different kinds of subjects and Foucault's examination of the discourses that create madness and sexuality both constitute geneologies of the subject in the discourse of the west.

Despite her criticism of the subject, however, Kristeva rejects the notion that we should abandon the concept of the subject. She writes: "Far from being an 'epistemological perversion,' a definite subject is present as soon as there is consciousness of signification" (1980a: 124); and "Let us assume that it is legitimate to speak of a 'subject' as long as language creates the identity of a speaking agency and ascribes that agency an interlocutor and referent" (1987: 8). The question arises, however, as to the nature of the "subject" that Kristeva is retaining. It bears no resemblance to the Cartesian subject; it is not a knower, a producer, but, rather, is a construct of discourse. It has nothing in common with the subject that is the necessary foundation of the metalanguage of science and philosophy. This sense of the subject is clearly expressed in the following passage:

> We are no doubt permanent subjects of a language that holds us in its power. But we are subjects *in process*, ceaselessly losing our identity, destabilized by fluctuations in our relations with the other, to whom we nevertheless remain bound in a kind of homeostasis. (1987: 9)

Despite Kristeva's retention of the subject, then, it is possible to argue that her position comes to much the same thing as Foucault's deconstruction and decentering of the Cartesian subject. Both see the subject as a linguistic construct, both reject the knowing Cartesian subject that occupies an Archimedean point outside discourse, and both are concerned to explore the different ways in which subjects are constituted in the discourses that have dominated the western intellectual heritage.

From this perspective Kristeva's "subject" is not a reconstitution or reconceptualization of the Cartesian subject but is a radical departure from the subject as it has been known in the tradition of phallogocentrism – it is a different entity entirely. But the constituted subject that Kristeva describes, like that of Foucault, is not a passive dupe of social forces. Rather, she claims that this subject possesses revolutionary potential. She argues that each new subject that is constituted transforms and revolutionizes the subject that precedes it; it contains the potential of deconstructing the subject that it challenges. Kristeva discusses this revolutionary potential most extensively in her analysis of the poetic subject in *Revolution in Poetic Language*. Avant-garde writing since the end of the nineteenth century, she claims, possesses the potential of transforming the signifying process of unifying conceptual thought that previously constituted the subject (1984: 185). It creates the possibility of what she calls in another context "traversal" (1980b: 165). Poetry is able to accomplish this by penetrating the symbolic order, thus creating a revolution not only in the linguistic sphere, but, she emphasizes, in the social sphere as well (1984: 83).

Kristeva's description of how this "traversal" takes place brings her to an analysis of the feminine in language. The presupposition of Kristeva's discussion of the feminine is a corollary to that which informs her discussion of the subject. She rejects the notion of an essentially feminine and argues instead that women and the feminine, like the subject, are linguistic constructs. She writes:

> In other words, if the feminine *exists* it only exists in the order of significance or signifying process and it is only in relation to meaning and signification, positioned as their excessive or transgressive other that it *exists*, *speaks*, *thinks* (itself) and *writes* (itself) for both sexes. (Kristeva in Moi, 1986: 11)

She moves from this position to assert that the body itself is not an essential unity, a pre-existent given. Rather, the body, like the subject, is in process, it has no unity without a signifying process to articulate it (1984: 101)

The linguistically constructed concept of the feminine is the focus of some of Kristeva's most powerful commentaries on the subject and the revolutionary potential of the new subject she is discussing. In *Revolution in Poetic Language* Kristeva argues that we need a new theory of the subject that can encompass elements that the Cartesian theory of the subject ignores (1984: 27). The basis of her theory of the subject is the division between the symbolic and the semiotic. The signifying process that constitutes the subject, she asserts, is always constituted by the dialectical relationship between the symbolic and the semiotic. She argues that the different ways in which this dialectic is played out will result in a different form of discourse and, hence, a different constitution of the subject. Thus although the subject is always both semiotic and symbolic, these elements will combine in different ways in discourse to constitute different subjects (1984: 24). The major thesis advanced in the book is that the signifying practice of modern literature constitutes a new subject by changing the dialectic between the symbolic and the semiotic, resulting in an explosion of the subject and its ideological limits (1984: 15).

Central to this thesis is Kristeva's definition of the difference between the semiotic and the symbolic. The semiotic is concerned with specifying the signifying practices such as art, poetry and myth that are irreducible to the language object. To characterize the semiotic she refers to the *chora* in Plato's *Timaeus* that denotes mobile and provisional articulation. The *chora* can never be definitively posited, it has no axiomatic form, no unity or identity; Plato refers to it as nourishing and maternal (1984: 21–6). Kristeva uses this definition of the semiotic to argue for a new understanding of how the subject is constituted. The semiotic, she claims, precedes the positing of the subject and the distinction between subject and object. The Cartesian subject ignores the semiotic element because it defines the subject as a fixed entity, the transcendental ego. Kristeva argues against this that we should see the subject as in process (1984: 27–40). The symbolic enters this picture in what Kristeva defines as the ''thetic'' phase, the deepest structure possible in enunciation. In the thetic phase subject is separated from object in the proposition and, as a result, the symbolic emerges. The separation from the maternal *chora* is accomplished first through language learning, but ultimately through the discovery of castration. It is the connection between castration and the symbolic, she argues, that entails that the phallic function is *the* symbolic function (1984: 42–7).

In the remainder of her book Kristeva is concerned with specifying how the semiotic and the symbolic interact in modern poetry. Her thesis is that art necessitates the re-investing of the maternal *chora* so that it transgresses the symbolic order (1984: 65). The thetic phase that establishes the symbolic attempts to deny the semiotic; it establishes its own "truth" that excludes the semiotic. Poetic language challenges this truth. By revealing the pretentions of the thetic, it "constantly tears it up" (1984: 62). Kristeva is careful to qualify these assertions with the claim that the signifying process always involves the dialectical interplay of semiotic and symbolic. The semiotic does not attempt to deny the thetic, but, rather, attempts to re-instate the semiotic function that the thetic ignores. Originally, she claims, the semiotic was considered a precondition of the symbolic. The fact that the role of the semiotic is denied by the Cartesian concept of the subject entails that today the semiotic functions within the symbolic as a transgression (1984: 68). It is through this transgression, Kristeva argues, that a new disposition of the subject can be articulated (1984: 51).

The dichotomy between the semiotic and the symbolic is central to an understanding of Kristeva's view of the subject. The opposition between these forces is the foundation of the other oppositions that structure the discourses of modernity: the semiotic is the Freudian unconscious, the realm of drives and instincts, the symbolic the realm of the super ego (1987: 5); the semiotic is nature, the symbolic culture; the semiotic is the realm of woman's *jouissance*, a realm that escapes day-to-day temporality, the symbolic is the realm of masculine time, patriarchal ordering (1986a). As Kristeva understands the workings of this dichotomy, art, and particularly poetry, becomes the scene of the confrontation between semiotic *jouissance* and the thetic (1984: 79). Perhaps her most unique discussion of this dichotomy is that presented in *The Power of Horror* (1982). In this work she posits an association between the abject and the feminine. *Jouissance* is counterposed to the realm of the symbolic, the realm that strives to suppress the powers of horror.

One aspect of Kristeva's theory of the relationship between the semiotic and the symbolic is particularly relevant to a feminist reading of her work: the revolutionary potential she subscribes to the role of the semiotic. In *Revolution* she identifies the working of the semiotic as a "transgression." The artist who employs the semiotic represents an asocial drive; the semiotic *chora* is the other side of the social frontier. Kristeva's purpose here is to argue that the debate between poetic language and the thetic takes place on the social and ideological sphere as well as the linguistic (1984: 61–78). Kristeva identifies a close connection between the revolution in language that she is describing and political revolution:

> We shall therefore say that the explosions set off by practice-process within the social field and the strictly linguistic field are logically (if not

chronologically) contemporaneous, and respond to the same principle of unstoppable break-through; they differ only in their field of application. (1984: 104)

If the semiotic provides a revolutionary potential in politics as well as in language, then it follows that the feminine is the locus of this revolutionary potential. If, as she has asserted, the semiotic is identified with the feminine, then it is women themselves who are the revolutionaries who explode the Cartesian subject and create the possibility of social and linguistic revolution:[5]

> The avant-garde has always had ties to the underground. Only today, it is a woman who makes this connection. This is important because in social, sexual, and symbolic experiences, being a woman has always provided a means to another and to becoming something else: a subject-in-the-making, a subject on trial . . . The moment of rupture and negativity which under-lies novelty we call ''feminine.'' No ''I'' is there to assume this ''feminin-ity'' but it is no less operative, rejecting all that is finite and assuring in (*sexual*) *pleasure* the life of the concept. ''I,'' subject of a conceptual quest, is also a subject of differentiation – of sexual contradictions. (1980b: 167)

Kristeva is very clear about how women, the semiotic, are to go about fomenting this revolution. Since the symbolic order is masculine, patriarchal, women cannot identify with this order. Nor should they try to reverse that order or set up an order of their own. Rather, their function is to subvert the order from within.

Kristeva's theory of the subject is bold, innovative and exciting. Many commentators have noted that she develops a position located between the outright rejection of the subject by postmodern philosophers and the attempt by some feminists to reconstitute the humanist subject (Feral, 1978: 8; Moi, 1986: 13; Jardine, 1985: 228; Nye, 1987: 673). Kristeva asserts that the solution to the Death of Man that the postmoderns have announced is neither resurrection nor renaissance. The strategy she espouses is, rather, that

> through the efforts of thought in language or precisely through the excesses of the languages whose very multiplicity is the only sign of life, one can attempt to bring about multiple sublations of the unnameable, the unrepresentable, the void. This is the real cutting edge of dissidence. (1986b: 300)

The emphasis in this passage should be on the word ''in.'' What Kristeva is trying to do is not to define a female essence, or to create a feminine language opposed to masculine language. Rather, she is trying to define the feminine *in* language and its potential for creating a new subject, a subject in process (Spivak, 1981: 171).

The reconstitution of the subject proposed by Kristeva constitutes a radical departure from the Cartesian subject because she challenges its constituting role. She replaces the constituting Cartesian subject with a subject that is constituted by discourse, but one that is by no means passive. Opposed to the fixed entity that is Descartes' knowing subject, she presents a subject in process, one that is constituted differently by different forms of discourse. The affinity between her position and that of Foucault that was posited above should now be evident. Like Foucault, Kristeva rejects the dichotomy between the constituting Cartesian subject and the passive constituted subject. Instead she explodes these categories by describing a subject that is both constituted and revolutionary. The difference between her reconstitution of the subject and that of the American feminists discussed above should also be clear. The reconstituted subject of Kristeva's theory is much more radical than that posited by the American feminists. These theorists wanted to fuse elements of the Cartesian subject onto that of the constituted subject in order to overcome its passivity. As a result their reconstitution fails because it does not break through the epistemology of the Cartesian subject. Kristeva's reconstitution, because it rejects the fundamental epistemological basis of the Cartesian subject, is more successful.

This is not to say, however, that there are no problems with Kristeva's formulation. One of the most serious is that there are essentialistic overtones to her position. Following Lacan, she asserts that the phallic or symbolic is not inherently masculine nor the semiotic inherently feminine but that they have been gendered by the discourses that created them. But in her own discourse Kristeva not only perpetuates but relies on this dichotomy. Unlike Derrida and Foucault she makes no attempt to move beyond the bipolar logic that she claims to be "transgressing." An equally serious problem is her assumption that although the subject is constituted differently in different discourses, there is a universal foundation that informs the constitution of the subject in all discourses: the dialectic between the semiotic and the symbolic. Moi claims that Kristeva needs some basic identity for the subject because she is a practicing psychoanalyst and cannot completely abandon the notion of an identity and a truth for the subject (1986: 17).

These two elements of Kristeva's approach, her reliance on the polarity of the semiotic and the symbolic and her assertion of a universal foundation for the constitution of the subject, represent her inability to break free from the Cartesian epistemology that she claims to be revolutionizing. Although she is willing to reject the centerpiece of Cartesian epistemology, the constituting subject, she is not willing to complete her radical deconstruction by attacking the polarity of masculine/feminine that is also central to that epistemology. Nor is she willing to argue, as does Foucault, that subjects are entirely constituted by discourses. Rather, she wants to retain at least a vestige of a foundation. Despite these problems, however, Kristeva has made a significant contribution to the theory of the subject. She has so radically attacked the basis of the Cartesian subject that it is difficult to label the entity that she discusses a "subject" at all. The all-knowing, constituting Cartesian subject stripped of his constituting ability and pulled down from his Archimedean point is no longer the "subject" of western philosophy. The "subject" that Kristeva presents, despite its residual Cartesianism, bears more resemblance to the Foucaultian entity than that of Descartes. Kristeva's approach, furthermore, offers another advantage: her stress on the revolutionary character of the feminine within language. Like Foucault and Derrida she rejects the attempt to reverse the polarity of phallogocentrism by privileging the feminine over the masculine. She also refuses to argue for the creation of an oppositional, feminine language. Instead she claims that the semiotic transgresses the symbolic from within by exploding the discourse that creates patriarchal order. Foucault claims that the decentering of the subject will create a new linguistic and, hence, political order. Kristeva's claim about the semiotic is very similar. Both emphasize that the displacing of the present patriarchal order of language will have both theoretical and practical political results.

The works of Irigaray, Cixous and Kristeva do not present a monolithic position on the question of the subject. There are, however, a number of commonalities among them that are significant for feminist theory. All challenge the hegemony of the Cartesian subject. All court the danger of essentialism, a tendency that many of their critics have noted (Moi, 1985b: 110; Wenzel, 1981: 284; Plaza, 1978; Sayers, 1986: 42). Most importantly, each defines the philosophy of the subject as fundamental to the definition of women as inferior and attempts to explore what lies beyond the Cartesian subject. Although this attempt, particularly in the case of Kristeva, still retains elements of Cartesian epistemology, it nevertheless indicates that, for these writers, the future of feminist theory lies in the rejection of the Cartesian subject.

This overview of the feminist critiques of the subject suggests several conclusions. First, it reveals that the feminist and postmodern critiques converge on several significant points. Central to both critiques is an explicit attack on man the subject. The focus of both the feminist and postmodern critiques of the subject is to expose the privileging of the subject that is at the root of the modern episteme. Second, the analysis reveals that the feminist critique extends and reinforces the postmodern critique of the subject. While postmodernism deconstructs the privileging of the subject in the modern episteme it fails to reveal the gendered character of man the subject. The feminist critique supplies this missing element in the postmodern critique. Feminists argue that man the subject is also the basis of an epistemology that excludes women from the human sciences. Women, who can only be objects, do not fit into the subject-centered discourse of the human sciences. This analysis reveals why the activity of women has not been conceptualized by the human sciences since their inception. But in a broader sense it reveals why women have been excluded from all realms of the modern episteme. Women, who cannot be subjects, cannot acquire knowledge in the subject-oriented epistemology of modernity.

Feminist thought extends postmodern analysis in another direction as well.

Foucault confidently proclaims the "death of man" and the arrival of a new episteme that is not "man-centered". Although Foucault thinks he is declaring the end of generic man in this statement, the feminist critique reveals that he is in actuality proclaiming the end of gendered man. The problem with the subject-centered epistemology of modernity is not just that it is problematic for the human sciences. More importantly it is problematic because it excludes women from the epistemology of modernity. Foucault is concerned that "man" is both subject and object in the modern episteme. Feminists, on the other hand, are concerned that women can only be objects. The conclusion of Foucault's analysis is his advocacy of an epistemology that does not have man as its center. Feminists extend this critique by arguing for an epistemology that is not exclusive of women.

The third conclusion of this analysis is that although the feminist critique is broadly consistent with the epistemological insights of postmodernism, the two critiques diverge on an important point: the reconceptualization of the subject. While the postmoderns call for the displacement of the Cartesian subject, most feminist critics of the subject do not take this radical position. The reconstitution of the subject suggested by Alcoff, Smith and De Lauretis attempts to retain what they consider to be the positive aspects of the Cartesian subject while rejecting its negative aspects. Kristeva's reconstitution of the subject is more radical because it completely replaces the constituting Cartesian subject with a constituted subject. Her position, however, is flawed because it retains a universal foundation for the constitution of subjectivity. Yet both attempts are informed by a position that is central to postmodernism: the bankruptcy of the Cartesian subject. Like the postmoderns, both attempts are efforts to conceptualize a subject that is both constituted and capable of resistance, linguistically constructed yet revolutionary. Like Foucault's subject, both are attempts to displace the active/passive dichotomy that informs the modernist distinction between the constituting and constituted subject.

Many feminists have suggested that at this point in its development feminist thought is not ready to embrace the death of the subject. The argument that women have been denied subjectivity for too long for them to reject it just when women are successfully challenging their inferiority is a compelling one. But the postmodern argument is even more compelling. The subject/object dichotomy that has characterized western thought and social structure defines women as inferior, and unless this dichotomy is displaced that inferiority will persist. A postmodern approach to feminism thus calls for a total rejection of the epistemology that rests on the subject/object dualism. It also calls for an approach that eschews any notion of the essentially feminine or a universal feminine sexuality. Instead of looking for ways to reconceptualize the Cartesian subject, feminists should be looking for ways to talk about the self and resistance to domination without reference to the constituting subject. In a passage from *Power/Knowledge* that is relevant to the feminist critique of the subject Foucault expresses what is involved in this attempt to move beyond the subject:

> One has to dispense with the constituent subject, to get rid of the subject itself, that's to say, to arrive at an analysis which can account for the constitution of the subject within a historical framework . . . genealogy . . . is a form of history which can account for the constitution of knowledges, discourses, domains of objects, etc., without having to make reference to a subject which is either transcendental in relation to the field of events or runs in its empty sameness throughout the course of history. (1980: 117)

III Subjects, Objects, and the Social Sciences

The subject/object dichotomy that excludes women from the realm of the subject has had a profound effect on the status of women in the modern era. Because only subjects can constitute knowledge, the exclusion of women from the realm of the subject has been synonomous with their exclusion from the realm of rationality and, hence, truth. Although this characterization of women has defined their status in all aspects of cultural life it has had a particular impact on women's efforts to engage in intellectual pursuits. Because women are defined as incapable of producing knowledge, they are therefore defined as incapable of engaging in intellectual, and, specifically, scientific activities. This exclusion has had a particular effect on women's participation in the natural sciences, but it has also affected the status of women in the social sciences precisely because it is the task of these disciplines to study human behavior, presumably including that of women.

Foucault claimed that the human sciences do not fit into the modern episteme because in these disciplines human beings are both the subjects and objects of knowledge. In this assessment, however, he was only half right. Men are both subjects and objects of knowledge but women have been only objects. The exclusion of women from the realm of the knower is an issue that many feminist critics of the social sciences have noted (Smith, 1979: 182; 1977: 15; Westkott, 1979: 426). Although the issue of women has become a popular social scientific topic in recent years and discussions of women's role in society, politics, and the economy abound in contemporary social science, a careful look at this literature reveals that the current burst of interest in women has been exclusively in women as *objects* of knowledge. The contemporary researcher who studies women's social or political roles is adhering to the subject/object dichotomy that has informed the social sciences since their inception: the social scientist is the knower (subject), the object of his study is the known (object). Several recent articles by feminist social scientists have noted that the social sciences have failed to effect a methodological or epistemological revolution that would dethrone the present male-centered paradigm (Stacey and Thorne, 1985; Cook and Fonow, 1986; Keohane, 1981). Some of these authors have called for a new methodology for the social sciences, one that displaces the subject/object dichotomy (Acker et al., 1983; Hochschild, 1975).

One of the themes of the feminist critique of the social sciences is that the categories of these disciplines exclude women and, thus, their experiences become invisible (Hooyman and Johnson, 1977; Smith, 1977: 18; Millman and Kanter, 1975). A good example of this critique is Delphy's analysis of social stratification studies. She argues that because these studies classify individuals according to jobs they render the experience of women who do not have "jobs" invisible; women are classified by the jobs of the males with whom they are associated (1984: 28–39). Delphy's observation is just one instance of a larger problem that informs the social scientific treatment of women: because women cannot be subjects they also cannot be actors in the social scene. Women who cannot act cannot create a social life, they cannot constitute knowledge or reality. This exclusion of women from the realm of action is particularly significant because of the pervasive influence of theories of action in defining the scope of the social sciences. In sociology, for example, Parson's model for the social sciences divides the social world in terms of actors making choices and selecting means to achieve rationally derived ends. The barriers between women and this world are three-fold: she cannot be rational, a subject, or an actor. The result is that her experiences are not conceptualized in the categories of social analysis.

The question of why the feminist revolution has not had more of an impact in the social sciences, that is, why, instead of radically restructuring social scientific methodology it has been "ghettoized" is a question that many feminists have raised (Stacey and Thorne, 1985: 308). To be fair, failure to create a revolution in social scientific methodology lies partly with some of the feminist critics themselves. Many feminists, although they perceive the liabilities of the masculinist approach to the social sciences, fail to make a clean break with the epistemology that informs that approach. This failure is particularly apparent in the discussion of "objectivity" in the social sciences. Some feminist critics have noted that what passes for "objectivity" in the social sciences is simply another word for the masculinist viewpoint. MacKinnon labels objectivity the "male epistemological stance" (1982: 23–4), others refer to it as the name we give to male subjectivity (Spender, 1981: 5; 1980: 61; Harding, 1977: 352; Farganis, 1986: 63; Grimshaw, 1986: 95). Although these criticisms are undoubtedly true, they are nevertheless limited as a critique of objectivity. Such criticisms can easily lead to the assertion that we should continue to seek the goal of objectivity simply by adding the female perspective to the inadequate and incomplete male perspective. They imply that what is wrong with the male perspective is simply its partiality but that this partiality can and should be overcome through the addition of the female perspective. This assertion is self-defeating because it merely perpetuates the objectivity/

subjectivity dualism and the presupposition of the autonomous, noninvolved subject on which it rests. Unless feminists can displace the epistemological presupposition of the subject they will continue to search for the chimera of objective knowledge.

The underlying cause for the failure to overcome the masculinist epistemology of subject/object, subjectivity/objectivity, however, lies in the centrality of these dichotomies to the very constitution of the social sciences. The desire for an objective knowledge of the social world rooted in the knowing rational subject is the basis of the epistemology of the social sciences. Although the definition of objectivity in the social sciences has been challenged by Weber and other critics of positivist social science, their critique did nothing to dislodge the epistemology of subject/object, subjectivity/objectivity. Weber and the anti-positivists did not seek to reject the goal of objectivity in the social sciences, they sought only to redefine it for these disciplines. As a result they failed to relieve the inferiority of the social sciences or their anomolous status in the modern episteme.

A feminist perspective informed by postmodernism yields two insights into the issues of this debate that are missing from the discussions of the methodology of the social sciences. First, it reveals why the attempt by some feminists to overcome "male subjectivity" with a feminist perspective that will produce "true objectivity" is futile. The attempt to redefine or even to perfect objectivity will not succeed in displacing the epistemology that relegates women and the social sciences to an inferior role. Second, it reveals why the goal of objectivity has been so important to the social sciences and, thus, why even the critics of positivist social science refused to relinquish it. "Objectivity" is, as MacKinnon put it, a specifically male epistemological stance. To abandon objectivity in the social sciences is tantamount to conceding that they are "feminine" discourses. Such a concession was anathema even to those social scientists who saw, long before Foucault, that the social sciences did not fit into the modern episteme.

Foucault's argument that the social sciences have no place in the modern episteme is powerful and insightful. But the feminist critique of subjects and objects extends that critique in significant ways. It reveals that the social sciences are anomolous not only because the "subject" of the modern episteme is both subject and object in these disciplines but also because they fail to conceptualize the experience of what should be half of their object of study: women. It also reveals why the social sciences have been so concerned to establish their conformity to the standards of positivist science, particularly with regard to objectivity. Adherence to the subject/object, subjectivity/objectivity dichotomies dictates that if the social sciences abandon the pursuit of objectivity they will be relegated to the sphere of "feminine" enterprises. This fear has informed the obsessive pursuit of objectivity in the social sciences from its inception to the present.

A brief look at some of the founding fathers of the social sciences provides insight into the way in which the subject/object dichotomy has produced not only the anomolous epistemological position of the social sciences, but also their inherent sexism. An examination of the work of three men who have figured prominently in the history of the social sciences, Weber, Freud, and Simmel shows that each of these theorists closely adheres to the subject/object dichotomy at the root of social scientific inquiry. But each of these writers illustrates in a particularly graphic way the confusions and liabilities caused by the subject/object split in the social sciences.

Max Weber's status as one of the founding fathers of the social sciences is indisputable. The influential "action sociology" of Parsons as well as the contemporary interest in charisma and bureaucracy attest to Weber's influence in the social sciences. It is not difficult, furthermore, to identify the basis of Weber's sociology in the realm of the subject. Weber effected a revolution in sociology by arguing that the basic category of sociology, social action, is constituted by the bestowal of subjective meaning by the social actor. In his words,

> Sociology . . . is a science concerning itself with the interpretive understanding of social action and thereby with a causal explanation of its course and consequences. We shall speak of action insofar as the acting individual attaches a subjective meaning to his behavior . . . Action is "social" insofar as its subjective meaning takes account of the behavior of others and is thereby oriented in its course. (1978: 4)

For Weber the subjective bestowal of meaning that constitutes social action is the essence of human activity. Reactive behavior, which is defined by its lack of meaning bestowal, is, on the other hand, only marginally human.

Weber organizes his massive corpus of sociological categories and empirical analyses around this definition of social action. His discussion of the different possible "motivations" of action is rooted in the definition of motivation as a complex of subjective meanings (1978: 11). One of his central organizing concepts, legitimate order or domination, is defined in terms of the subjective belief by the social actors in the legitimacy of the order (1978: 31). When it comes to the constitution of the concepts of the social scientists, the emphasis on subjective meaning bestowal becomes, if anything, more central. The ideal type, which Weber defines as the fundamental tool of analysis in the social sciences, is constituted by the subjective meaning bestowal of two different categories of actors. First, the meaning bestowal of the social actors create the raw material out of which the ideal type is constructed, and, second, the subjective meaning (interest) of the social scientist defines the parameters of the ideal type: "without the investigator's evaluative ideas there would be no principle of selection of subject-matter and no meaningful knowledge of the concrete reality" (1949: 82).[6]

It is easy to see from just these few references that Weber's influential sociological categories are firmly rooted in the subject/object dualism. The exclusion of women from the realm of social action, as with Parsons, is a foregone conclusion.

But another problem plagues Weber's sociology as well, a problem that is central to the definition of the social sciences as sciences within the modern episteme. Weber was very concerned with the issue of the degree to which the social sciences can obtain objective knowledge. In a long and involved dispute with the subjectivists on one side and the positivists on the other Weber attempted to argue for a different kind of objectivity in the social sciences, an objectivity that rests on the study of subjective meanings and the subjective choices of social scientific investigators. Although many of the issues in this debate are no longer timely, what is relevant about it is the fact that Weber's attempt to define objective knowledge for the social sciences indicates a fundamental problem that these sciences face in the modern episteme. The Enlightenment defines objective knowledge as definitive of the scientific realm: unless subjectivity can be eliminated, knowledge cannot be defined as objective and scientific. Weber's admission that social scientific knowledge has an unavoidably subjective basis thus calls into question the scientificity of the enterprise, a problem of which he is well aware. This is further complicated by the fact that ideal types, the basic category of social scientific knowledge, are, by his own admission, fragmentary and partial rather than, as with scientific knowledge, whole and complete. What this comes to is that, by the definitions of Enlightenment knowledge, and particularly due to the dichotomies between subject/object and subjective/objective, the social sciences do not fit into the realm of scientificity to which they aspire. Rather, much to the horror of their practitioners, they fall into the category of subjective, partial, i.e., feminine knowledge. Although Weber was aware of the anomolous position of the social sciences, he was not willing to relinquish the search for objectivity that, for him as well as the Enlightenment, defined scientific knowledge. He was unable to accept the "feminine" status of the social sciences or to challenge the dichotomies at the root of his dilemma.

The problem of the fragmentary, and, hence, feminine character of social scientific knowledge posed a problem for Freud as well as Weber. Freud's discussion of this problem is particularly urgent because, unlike Weber, he was immediately concerned with the issue of sex and the symbolic meaning of the sexual in human life. But, like Weber and his fellow social scientists, Freud unquestioningly believed that males are subjects, females objects, and that objective scientific knowledge is masculine while fragmentary, incomplete knowledge is feminine. While these associations are problematic for the social sciences as a whole, Freud's acceptance of them in his attempt to create a science of psychoanalysis led him into difficulties that are peculiar to his work.

That Freud was very ambivalent on the subject of women and their nature is evident in the vast feminist literature on the relevance of Freud for feminism.[7] On one hand Freud is not hesitant to make sweeping generalizations about women's nature. He identifies narcissism and physical vanity as "psychic peculiarities" of mature femininity and argues that women's lack of a sense of justice is due to the predominance of envy in women's mental life (1971: 596–8). Little girls are declared to be less aggressive, more dependent and pliant, livelier and more intelligent (1971: 581). Freud specifically objected to Mill's argument for the equality of women, asserting that it violates nature and is an "absurd" idea (Gay, 1988: 38–9). But, on the other hand, Freud concedes that these sexual differences are of "no great consequence" (1971: 581). He leaves open the question of whether these characteristics are inherent or a product of conditioning and, thus, begs the question of whether the present state of women is fixed. Even though he characterizes women as passive, men as active, he argues against equating the masculine with the active, the feminine with the passive. This association, he states, "seems to me to serve no useful purpose and adds nothing to our knowledge" (1971: 579). But, most importantly, he admits that his knowledge of the feminine is incomplete. What has been said on femininity, he argues, relates only to women in so far as their nature is determined by their sexual function. Although this influence extends "very far," an individual woman "may be a human being in other respects as well." Finally, he concludes that for more information on femininity we must consult the poets or "wait until science can give you deeper and more coherent information" (1971: 599).

This ambivalent attitude toward women causes Freud significant problems in his effort to construct a science of psychoanalysis. One of these problems is that of fragmentary knowledge. Like Weber, Freud equates masculinity with complete, objective knowledge, femininity with incomplete, fragmentary knowledge (Marcus, 1985: 66). The fact that psychoanalysis, on Freud's own account, seemed only capable of yielding fragmentary knowledge created what amounted to a sexual crisis for Freud. Toril Moi argues that fragmentary knowledge implied impotence for Freud and that castration anxiety dominated his epistemological quest for phallic omnipotence (Moi, 1985a). The effort to create a science of psychoanalysis that could hold its own against the hard, masculine sciences was one of the principal aims of Freud's work. It was an aim, however, that he perceived to be doomed to failure.

The subject/object dichotomy that informs Enlightenment thought posed another problem for Freud as well, a problem that is unique to psychoanalysis. In psychoanalysis knowledge is gained through text analysis and, in the analysis, the patient not only provides the text, but *is* the text (Marcus, 1985: 81). Since in the vast majority of Freud's cases the patient was a woman, this posed a problem: women, who are objects, cannot be subjects in textual narratives. Freud's problem here is that which de Beauvoir discussed in her work: women, who cannot be subjects, cannot construct their own narratives. Although de Beauvoir saw this as a barrier to woman's achievement of transcendence, Freud must deal with it in terms of the psychoanalytic situation. Unless he can overcome this problem he cannot proceed with psychoanalytic therapy.

The way in which Freud surmounts this problem has been extensively analyzed by feminist theorists in one of Freud's most famous cases: the case of Dora. A number of factors make Dora's case particularly problematic for Freud. Dora, who is relating the narrative to Freud, tells a tale in which she is an object in a complex exchange between her father, his lover, and his lover's husband. A central problem that Freud fails to surmount in this case is that he never deals with the question of how an object can tell a story (Kahane, 1985: 21). Dora's position is one of object in two senses: first, she is a woman, and, second, she is an element of exchange in the lovers' scheme. One commentator argues that Freud resolves this problem by himself becoming the central character (subject) in the case (Marcus, 1985: 83). This is, of course, a poor solution. It is Dora, not Freud, who is seeking therapy and is caught up in the complex web of relationships that is causing her psychological problems.

Feminist commentators on the Dora case have pointed out that Dora thwarted Freud's intentions in the analysis in at least two ways. First, she refused to accept her object role in the exchange proposed by her father and his lover's husband, an exchange that was also endorsed by Freud. Her refusal of this object status has endeared her to feminist critics who see her as a proto-feminist who stands up to Freud's masculinist scheme. Second, and just as importantly, she thwarts Freud's intentions by breaking off the analysis prematurely. Thus Freud, who was, as always, concerned with the fragmentary character of his knowledge, was quite unavoidably left with a fragment of an analysis. Significantly, he later published the case under the title *Fragment of an Analysis of a Case of Hysteria*. The case of Dora illustrates that Freud, like Weber, was confronted with a "science" that exhibited unavoidably "feminine" characteristics. Although Freud acknowledged these characteristics he was unwilling to accept them because to do so meant abandoning the scientificity of his enterprise.

It is Weber's contemporary, Georg Simmel, who has most explicitly explored the exclusion of women from the realm of objective knowledge. Several aspects of Simmel's discussion of women make his account particularly relevant. Simmel sees his work as a direct challenge to the concept of reason dominant in Enlightenment thought (Oakes, 1984: 36) and, Simmel, like Nietzsche, casts his discussion of women in the context of the feminist movement of his day. These two factors inform his discussion of the role of women in society. His reaction against the Enlightenment leads him to employ what he defines as a different form of logical analysis and his awareness of the women's movement leads him to consider the *potential* contribution of women in society.

Simmel's challenge to Enlightenment epistemology consisted of his argument that human experience is defined and molded by a plurality of independent and irreducible forms. Against the Enlightenment's reduction of all knowledge to reason, Simmel argued that cultural forms are plural and incommensurable (Oakes, 1984: 36). Although this sounds as if Simmel is a precursor of postmodernism, this is not the case. Simmel's reaction against the Enlightenment leads him not to the antifoundational position of postmodernism but, rather, to the assertion of a series of dichotomies which perpetuate the dualism of Enlightenment thought. One of the central dichotomies he employs is that between men and women. He argues that one of the irreducible forms of human experience is being a woman and his discussion of women is structured around the contrast between the forms of manhood and womanhood in culture. Although he claims to reject the monolithic reason of the Enlightenment, his adherence to this dichotomy perpetuates one of the central tenets of Enlightenment rationality: the association between the masculine and the logical. In effect he assigns the qualities of reason and logic to men and leaves women in an ambiguous realm that excludes them from culture itself.

Simmel begins his discussion of women by noting that the women's movement represents an attempt to bring women into the "forms of life and achievements of men" (1984: 66). The question he attempts to answer in the course of his analysis is whether women are capable of making a contribution to "objective culture" which, he argues, has been defined by men. His first answer to this question is consistent with his avowed aim to challenge the monolithic reason of the Enlightenment. He states:

> The naive conflation of male values with values as such can give way only if the female existence as such is acknowledged as having a basis fundamentally different from the male and a stream of life flowing in a fundamentally different direction: two autonomous totalities, each structured according to a completely autonomous rule. (1984: 72)

This "naive conflation" of male values with values as such, Simmel claims, is a result of the dual meaning of "objective." It is both above male and female principles and "the specific form of achievement that corresponds to the distinctively male mode of being" (1984: 72). On the basis of these definitions, Simmel advances his first thesis: women have something to contribute to male culture because women's nature is fundamentally different from that of men. Women, unlike men, have a unity at the root of their being that contrasts with the detachment characteristic of men. Woman cannot relate to objects detached from her; she must have a concrete relationship to them. This connectedness derives from the fact that women are more attuned to their nature, that is, their specific humanness. It follows that woman is the "authentic human being," a being that is situated in the human in an unqualified way. Man, on the other hand, remains "half animal, half angel" (1984: 112).

The ambiguity informing this description of essentially female nature begins to surface as Simmel moves into a discussion of culture itself. Up to this point he seems to be criticizing the association of objectivity with the male. He asserts, for example, that *in our culture* the objective is defined as the male (1984: 102). But in the course of his discussion of this cultural association the tenor of his analysis changes. Women, we are told, due to the unity at the root of their being, are incapable of distinguishing between subject and object, subjective and objective; they cannot constitute themselves as subjective beings (1984: 86). But since the possibility of all culture rests on the objectivation of subjective contents it follows that women, because of the unitary nature of their being, may be incapable of the objectivation necessary for the creation of culture. In other words, objective female culture may be an oxymoron (1984: 99–100).

The inability of women to objectify sets the stage for the remainder of Simmel's analysis. His general thesis is that there is an elective affinity between objectivation and masculinity and that the reification on which culture rests is inherently masculine. In his discussion of the contrasts between male and female in this regard he seems to be arguing for a separate but equal status for the two realms and, at times, even for the superiority of the female model. He asserts that women, because of the unity of their being, cannot distinguish ideas from existence. Thus, although they are incapable of the intellectual feats of men, they, unlike men, do not succumb to relativism. The so-called logical deficiency of women, he concludes, is not a defect but a product of women's mode of being (1984: 119). Against the feminists of his day he argues that women, because of their inability to objectify cannot enter the male world of culture. Her only possible sphere of culture is the home which remains her "supreme cultural achievement" (1984: 97). While these characteristics of women might be defined as liabilities, Simmel concludes that they entail that women's mode of being is superior to that of men. Woman is connected to absolute being, the ground of existence and thus has an inner unity that "transcends logic." Man, who is divided by his power of objectification lacks this inner unity (1984: 121). Woman, who is one with nature, has no need of reason but man, who is divorced from nature, is forced to employ this artificial tool.

Despite his attempt to praise the "female form" in cultural life, Simmel's attempt to define both women and some version of feminism ultimately fails because of its adherence to the very epistemology he is attempting to refute: Enlightenment dualism. Simmel's attempt to portray the female mode of being as irreducible and in some senses superior is not successful precisely because of his assumption of separate male and female spheres. Two problems with his analysis are paramount. First, his claim that women are superior to men yet are barred from "objective culture" contradicts his assertion that objectivity is the highest achievement of the cultural history of the west. His equation of women with nature permanently excludes women from this realm of culture and objective knowledge. Second, although he claims that his analysis is feminist because it shows, at the very least, the separate value of the feminine sphere, his position defeats the fundamental purpose of feminism: bringing women into the wider sphere of culture as equal members. If culture is objective and hence masculine then the Simmelian feminist must be content with her "inner unity" that transcends logic. Simmels' association between women and nature in this regard is, of course, nothing new. But his claim that woman's inner unity makes her superior to men is ultimately defeated by its adherence to the dualism of male and female.

In his commentary on Simmel's thesis Guy Oakes argues that Simmel's position is very similar to that of Carol Gilligan. Both Gilligan and Simmel, he claims, assert that there are paradigmatic male and female ethical realms (1984: 47). But Oakes fails to see the important point of difference between the two accounts. Simmel defines the female mode of being as an *irreducible form* of cultural life and, furthermore, one that excludes women from culture itself. Gilligan, on the other hand, tries to show how women's socialization produces different ethical norms than those of men and, further, how the male norms have come to be regarded as universal. The difference lies in the fact the Gilligan shows how men and women develop different ethical patterns rather than accepting these patterns as irreducible and unalterable. In contrast Simmel assumes a fundamental difference between men and women and focuses his analysis on the articulation of that difference. This effort opposes the feminist effort to define, in de Beauvoir's phrase, how women are made, not born.

The point of this analysis of the subject/object dichotomy in the social sciences has been to emphasize that the adherence to this dichotomy is problematic for both the social sciences and feminism. The modern episteme that informs the subject/object dualism places both women and the social sciences in an anomolous position. With regard to women it entails that women can only be objects, not subjects, that their experience as social actors is invisible, and that they are incapable of objective knowledge. With regard to the social sciences this dualism entails that the scientific status of these disciplines is called into question by the "feminine" nature of knowledge that they produce. Simmel's attempt to give women separate but equal status by associating women with nature does nothing to remove women's inferior status. If anything, as the next chapter illustrates, it increases their subordination. The analysis of the significance of the subject/object dichotomy for feminist thought leads to a conclusion inspired by Foucault: it is only through the death of gendered *and* generic man, that woman's inferiority can be overcome.

Notes

1   Although it is not directly relevant to the thesis being argued here, the rejection of subject and object has had a profound effect on literary criticism as well. The notion of the objectivity of the text has been definitively rejected by postmodern critics (e.g., Fish, 1980).

2   Gadamer's rejection of authorial intention as the locus of meaning has come under heavy criticism (Hirsch, 1967).

3   MacKenzie also notes this contradiction (1986: 153). Firestone argues that de Beauvoir should, but does not, identify the category of Other as sexual in character (1979: 16). For other discussions of de Beauvoir see Evans (1987: 78), Gatens (1986: 17–20), and Donovan (1986: 123).

4   This argument is echoed in Hartsock (1987) and Brown (1987).

4

Nature/Culture

I Postmodernism and Science

The dichotomy between nature and culture and the association of woman with nature, man with culture is, like the other dichotomies that have been discussed here, not an isolated phenomenon. The association between women and nature is closely related to the identification of women as irrational and their exclusion from the sphere of rationality. Rationality is definitive of culture, a sphere in which men have been identified as the creators, women the passive recipients. Likewise, woman's exclusion from the realm of subjectivity, and what de Beauvoir identified as her "immanence," is a function of her association with nature. As de Beauvoir showed so clearly, woman's failure to achieve transcendence, her inability to be a subject, and her association with nature through reproduction are closely tied. Simmel's examination of the link between culture and objectivation and, consequently, the incompatibility of women and culture is only one instance of this association.

The dichotomy between nature and culture, like those between rational and irrational, subject and object, is not unique to Enlightenment thought. The association between women and nature can be traced to the very beginnings of western thought. Feminist anthropologists have pointed out that although the association between women and nature is a pervasive phenomenon in human culture it is not universal. Although the association between women and nature may seem "natural" to us and, indeed, many feminists have argued for the universality of this association, it is in fact a historical phenomenon. As a historical phenomenon it has specific roots and can be identified as the product of particular social forces. For the purpose of understanding the implications of the association between women and nature in contemporary society, one of the most important facts in its historical development is that with the advent of the Enlightenment the meaning of this association changed significantly. With the rise of modern science the connection between women and nature that had existed since the Greeks was reinforced but it assumed a distinctly different dimension. The domination of nature that is characteristic of modern science significantly altered the woman–nature association that had been a common denominator in western thought as well as most other cultures. In premodern thought, woman's association with nature was conceptualized in terms of a nature that was a mysterious but nurturing mother. With the rise of modern science this conceptualization of nature was changed to that of a wild force that must be subordinated to a dominant mankind. This new conception of nature that was fostered by the rise of science entailed a new conception of the relationship between the man of culture and the natural world he sought to dominate.

Both postmodernism and feminism have made significant contributions to the discussion of the nature/culture dichotomy. The most relevant contribution of postmodernism is its critique of the rationalist philosophy of science. The postmodern's rejection of the Enlightenment's definition of science has important implications for feminist thought about nature, science, and women. It both reinforces and extends the feminist critique of science that has been advanced in recent years by calling into question the absolutism of scientific knowledge. The feminist literature that discusses the relationship between women and nature and the implications of this relationship for the role of women in science is both extensive and insightful. One of the central aspects of this literature is a discussion of what a ''feminist science'' would entail and how it would differ from the masculinist science that evolved out of Enlightenment thought. Finally, the discussion of women and nature must include an issue that is one of the most controversial topics in contemporary feminism: is there such a thing as woman's ''nature''? On the surface the question of woman's nature seems to raise a wholly different topic than the association of women and nature. The sense of the word ''nature'' employed in the two discussions is significantly different. Despite this difference, however, there is a close connection between the two issues. Both radical and conservative feminists who argue for a distinct nature for women ground their arguments in woman's close association with nature. The notion that woman *has* a distinct nature and that her nature is tied in a special way to the natural world is thus central to a discussion of the implications of the nature/culture dichotomy that has permeated western thought. Rejecting the notion that women have a distinct, universal ''nature'' and the essentialism entailed by that notion is crucial to a deconstruction of the nature/culture dichotomy.

Although Gadamer, Foucault, and Derrida have not explicitly discussed the issues raised by the feminist discussion of women, nature and science, their perspectives, and that of postmodernism in general, can be useful in resolving some of the questions raised by an examination of the nature/culture dichotomy. Gadamer's central work, *Truth and Method*, is aimed at elucidating the character of knowledge in the human sciences. It does not specifically deal with knowledge in the natural sciences nor does it even mention the issue of the relationship between women, nature, and science. Yet Gadamer's perspective in this work can shed light on the contemporary feminist discussions of women, nature and science. Because of women's exclusion from the sphere of rationality due to their supposed emotional and irrational qualities women are barred from the realm of knowledge in general. This exclusion, however, has particular impact in its application to the realm of science. Science, especially since the Enlightenment, has been defined as the highest expression of man's rationality. For the Enlightenment, rational man *is* man the scientist. It follows that woman, who is barred from even the lower reaches of the sphere of rationality, is most definitively excluded from its highest expression – science.

Although Gadamer does not discuss the gendered connotations of the Enlightenment conception of science, he attacks the very root of the conception and thus undermines the reasons given for the exclusion of women from science. At the heart of the Enlightenment conception of science is the notion of objectivity, that is, the ability of the scientific observer to remove himself from what is being observed and to analyze rationally the data that he gathers. Gadamer attacks this notion by arguing that *all* human understanding, in the natural sciences, the human sciences, art, and every other sphere of human knowledge, is always hermeneutic. He argues that the ideal of abstract, objective knowledge and the notion of the Archimedean point that is definitive of the Enlightenment conception of science is a false ideal. It is not only unattainable but also undesirable. Against this he argues that all human understanding is rooted in prejudice, in the preconceptions that order human life and make human understanding possible. His thesis that all human understanding is contextual, perspectival, prejudiced, that is, hermeneutic, fundamentally challenges the conception of science as it has been articulated since the Enlightenment.

It also undermines the conception of science that provides the justification for the exclusion of women from the realm of rationality and, hence, science. On the Enlightenment view, women are excluded from science because they are unable to abstract from their particular situation and thus are unable to make the conceptual leap to the Archimedean point that is the necessary precondition of scientific thought. In his discussion of women's intellectual qualities Mill emphasized this inability of women to engage in abstract thought. But if, as Gadamer argues, this ideal of abstract thought is a chimera, then the position of women *vis-à-vis* science is significantly altered. If all thought, including that of science, is by definition contextual and perspectival, then even if we accept that women are, in fact, defined by these qualities, it no longer follows that they can be excluded from the sphere of science. What this comes to is that Gadamer's critique has turned the tables on the Enlightenment conception of science and eliminated its rationale for excluding women from this realm.

Another aspect of Gadamer's thought is also relevant to the feminist approach to the nature/culture dichotomy. One of the principal aspects of Gadamer's work is his rejection of the Enlightenment's attempt to ground knowledge in some indubitable realm. Gadamer's antifoundational philosophy challenges this impulse with the thesis that all knowledge is contextual, historical, and social. His argument against essentialism and absolutism can be used to refute contemporary feminist arguments for an essential female nature. Several schools of contemporary feminism follow the Enlightenment's lead in attempting to identify an essential female nature, frequently defined by woman's closer ties to the natural world, that can serve as a ground for the knowledge of women and their role in society. This essentialist impulse, however, leads feminism to the same sterile dichotomies of Enlightenment thought that have been used to keep women in an inferior position. Gadamer's critique of essentialism and foundationalism reveals the danger of retreating into a universalistic conception of human nature. His emphasis on historicity and linguisticality serves as a necessary antidote to the effort to establish the "essentially female." Lyotard put this point very graphically when he stated that the whole question of the "essential" differences between men and women is a phallocratic question, that is, it is a question that can only be posed in the metalanguage of a philosophy the aim of which is to discern the one, true answer (1978: 15).

Foucault, like Gadamer, does not explicitly discuss the exclusion of women from the realm of science. But, also like Gadamer, Foucault effectively undermines the Enlightenment conception of science and, hence, calls into question the exclusion of women from the scientific realm. Foucault's critique of Enlightenment rationalism, however, stresses different themes than that of Gadamer. His discussion of the transition from the classical to the modern episteme in *The Order of Things* reveals the relativity of the rationalist enterprise. Like Kuhn, Bachelard, and Althusser, Foucault criticizes the Enlightenment conception of science as an abstract activity, rationally progressing from error to truth. He reveals, instead, that the progression from the classical to the modern episteme involved an epistemological break, a kind of conversion to a new way of conceptualizing the world. He thus reveals that modern science, far from offering the one true model of knowledge, is, like its predecessors, rooted in certain historically specific assumptions about the way the world is, assumptions that, contrary to the claims of the rationalists, are not universal. Like Gadamer, Foucault shows that the conception of science definitive of Enlightenment thought, a conception that excludes women from the scientific realm, is not monolithic or infallible.

Foucault's argument concerning the relationship between knowledge and power and his emphasis on the historical specificity of discourses that constitute subjects in particular ways also contributes to the feminist discussion of women, nature, and science. Foucault's perspective allows us to see, first, the mechanism by which the discourse of rationalist science creates a scientific world that excludes women. The discourse of science defines women as incapable of acquiring knowledge that can lead to the domination of nature implicit in the scientific enterprise. By pointing to the historical specificity and relativity of this conception Foucault undermines the universalistic claim of this knowledge–power nexus. Second, Foucault's emphasis on historicity, like that of Gadamer, calls into question the universalistic and essentialist tendencies of contemporary feminism. Foucault's antifoundationalism points to the error of attempting to define woman's "nature." His discussion of the historical constitution of the notion of "sexuality" reveals the folly of searching for a "true female nature." The theme of Foucault's extended discussion of the evolution of notions of the self and sexuality in the west is precisely to dispel the notion that there is an essential sexuality that all human beings share. Rather, he establishes that what we regard as our sexuality is a product of particular discourses that evolved from identifiable social and historical influences. While his approach encourages us to study the technologies of sex that structure the sexuality of women, it discourages us from attempting to define an essential female sexuality or nature.

Derrida, like both Foucault and Gadamer attacks the universal validity of the modern episteme, and, by extension, the basis for the exclusion of women from the realm of science. But Derrida's critique of modern thought is much more comprehensive than that of either of the other two theorists. Derrida's attack on what he calls the "metaphysics of presence" challenges the very roots of western thought. He is concerned not just to show the errors of the modern episteme, including that of rationalist science, but the errors of philosophical thought since its inception. Thus his work offers fewer arguments that are directed specifically against the rationalism of science. In the course of his attack on the metaphysics of presence, however, Derrida advances one argument that is specifically relevant to the issues of women, nature and science. In several of his writings Derrida argues that the nature/culture dichotomy is one of the central dualisms of the metaphysics of presence that he is attempting to deconstruct. In *Writing and Difference* (1978b) he discusses the distinction between nature and culture in the work of Lévi-Strauss, commenting that Lévi-Strauss sees the opposition between nature and culture as universal and spontaneous (1978: 283). Against Lévi-Strauss Derrida argues that this opposition is not universal, but, rather, is "congenital to [Western] philosophy", having originated with the Greek sophists. The Greeks saw nature as opposed to law, education, art, technics, and liberty, in short, the achievements of human culture (1978b: 282–3). In *Of Grammatology* (1976) Derrida extends this critique of Lévi-Strauss to argue that his distinction between nature and culture hid an ethnocentrism, but an ethnocentrism that was *thought* as an anti-ethnocentrism. The ethnocentrism that led Lévi-Strauss to see the nature/culture distinction in western thought as universal is the same ethnocentrism that informs the principal distinction in the metaphysics of presence: the privileging of speech over writing (1976: 106–21). Although Derrida does not devote much attention to the discussion of the nature/culture dichotomy he nevertheless argues that we must transcend the opposition between nature and culture and the ethnocentrism that it indicates. Derrida's intent in this analysis is not to free women from the association with nature, but his attack on the nature/culture dichotomy reinforces the feminists' efforts to transcend this association.

Derrida's approach is also relevant to feminist discussions of woman's "nature". Like Gadamer and Foucault, Derrida rejects essentialism and thus would oppose the attempt to define an essential female nature. But Derrida's relevance goes beyond this. He challenges the metaphysics of presence, an epistemology organized in terms of dualisms and hierarchies, with his notion of *différance*. The metaphysics of presence casts all distinctions in black and white terms; all dichotomies are hierarchical and absolute and thus end up repressing or denying difference rather than expressing it (Young, 1986a: 4). Derrida's thesis of *différance*, on the other hand, encourages us to think of the differences between men and women not in terms of absolute hierarchies but in terms of chains of signification expressed in language, subtleties and shadings rather than absolute oppositions. *Différance* thus offers a way of talking about sexual difference that displaces the oppositions of the metaphysics of presence without denying the differences between the sexes. It offers a way of talking about sexual difference in terms of multiplicity and plurality rather than hierarchy.

In their different ways, then, Gadamer, Foucault and Derrida are all undermining the Enlightenment/modern episteme that not only establishes a dichotomy between nature and culture but also effectively excludes women from the realm of science. There is, however, another aspect of postmodern thought that reinforces their critique of the Enlightenment conception of science by attacking the rationalism of the natural sciences. In recent decades philosophers of science have launched a frontal attack on the Enlightenment conception of science, stressing many of the themes that Gadamer, Foucault and Derrida articulate. Following the pathbreaking work of Thomas Kuhn, these philosophers of science have re-examined the rationalist basis of science and found it to be wanting. The clearest statement of the significance of this "revolution" in the philosophy of science is that in Mary Hesse's *Revolutions and Reconstructions in the Philosophy of Science* (1980). Hesse points out that the three premises of the rationalist (empiricist/positivist) conception of knowledge – naive realism, universal scientific language, and the correspondence theory of truth – are all questionable (1980: vii). She argues that most philosophers of science would now assert the "theory-laden" character of facts in the natural sciences as well as the social sciences. They would agree, that is, that data are not detachable from theory and that meaning is determined by theory, not theory-free observation (1980: 172–3). The point of Hesse's argument is to assert that the debate between the social and the natural sciences as to the scientificity of the social sciences is moribund. If, as she claims, both the social *and* the natural sciences are hermeneutic, that is, contextual and perspectival, then the long-standing debate over the scientific status of the social sciences is no longer tenable.[1]

Hesse's arguments are echoed by a broad range of authors. Among postmodern philosophers both Rorty (1987) and Lyotard (1984) argue that postmodernism entails a crisis in metanarratives, particularly the metanarrative that is constitutive of the natural sciences. Lyotard argues that the "condition of knowledge" in the postmodern age obviates the legitimizing role of the metanarrative of science and that postmodern science must define itself in a radically different way. Social theorists have been quick to see that the postmodern critique of science removes the inferior status of the social sciences that was fostered by the Enlightenment conception of science. Furthermore, radical critics of scientism have used this argument to reinforce their assertion of the oppressive nature of modern science and technology (Rose and Rose, 1976). These arguments have a particular significance for the feminist critique of science. The most incisive feminist critiques of science have relied explicitly on the arguments of Hesse and the approach to the philosophy of science that she represents (Curran, 1980; Rose, 1983; Longino and Doell, 1983). If, as Hesse and Gadamer claim, all human knowledge and understanding is hermeneutic, contextual, and "prejudiced" then the reason for excluding women from the realm of science is obviated. This attack on the abstract universalism of Enlightenment science offers a radical and effective means of challenging the exclusion of women from the realm of the scientific.

II Nature and Culture

In "The Greek Woman" Nietzsche expresses the relationship between woman and nature that has been a theme of western thought since at least the time of the Greeks:

> Woman is more closely related to nature than man and in all her essentials she remains ever herself. Culture is with her always something external, a something which does not touch the kernel that is eternally faithful to Nature, therefore the culture of woman might appear to the Athenian as something indifferent, yea – if one only wanted to conjure it up in one's mind, as something ridiculous. (1964a: 23)

Lest we think that this association between women and nature was only true for the Greeks, Nietzsche goes on to assure us that today the nature of woman remains unaltered. She is still the instrument out of which nature speaks, an instrument foreign to the masculine world of culture (1964a: 24–5). In these passages Nietzsche is expressing an understanding of the association between women and nature, man and culture, that has dominated western thought. Nietzsche, like many contemporary feminist scholars, traces these associations to the Greeks but the assumptions on which these associations rest pervade western thought until the present. Plato's cave analogy, in which knowledge is defined as the masculine thrust out of the depths of mother nature, is echoed in Freud's claim that culture is dependent on men because men, not women, are capable of the repression of their sexual nature which is the foundation of civilization (Griffin, 1978: 5; Sayers, 1982: 111).

From Plato onward, the association of women with nature, men with culture, has been understood as a hierarchical dichotomy with men, as usual, occupying the privileged side of the dichotomy. Despite this, however, there has always been a certain amount of ambiguity associated with the dichotomy. Many of those who discuss the dichotomy, both men and avowed feminists, argue that woman's association with nature in some senses privileges her over the man of culture. Simmel's work is a good example of this position. For Simmel, woman's inability to enter the male world of culture is not strictly a liability. Although woman is excluded from the masculine world of culture, this is an advantage in that she is more "natural" than man, more attuned to what he defines as essential human nature. Nietzsche echoes Simmel's sentiments in his statement that woman's nature is more "natural" than man's because she lacks the artificiality of man's cultural "achievements" (1964b: 190). Both Simmel's and Nietzsche's comments are indicative of the fact that, in addition to the disprivileging they have experienced due to their exclusion from culture, women have also been praised for exhibiting a kind of naturalness through which the artificiality of civilization can be transcended. The ambiguity has led some to conclude that the male/culture, female/nature relationship is a complex one with good and bad on both sides of the dichotomy (Jordanova, 1980). This is true, but must be carefully qualified. Although woman's association with nature has more positive connotations than her associations with irrationality and an object status, it is nevertheless erroneous to conclude that this association has been, on the whole, an advantageous one for women. It is important to note that those who define the association of women and nature as positive are always critics of the status quo, that is, the cultural institutions of their day. Both Nietzsche and Simmel are advocating an overthrow of the dominant culture of the time. Even more significantly, the contemporary feminist school that promotes the association of women and nature as a positive good, the eco-feminists, also define themselves as radical critics of the cultural status quo. For those who support the status quo, in contrast, there is no ambiguity in woman's association with nature; it is quite clearly conceived of as a liability.

One of the most lyrical expressions of the association between women and nature and the ambiguity present in that association is that provided by Susan Griffin. In *Woman and Nature: the roaring inside her* (1978) and *Pornography and Silence* (1981) Griffin expresses in poetical language the nature/culture dualism and its effect on the bodies and minds of women. Although she praises the association of women and nature, Griffin denounces the culture of men that leads to the domination of both women and nature. She claims that women are, in fact, closer to the earth than men, but what this means is that, for men, women are something to be penetrated by the power of reason (1978: 7–14). Women learn two kinds of knowledge in infancy, knowledge of the body from their mothers and knowledge of culture from their fathers (1981: 135). But it is the father's, not the mother's, knowledge that has negative results: "Culture has created a male mind which would exercise absolute power both with kindness and cruelty, over nature in the body of a woman" (1981: 141). In *Woman and Nature* Griffin documents how the masculine, cultural knowledge has led to the rape of nature in the modern world. In *Pornography and Silence* she extends this argument by connecting man's denial of the erotic in culture with the phenomenon of pornography and even with fascism. She argues that the pornographer places himself above the woman as culture over nature. His final solution is to erase nature and replace nature with culture (1981: 125–6).

Griffin's work reveals a number of themes that are important for an understanding of the association between women and nature. She articulates three assumptions that inform not only the eco-feminist movement but also the position of those feminists who want to define woman's nature as more closely tied to the natural world than that of men: first, that women have an essential nature, second, that it is defined in terms of a closeness to the natural world, and, third, that it is vastly superior to that of men because men are associated with culture and culture entails domination. For Griffin, men, who created culture and excluded women from it, use cultural tools to dominate both women and nature. She concludes that, in the name of culture, men have attempted and largely succeeded in the rape of both women and nature.

All of Griffin's assumptions are important for understanding how feminists approach the question of women and nature in contemporary discussions. But for the purpose of understanding the particular attitude toward women and nature that has created the exclusion of women from the realm of science, the aspect of Griffin's work that is most significant is her assumption that men, through their control of culture, seek to dominate nature and, by extension, women. Although Griffin presents this attitude as a universal, it is, in fact, an attitude that is of fairly recent origin. The dominating attitude toward both nature and women that Griffin denounces is a product not of the inherent nature of men, but, rather, of Enlightenment thought and the rise of modern science. Although the association of women with nature predates the modern world, an important shift in that conception occurred around the time of the Enlightenment. In western thought nature has always been conceptualized as female, but the conception of what kind of female nature represents altered radically with the birth of modern science. In the premodern era nature was equated with two kinds of females: the nurturing mother and the wild and untameable temptress. As a result the female image of nature was likewise two-sided: peace, serenity and nurture on one side; plagues, famines and tempests on the other. This two-sided image generated opposing attitudes toward nature. On one hand the association between nature and nurture fostered a benign attitude toward nature and created a cultural constraint on the exploitation of nature. On the other hand, however, the wild side of nature created a desire to tame its excesses, to control the power of nature (Merchant, 1980).

Around the time of the Renaissance the ambiguity inherent in these two images of nature began to be problematic. Hanna Pitkin's analysis of Machiavelli's thought (1984) illustrates this ambiguity toward women and nature that characterized premodern and particularly Renaissance thought. Machiavelli's understanding of *Fortuna* is that of a cruel goddess whose power must be trapped by man for his use in culture (1984: 234). Through the concept of *Fortuna* Machiavelli reveals his attitude toward women: they are dangerous, inferior, and dependent. Pitkin's analysis of *Fortuna*, however, goes beyond the commonly held view that Machiavelli sees women as wild forces to be controlled. She argues instead that Machiavelli's attitude toward women and nature reflects his concern with his manhood (1984: 25). Manhood, for Machiavelli, is equated with autonomy, while feminity equals passivity and dependence. The concept of *virtu* that is at the center of his political writings, furthermore, is equated exclusively with manliness (from the Latin *vir* meaning man). The masculine realm of humanness, politics and autonomy is contrasted to the feminine opposites of these qualities (1984: 109). Pitkin argues that the central theme of Machiavelli is the problematic relationship between the masculine political world and the feminine world of nature (1984: 131).

This ambivalence toward nature that characterized the Renaissance disappeared with the birth of modern science. The two-sided view of nature as either nurturing or disorderly and chaotic share an important quality: they are organic images. As such they are in sharp contrast to the mechanical conception of nature that emerged in the modern period. Paving the way for the appearance of the mechanical conception of nature was a change in the organic conception of nature that occurred in the early modern era: the disorderly side of mother nature began to be emphasized over her nurturing side. The emphasis on disorderliness carried with it the desire on the part of men to tame that disorder, to control nature. This desire set the stage for the attitude toward nature characteristic of modern science, but in itself this attitude was not sufficient. The pre-modern desire to control nature still assumed that nature was wild and mysterious, an organic or super-organic force. The mechanistic conception of science that arose in the seventeenth century, however, brought with it a new conception of nature that significantly changed the premodern conception. In the modern conception nature was still seen as female, but she was now defined as a female that was passive and subject to domination by the (male) scientist. Most importantly, nature was no longer seen in organic, but, rather, in mechanistic terms. Nature the nurturing mother or the wild, insatiable *Fortuna* was transformed into a mechanistically conceived universe that could and should be manipulated and dominated by the scientist. In the organic conception of nature, woman, although feared, played a key role. This was replaced by a mechanical conception in which she was completely passive (Merchant, 1980: 2).

The work of Francis Bacon best expresses this new attitude toward nature. Bacon, both by his writing and the example he set as a scientist, wanted to vanquish the errors of scholasticism and alchemy and establish a "New Philosophy" that would inaugurate the "Masculine Birth of Time" (Bacon, 1963: 92; Farrington, 1964: 13). In his attempt to define this New Philosophy Bacon makes it clear, first, that nature is no longer to be conceived in terms of a nurturing mother, but, rather, in terms of a machine the mechanism of which must be exposed and understood. Second, he asserts that nature is female while the scientist and his New Philosophy are male. The impetus for Bacon's New Philosophy is rooted in an attempt to subdue nature and subject her to the needs and desires of human life: "I am laboring to lay the foundation, not of any school of thought, but of human utility and power" (1964: 9). Bacon's conception of science is an instrumental one in which utility is the central principle, a principle that requires the domination of nature: "I am come in very truth to lead you to Nature with all her children to bind her to your service and make her your slave" (1964: 62). "My only wish," he claims, is "to stretch the deplorably narrow limits of man's dominion over the universe to their promised bounds" (1964: 62). What is needed in order to effect this extension of knowledge, Bacon asserts, is a new conception of truth that is rooted in the scientific method (1964: 71).

The means by which men can establish this New Philosophy and achieve this new truth, Bacon claims, is through a "chaste, holy, and legal wedlock" with the "things themselves," that is, nature (1964: 72). The metaphor of a sexual union between the male scientist and female nature dominates Bacon's discussion of the New Philosophy. But this discussion contains a basic ambiguity. On one hand Bacon emphasizes the chaste, even holy aspect of this union, a union that will produce a "blessed race of Heroes and Supermen" who will overcome the miseries of the human race and secure happiness and prosperity (1964: 72). This marriage, he claims, will have "divine Mercy" as the bridegroom (1964: 131). But in other passages he uses violent and even rapist metaphors in order to describe this union. He asserts that "nature herself, in great part, nay, in her best part, is despised by man" (1964: 120). Man and nature are not on such good terms, he argues that "in response to a casual and perfunctory salutation she would condescend to unveil for us her mysteries and bestow on us her blessings" (1964: 129). It follows that nature must be taken by force: "Nature must be taken by the forelock, being bold behind." We must "lay hold and capture her" (1964: 130). These passages suggest that Bacon's conceptualization of this union comes closer to a gang rape of nature rather than a legal marriage (Easlea, 1980: 84).

The sexual metaphors that dominate Bacon's work are not merely rhetorical devices that can be overlooked or replaced. Rather, the gendered associations of the scientist and the nature he studies constitute the essence of Bacon's mechanical philosophy. As Lloyd puts it, these metaphors give a male content to what it is to be a good knower (1984: 17). The link between modern science and Latin, the abstract and exclusively male language, also ensured that this activity remained a solely masculine preserve (Ong, 1977: 38). The new conception of nature propounded by Bacon, although it is still female, profoundly changed the treatment of nature in modern science. It also profoundly changed the treatment of women. A new image of the female emerged in the modern world, a female to be controlled and dissected (Merchant, 1980: 189) This image legitimated not only the domination of nature but that of women as well. To match this new image of the female a new image of masculinity also emerged. The man of science that is a product of the mechanistic philosophy is a man who must prove his virility by penetrating the secrets of nature. The scientist is a "master, active with his own instruments" who "penetrates" the secrets locked in the bosom of nature (Easlea, 1980: 248). The man of science who is unlocking the secrets of nature, however, is engaged in an activity devoid of sensuousness. Despite the dominance of sexual metaphors in Bacon's work, his New Philosophy is divorced from the sensuousness of the world of the nurturing mother. The consummation of the union between scientist and nature is achieved through reason, not feeling. In her discussion of the relationship between gender and science Evelyn Keller claims that this emphasis on reason has distorted the nature of the scientific enterprise since Bacon (1983b: 191). The result has been the de-sexualization of both nature *and* women (Keller, 1985: 63; Easlea, 1980: 252). The machine imagery that dominates mechanistic philosophy creates a science the goal of which is to extract what is useful from nature in order to foster economic advance (Merchant, 1980: 165). Both the nurturing and the mysterious qualities of women and nature are lost in this mechanistic world.

Several scholars have argued that the mass execution of women as witches in the sixteenth and seventeenth centuries and its cessation at the beginning of the eighteenth century is one of the best indications of the changing attitude toward women and nature in this period (Merchant, 1980; Easlea, 1980). Part of the ideology of both women and nature in the premodern era was a belief in their capacity for unlimited evil. When, in the period immediately before the establishment of the New Philosophy, attention began to be focused on the control of the untameable side of nature, the issue of controlling her evil side also came to the fore. One of the manifestations of this effort was the widespread execution of witches in this period. Witches represented the collusion of women and nature and their combined capacity to wreak havoc in human affairs. It was logical, then, that the premoderns' efforts to control nature should focus on the uniquely threatening force of witches. What is most significant about this witchcraze from the perspective of the development of science, however, is not the fact of its occurrence, but, rather, the fact that is ceased quite abruptly at the beginning of the eighteenth century. One of the principal aims of the mechanical philosophy that was beginning to be established in the early eighteenth century was to defeat the belief in evil powers such as Satan and, more generally, the belief that nature is ruled by mysterious, unknowable forces. Instead the New Philosophers wanted to present nature as a smoothly working mechanical model, one that could be understood, controlled, and dominated by the knowledge acquired by the scientist. This meant, among other things, that women could no longer be conceived as the agents of the devil. The irony of this development is that the philosophy that was to legitimate the domination of both women and nature experienced one of its first triumphs in terminating one of the most overt attacks on women, the witchcraze of the early modern period.

Reinforcing the mechanical view of nature that was developing in the natural sciences was the rise of Cartesian rationalism in philosophy. The subject-centered philosophy of Descartes is closely connected to the New Philosophy that Bacon developed for the natural sciences (Megill, 1985: 139; Bordo, 1986; Lloyd, 1984: 50; Easlea, 1981: 72; Lovitt, 1977: xxvii). In defining himself as a subject and, as such, the source of all possible certainty, Descartes accomplished two things. First, he turned that which is not subject, object, into something external to himself. He in effect cut himself off from the sensuous, female universe of the Middle Ages. In her analysis of Descartes, Bordo argues that although in the Middle Ages certain "feminine" elements were present in the conception of knowledge – merging with the known object, bodily identification – Descartes banished these elements (1987: 9). Cartesian objectivism thus can be seen as a kind of denial of the feminine sensuous world. Secondly, Descartes created an object world of nature that is devoid of mysterious *or* sensuous forces. It is a world that is ruled entirely by cause and effect forces, a world that can be explained, dominated, and controlled. This object world is still a feminine world but it is a world that is passive and mechanical, not mysterious and unpredictable. The world that Descartes created through the subject/object dualism is, in short, the world that Bacon envisioned as the object of the natural sciences.

Although the distinction between nature and culture and the association of women with nature did not originate with Enlightenment thought and the rise of modern science, the dichotomy changed definition and gained importance in this period (Bloch and Bloch, 1980: 27). The association of nature with the nurturing mother and the mysterious force that characterized the Middle Ages gave way to an ideology in which both women and nature were systematically devalued. Although the organic conception of nature that prevailed in the premodern era allowed individuals to decry the injustice of nature, it did not allow them systematically to exploit her in the way that has become one of the hallmarks of modern science. The objectivation of both nature and women that was a result of the New Philosophy not only allowed but encouraged such exploitation. One of the results of this changing conception is that it set the stage for the connection between the women's liberation movement and the ecology movement (Merchant, 1980: 294). The exploitation of women and that of nature are indissoluably linked in the New Philosophy, as Bacon illustrates so clearly. This connection has led feminists in the twentieth century to argue that it is only by overcoming the objectification inherent in the masculine epistemology of the modern era that we can overcome both the rape of nature and the domination of women. In *Beyond God the Father*, for example, Mary Daly argues that we must replace the male objectification of nature with a "covenant" relationship (1973: 177–8). Feminist scholarship on the association between women and nature and its changing aspect in the modern era has had a profound effect on contemporary feminist thought. It has led to the rise of the eco-feminist movement. It has also led feminists to advocate a radical change in the epistemology of the sciences and to call for a feminist science. But this historical analysis of the relationship between women, nature, and science, also indicates the difficulty of effecting such a change. Modern science has for several centuries dominated the world view not only of the west but of the developed world as a whole. The conception of both women and nature that is central to the scientific enterprise is firmly entrenched and will not yield easily.

One of the important conclusions that emerges from this analysis of the relationship between the conceptions of women and nature is that the understanding that we have of this relationship in the twentieth-century west has specific historical and ideological origins. It arose as a direct result of a series of influences and developments in the seventeenth and eighteenth centuries. It is, as Foucault would put it, a particular discourse that deploys a particular regime of knowledge/power. This insight is an important counter to the tendency among some feminists to universalize the nature/culture dichotomy. Many eco-feminists, for example, want to posit an essential connection between women and the natural world that transcends history and culture. This thesis has become one of the fundamental tenets of the movement. The debate about the ''naturalness'' of this connection between women and nature, however, has been hotly disputed in the discipline of anthropology. Anthropologists have, for obvious reasons, long been concerned with this distinction. Interestingly, one of the first attempts to identify the cultural roots of women's oppression, Engels' *The Origin of the Family*, utilized anthropological evidence to establish that the overthrow of ''mother right'' and the rise of property led to the ''world historical defeat of the female sex'' (1985: 87). More recently, anthropologists have turned specifically to the nature/culture distinction and its relationship to women's oppression. Lévi-Strauss defined the nature/culture distinction as universal and central to the organization of human societies. Feminist anthropologists have subjected this distinction to particular scrutiny. In an influential article Sherry Ortner argues that women are devalued in every culture because they are associated with something that every culture devalues: nature (1974: 72). She asserts that every society posits a dichotomy between nature and culture and in every society nature is devalued. Her reasons for this conclusion echo the assumptions about women and nature that have dominated western thought: woman is closer to nature because of her reproductive function; the world of culture is a world created by men.

Recently, however, several anthropologists have challenged the validity of Ortner's thesis. Sanday (1981) argues that Ortner has overstated her claim. Although Sanday argues that women are *usually* associated with nature, men with culture, she asserts that this is not always the case. She claims that the male dominance that is implicit in Ortner's thesis is in error. Rather, she argues that there are societies in which male dominance is not universal. This challenge to Ortner's thesis is echoed in the collection of articles edited by MacCormack and Strathern (1980). Many of the authors of these articles argue that our conception of the nature/culture distinction is not universal nor is our association of the male with culture and the female with nature. MacCormack states this thesis very precisely in her article:

> There is no way absolutely to verify that the nature–culture opposition exists as an essential feature of universal *unconscious* structure, and there is ethnographic evidence to suggest that in the form in which Europeans now conceive it, the contrast is not a universal feature of consciously held folk models. (1980: 80)

Another theme that emerges from this challenge to Ortner's thesis is the claim that there are cases in which the dichotomy is reversed: women are defined as morally superior, civilized beings while men are portrayed as wild and untamed (Rogers, 1978; Strathern, 1980). Rousseau's idealization of nature as morally superior and the ideology of the American West which defined woman as a civilizing force are instances of this reversal.

The exceptions cited by these anthropologists destroy the neatness of Ortner's thesis. They stress that the assumptions that we have of the nature/culture dichotomy are historically specific, not universal. They emphasize the fact that the link between women and nature is not an unchanging absolute that determines the role of women in society, but, rather, a specific historical and cultural association, an association which has been used by a particular society to control women and rationalize their devaluation. Focusing on the specific and the historical rather than the universal and the abstract is of crucial importance in reassessing the relationship between women, nature, and science. Feminist theorists who try to explain the role of women by reference to abstract universals such as the "naturalness" of woman's connection with nature are reverting to the epistemological assumptions of Enlightenment epistemology. Enlightenment epistemology aims at exploring phenomena in absolute, universal terms, ignoring the historical and social variables that determine the existence of these phenomena. By objectifying and abstracting phenomena in its attempt to define universal laws, Enlightenment thought fostered the oppression of women and nature that feminists are challenging. That challenge should not employ the same epistemology. Rather, the feminist challenge to the nature/culture dichotomy must focus on its historicity. Although the association between women and nature and the objectification and exploitation of both is widespread and influential, it is the result of a particular ideological conformation, in this case, Enlightenment science, that has affected women in a specific historical context. It must be challenged as such both theoretically and practically.

III A Feminist Science?

In *Three Guineas* Virginia Woolf remarks "Science, it would seem, is not sexless; she is a man, a father, and infected too" (1984: 263). Woolf's remark is indicative of many of the themes of contemporary feminist scholars. The Enlightenment conception of science has been carefully scrutinized by contemporary feminists who want to discover the roots of our attitudes toward women and science. Initially these investigations began with the question of why there are so few women scientists. Although this question is still debated, the discussion has long since transcended a narrow interest in issues of discrimination. Feminists have come to realize that asking why there are so few women in science and focusing on affirmative action programs in science is not going to eradicate the problem posed by the relationship between women and science. This problem is rooted in the distinctive Enlightenment conception of science, a conception that defines it as an inherently masculine enterprise.

That science has been defined as a masculine activity that women, because of the qualities associated with femininity, are incapable of, is obvious from the foregoing analysis of the work of Bacon and the tenets of his New Philosophy. Women, who are excluded from the sphere of rationality, are declared to be unfit to participate in the activity of science, the highest expression of rationality. In trying to explore why this exclusion is so pronounced in the sphere of science, several feminist writers have turned to the child-rearing literature discussed in chapter 2. They have argued that our child-rearing practices produce attitudes that effectively exclude women from the realm of science. Because mothers are the primary caretakers of infants, women come to represent nature and the flesh to both men and women. It follows that women cannot also represent the opposite of nature: civilization, history and, particularly, science (Dinnerstein, 1976: 210). Another result of women-dominated child care is the development of personality traits in both men and women that determine their respective aptitude for scientific work. Men, because they are forced to separate from their mothers develop the separation and ego detachment that have been defined as the central requirements of the scientific method. Women, on the other hand, because they do not separate from the mother, remain more connected to their world; their outlook is contextual and situational (Keller, 1983b: 198–9). Thus when women are confronted with the necessity to detach themselves from their situation and engage in the abstract, value-free analysis that is definitive of the scientific enterprise, they are unable to do so. The ego detachment that the Enlightenment defined as necessary to science is, because of these child-rearing practices, alien to women (Hein, 1981: 374). This literature is very effective in explaining why the attitudes that we have come to associate with science are rarely developed in women. It is flawed, however, by the assertion of universality on the part of some of these writers. Both of the phenomena under discussion, western science and the child-rearing practices that produce its sexism, are culturally and historically specific, a fact often overlooked in this literature (Fee, 1986).

The subject/object, subjectivity/objectivity distinction also exerts a powerful influence on the gendered character of contemporary science. The separations between subject and object, knower and known are central requirements of the scientific enterprise. Women fail to meet these requirements in two senses. First, they cannot be subjects and, as objects, can only be the ego-less objects of scientific study (Hein, 1981: 373). The active, knowing subject that is essential to science has been defined as exclusively masculine (Bleier, 1984: 196). Second, women cannot effect the distinction between knower and known that is the hallmark of the scientific method (Keller 1985: 79). Women, who tend to see things in perspectival terms, cannot abstract themselves as knowers from the known. In her excellent study of the biologist Barbara McClintock, Evelyn Keller (1983a) argues that McClintock's rebellion against the scientific establishment lay in her rejection of this model of knowing. Unlike her male colleagues, McClintock attempted to get a "feeling for the organism" that broke down the barrier between knower and known. This attempt to challenge one of the fundamental tenets of the scientific method, Keller argues, accounts for her difficulty in obtaining recognition in the scientific community.

For many feminists the issue of the reputedly objective stance of the (male) scientific knower has raised the question of the origin of the desire for dominance and control. Why is it, they ask, that modern scientific investigations are so closely tied to the dominance of nature? Does objectivity necessarily entail dominance? The answer that several writers give to these questions is that the cause lies, once again, in child-rearing practices. Balbus claims that the domination of nature is a direct outgrowth of mother-monopolized child-rearing. Nature, he claims, becomes a repository of our unconscious attitudes toward our mother, and thus men's attempt to dominate nature is an expression of their attempt to dominate their mothers (1982: 335). Another interpretation of the effect of these child-rearing practices is that the dream of domination echoes the dream of the son in identifying with the authority of his father. It separates the son from the mother and prevents him from knowing her except as an object of knowledge (Keller, 1985: 96–125). Another possibility is that the problem of domination has even deeper roots: it is a result of the dichotomized thinking that is the basis of the masculinist Enlightenment epistemology. The epistemology of science is an epistemology of dualisms: nature/culture, subject/object, knower/known. The dichotomizing of the world leads to a world of control and domination; dualisms always imply hierarchies and hierarchies always imply control (Bleier, 1984: 164; Haraways, 1978: 36). Woolf even goes so far as to argue that the dichotomizing of male and female and the assignment of an inherent nature to each is at the root of one of the cruelest systems of domination the world has seen, fascism (1984). The problem that none of these discussions confronts, however, is why it is only in modern science that the issue of control has come to the forefront. Both mother-dominated child rearing and dualistic thought predate the advent of modern science and its obsession with domination. Thus neither of these features of science can account for the dominance of nature that distinguishes it from earlier scientific activities. In trying to identify the roots of the sexism of modern science, therefore, it is much more profitable to turn to an analysis of the scientific method itself. Although child-rearing practices and dualistic thinking may contribute to the sexism of science, they cannot fully explain its masculinist character.

Feminists have no difficulty in agreeing that western science has an androcentric bias (Harding, 1986b: 100) or that the association of masculinity with scientific thought has the status of a myth that is rarely examined (Keller, 1985: 75). But although feminists agree on the masculinity of western science, they cannot agree on an alternative. The pattern here is the same as that noted in the discussion of the two previous dichotomies: while feminists may concur on the nature of the problem, they disagree significantly on its solution. Criticisms of the masculinist bias of scientific theories are prominent in feminist discussions of the scientific enterprise and calls for a "feminist science" abound. But there is very little agreement on what is entailed by a such a feminist science. In order to indicate the range of positions that feminists have articulated it is useful to begin with an examination of an issue that is central to many of the feminist critiques: sociobiology.

It is not surprising that the claim by Wilson and other sociobiologists that women's role as homemaker and child-rearer has genetic origins should evoke criticism from feminists. The criticisms that both feminists and non-feminists have advanced against the claims of the sociobiologists have effectively undermined most of their major claims, particularly their attempt to establish the genetic basis of social behavior. What is instructive about this debate, however, is not so much who makes the most telling point against whom, but, rather, the basis of the criticisms that have been advanced against sociobiology by feminist writers. The feminist criticisms of sociobiology fall into a pattern that is characteristic of most feminist discussions of masculinist science. On one hand, feminist critics of sociobiology argue that the sociobiologists are engaged in bad science, that is, that they do not adhere to the established canons of scientific method. On the other hand, however, they argue that the presuppositions of masculinist science are fundamentally flawed and must be replaced. The course of the discussion over sociobiology reveals that, ultimately, these two arguments are incompatible.

The feminists who argue that Wilson and his colleagues are engaged in bad science point to his faulty methodology, insufficient evidence, unfounded generalizations, and his use of hidden assumptions (Blee, 1979, 1984; Leibowitz, 1978; Reed, 1978; Hendler, 1976; Fausto-Sterling, 1985; Lowe and Hubbard, 1983; Lewontin et al., 1984). A good example of the arguments found in this literature is that of Rosser (1984). Rosser argues that the scientists who use sociobiology's false evidence are failing to use "objective methods." As feminists, she claims, our task is to point out to these scientists their lack of objectivity. She concludes:

Women in science must follow the lead of women in other disciplines who have provided innovative and more objective approaches which lead to alternative interpretations of data and to new theories that enrich the discipline. (1984: 5)

It is interesting that not only women have criticized the sociobiologists for their faulty methods, but male scientists have jumped on the bandwagon as well (Gould, 1986; Kitcher, 1985). At this point in the debate both feminists and non-feminists seem to agree that the claims of the sociobiologists do not hold up to scientific scrutiny. In fact, reading through this literature, one wonders how any scientists could have taken these theories seriously in the first place. Perhaps the only explanation for the tenacity of the sociobiologists' theses is the fact that theories of women's biological inferiority have been a theme in biological science since Aristotle (Bleier, 1984: vii). Although we can hope that sociobiology is the last expression of this tradition, its popularity, despite its logical and methodological flaws, should not surprise us.[2]

What is important about this first group of critics is the fact that they do not challenge the established code of scientific method that, by sociobiology's own admission, informs the theory. Rather, it is a wholly internal critique; it finds sociobiology wanting in terms of the (unquestioned) standards of scientific method, particularly that of objectivity. There is however, another group of feminist critics of sociobiology that go beyond this internal critique. Several feminist writers have argued that instead of questioning the sociobiologists' application of the scientific method we should question the method itself. The most sustained criticism of sociobiology from this perspective is that offered by Joan Smith (1981–2). Smith argues that the feminist critique of sociobiology has not been successful because both feminists and sociobiologists share a set of basic presuppositions. These presuppositions include the belief that the essence of a phenomenon can be described independently of its particular manifestation, that phenomena can be treated apart from the social totality to which they belong, and that historical causation can be ignored. Against these assumptions Smith argues that what is wrong with both sociobiology and many of its feminist critics is that they share a biological reductionism. Smith argues that the essentialism at the root of these theories ignores the historical particularity of instances of male domination. Against the approach of both the sociobiologists and their feminist critics she argues for a method that is historical and situational rather than essentialist.

What Smith is claiming, in effect, is that the feminist critique of sociobiology calls for a new approach to science, not just an internal critique of the sociobiologists' methods. Her criticism is echoed in the work of several other feminist critics of sociobiology. Hendler (1976) attacks the fundamental criticism of biological development on which sociobiology rests: the competitive model. Against this he argues that a different understanding of biological development would result if we assumed cooperative interaction among organisms (1976: 8). Hendler is calling for what amounts to a new model for understanding biological evolution. Similarly, Fausto-Sterling, in her analysis of sociobiology, calls for a new approach based on her critique. She argues that sociobiology calls into question one of the basic tenets of science: the necessity and possibility of unbiased observation. She observes that although sociobiology is biased, it is difficult or impossible to be unbiased about something that affects one too personally (1985: 10). She claims that the discussion of sex roles is something that affects all of us very personally and that neither sociobiologists nor their critics can transcend this bias. Her point is that although we can and should criticize the sociobiologists for poorly done science, the critique must go further. In another context she expresses this point very clearly: "I have framed the issue as poorly done science, while at the same time undertaking to look beyond the existence of good science to something called feminist science" (1985: 208).

These criticisms, although sketchy in themselves, point to a feminist attitude toward science that holds much more promise that the charges of "bad science."[3] They point to the fact that challenging the validity of sociobiology's claims on their own terms is ultimately self-defeating. They indicate that if the canons of scientific method as they have been defined by the dominant tradition since Bacon are inherently sexist, then adherence to those methods, no matter how rigorous, will not produce results that will fundamentally alter the sexist character of the scientific enterprise. Although the sociobiologists may be engaging in bad science as it is defined by the scientific method, this criticism does not challenge the method itself. The criticisms of Smith and Fausto-Sterling, on the other hand, point to a different conception of science. They argue, first, that scientific truth is a-historical, second, that it is unitary, and, third, that it claims to be unbiased. This entails that feminist criticisms of science must move beyond an internal critique and begin the task of formulating an alternative conception of science. On the basis of their brief remarks we learn that a feminist science, unlike the masculinist conception, should be historical, plural and hermeneutic. But a much more positive advocacy of an alternative science is necessary. Although these authors are willing to criticize the dominant tradition in science, their criticisms are tentative and vague. The arguments they advance are consistent with many postmodern themes – plurality, historicity, etc. – but these themes are undeveloped. This pattern is characteristic not only of the critique of sociobiology, but of the call for a feminist science more generally. Much of what the feminist writers argue for is consistent with postmodernism but the connection to the postmodern movement is rarely made explicit.

Although many feminist writers have supplied what they consider to be exhaustive lists detailing the elements of a feminist science, little unanimity exists as to what should be included on this list. It is possible, however, to discern a number of themes that run through this literature. The first is an insistence that what is needed is more than an end to discrimination against women in the scientific establishment. In their call for a feminist science feminists have been careful to distinguish between two issues: the discrimination against women in science and the androcentric bias of the scientific enterprise itself. Although it is important to note, for example, that because there are few women in tenured positions at research universities, men have been able to define the direction of scientific research (Sherman and Beck, 1979: 5) this is not the fundamental issue. It is likewise significant to ask, as Kimball (1981) does, why the difference in participation rates of women and men in scientific fields is so large when sex differences in intellectual abilities is so small, but this question does not lead to an understanding of the problem with masculinist science. Feminist theorists have made it clear in their investigations that the question is not sexism in the scientific establishment, but a sexist science (Eichler, 1980: 118).

The second theme that unites the calls for a feminist science is a negative one: opposition to the principal attributes of masculinist science. Almost all of the basic elements of masculinist science have been attacked by feminist writers, although the alternatives that they propose to this orthodoxy are much less clear. One of the principal targets of these attacks is the competitive model. Lowe (1981) claims that feminist science would eschew the competitive drive at the root of masculinist science. In a feminist science cooperation rather than competition would be the rule. Another target is the ideals of absoluteness and abstraction. Morgan (1982) argues that relativity and interrelatedness should guide the feminist in the pursuit of truth. In a similar vein, Fee (1982) argues that we should create a feminist science that acknowledges itself to be historically determined rather than neutral. Although the term "hermeneutics" is rarely employed in these discussions, what these writers are arguing is very similar to the postmodern critique of positivist science. Like Hesse, these theorists are arguing that instead of trying to eliminate "bias" (values, gender, social forces) we should acknowledge its presence as a necessary part of the scientific enterprise (Bleier, 1986: 16; Hubbard, 1988: 14; Potter, 1988: 20).

Another focus of attack has been the dualistic, hierarchical model of knowledge at the root of the masculinist scientific enterprise. In attempting to formulate a feminist science, several writers have argued that we must reject the dualism that informs modern theories of knowledge because the science it produces is inherently hierarchical and, hence, leads to domination (Bleier, 1984: 200-1; Fausto-Sterling, 1981; Harding 1980: 305-6). Although dualistic thinking may not alone be responsible for the domination of nature in modern science, the attack on dualities has led feminists into some fruitful lines of thought. Fee (1981) argues that a feminist science would obliterate the distinction between thought and feeling, subject and object, subjectivity and objectivity. It would be a science that rejects a neatly dichotomized world and the attempt to catalogue the natural world into stereotypes (Hubbard and Lowe, 1979). A good example of how a non-dichotomized way of thinking would operate is offered by Birke (1986). Focusing on the nature/nurture dichotomy, Birke argues that this dualism has caused what appear to be insuperable problems in biological theory. What she proposes instead is an interactive model that eschews the dichotomy. Turning to the question of the relationship between sex and gender, she argues that biological sex is not separate from social constructions of gender, but, rather, women experience their biological sex in a social context that defines it (1986: 105). Feminists such as Birke who call for the rejection of stereotypes and dichotomies are rejecting the monolithic ideal characteristic of masculinist science. These feminists' call is for a pluralistic world view, one that eschews the closure that is representative of the scientific enterprise as we know it (Keller, 1982: 223). Finally, many writers have argued that the rejection of hierarchy should also extend to the internal organization of science. A feminist science would be a non-elite activity in which community participation would be both desired and encouraged (Bleier, 1986: 16; Hubbard, 1988: 14; Birke, 1986: 168).

These attacks on the roots of masculinist science and, particularly, the call for a transcendence of dualistic thought represent themes that are consistent with the postmodern position. They call for a feminist science that is de-centered, pluralistic, non-hierarchical and hermeneutic. Although the authors of most of these works claim to be unsympathetic to the postmodern stance, their positions nevertheless reinforce the themes of that position. This cannot be said, however, of another aspect of the call for a feminist science. A number of feminist critics of science, and masculinist epistemology in general, argue that we should replace the masculinist epistemology of science not with a de-centered pluralistic epistemology but with a distinctly "feminist epistemology." These arguments, which, since Hartsock's influential article (1983a), have been catalogued under the heading of "feminist standpoint epistemologies," entail the claim that women, because of certain aspects of their make-up, possess a privileged position which provides them with a unique perspective. The feminist standpoint epistemologies take a number of forms, but common to all of them is an appeal to woman's unique association with nature. Dinnerstein argues that women are less likely to participate in the plunder of nature that is characteristic of modern science because they feel closer to their first parent, their mother, who is linked to nature (1976: 103). Mary Daly echoes this sentiment when she states that "insofar as we are witches, women are in harmony with the rhythms of the universe" (1984: 90). Our task as feminists, she claims, is to re-establish the severed connections with these natural rhythms, connections that have been lost with the rise of modern science. Concluding her argument, she comments: "To the crone-logical mind it is no mere coincidence that Francis Bacon and Réné Descartes constructed sterile systems while women burned" (1984: 154).

The arguments of Rose (1983, 1986a, 1986b) and Hartsock (1983a, 1983b) are more oriented toward specifically scientific questions. In "Hand, Brain and Heart" (1983), Rose looks to the craft-organized areas of inquiry for a model of a feminist science that can counter the dualisms of Enlightenment thought. Her vision of a transformed, feminist science involves what she calls the unity of hand, brain and heart in the process of scientific inquiry. In a later paper (1986b) Rose broadens this argument to include a feminist epistemology in general. Following the basic Marxist principle that a materialist human knowledge must come from practice, Rose argues that their labor offers women a distinctive knowledge of the social and natural worlds. A feminist epistemology must come from this experience of labor:

> A feminist epistemology derived from woman's labor in the world must represent a more comprehensive materialism and a truer knowledge. Such an epistemology transcends dichotomies, insists on the scientific validity of the subjective and the need to unite cognitive and affective domains; it emphasizes holism, harmony and complexity rather than reductionism, domination and linearity. (1986b: 179)

Although in this passage Rose claims that her approach "transcends dichotomies" she qualifies this in another context. A feminist materialism, she insists, is necessarily dualistic, but this dualism provides a theoretical tension that is a better tool for analysis and a "more creative framework for struggle" (1986a: 68). Rose identifies the feminist materialism that she advocates as a "successor science" to the dominant masculine model. In conclusion, Rose contrasts this successor science to the postmodern vision of a science that rejects hegemony altogether (1986b: 180).

Rose is interested in formulating a feminist science that is true to Marx's materialism and, like Marxism, offers a "truer knowledge" of the social and natural worlds. Hartsock, who also argues for a feminist materialism, asserts that we must move beyond both Enlightenment and Marxist epistemologies. She claims that women's sensuous, relational and contextual perspective allows them to understand aspects of nature and social life not available to masculinist epistemologies. Although Hartsock's argument follows Marx in arguing that the unique perspective of a particular group affords them a "truer knowledge," she claims that her perspective also transcends that of Marx. Proletarian labor, for Hartsock, is not as basic as the labor of women because women's labor is closely tied to the necessary, sensuous existence of all human beings. Hartsock, like Rose, wants to offer a successor science based on this unique feminist standpoint. Like Dinnerstein and Daly, she appeals to woman's special relationship to nature to ground this distinctively feminist epistemology.

Feminist standpoint epistemologies have a great deal of appeal for feminists who are searching for an alternative to masculinist science. They combine a rejection of masculinist science with an emphasis on the strengths of qualities that have been associated with the feminine and, consequently, devalued. But the position of the feminist standpoint epistemologies is not the answer to the question of defining a feminist science. The first problem with this approach is that it reifies the nature/culture dichotomy that is at the root of the exclusion of women from the scientific enterprise. All of the theorists who argue for a distinctive feminist standpoint appeal in some way to woman's special relationship to nature to ground the feminist epistemology that they advance. The contradiction in this position should be obvious: they are appealing to women's special relationship to nature to advance an epistemology that is intended to counter Enlightenment epistemology, an epistemology that rests on the association between women and nature. In this sense feminist standpoint epistemologies do not counter Enlightenment epistemology but, rather, reinforce it. The second problem with this position is that the feminist standpoint epistemologies also reinforce another central aspect of Enlightenment epistemology: its universalism. Like that epistemology and the masculinist science that it produced, this approach overlooks historical and contextual elements. In attempting to present *the* women's perspective, these theorists perpetuate the monolithic universalizing tendencies of Enlightenment thought. To argue for a single, unitary women's perspective is to forget that women, like men, are always found in particular situations with varying social and historical contexts. What these theorists forget is that we cannot define *one* women's perspective, but, rather, must define as many different perspectives as there are different contexts in which women live. Finally, the feminist standpoint epistemologies, in their attempt to offer a "successor science," are attempting to substitute a new truth and, hence, a new authority, for the discredited masculinist science. But in doing so they once again are following the lead of Enlightenment thought. The desire to find "truer knowledge" will inevitably lead to the establishment of a new orthodoxy to replace the old, a new orthodoxy that will produce its own truths and its own hierarchies.[4]

A challenge to the fundamental principles of masculinist science unites all the feminist critiques of science. The question that most sharply divides these critiques, however, is how far that challenge should extend. Rose, for example, although she claims to be rejecting the Enlightenment conception of science, nevertheless maintains one principal element of that conception: the assertion of "truer knowledge." The question of truth and, particularly, objectivity, has become a kind of litmus test for feminist critiques of science because it is so central to the Enlightenment definition of science. Many feminists who are strong critics of the Enlightenment view of science as masculinist still balk at the prospect of abandoning or even redefining the concept of objectivity. For most of these critics rejecting objectivity seems to be tantamount to rejecting science itself. These feminists argue that the purpose of a feminist science is not to reject science altogether but, rather, to formulate a science that avoids the sexist bias of the Enlightenment conception of science. To these feminists objectivity is so central to the enterprise of science that to reject it entails a retreat to prescientific irrationality.

Although the question of objectivity, like many of the issues in the feminist critiques, is not always clearly expressed, it is possible to discern three different positions on this question that feminists have articulated. One group of critics argues that the bias of male science can be overcome by adding the woman's perspective to that of the male scientist and by correcting the logical errors ("bad science") of male scientists. This position, which was illustrated in the sociobiology debate, is what Harding labels "feminist empiricism" (1986b: 24). It involves the claim that the pursuit of objectivity is a valid one, but that male scientists have simply gotten it wrong all these years. The position espoused by this group is summarized in Dale Spender's comment that objectivity is simply male subjectivity. Feminist empiricists argue that the male pursuit of objectivity is not wrong-headed and that women can improve on this pursuit and thereby achieve the objectivity that men have failed to attain. The problem with this position is that it fails in the most basic way to challenge the Enlightenment conception of science. These writers fail to see that the concept of objectivity that they so unquestioningly embrace is an integral part of the masculinist conception of science that relegates women to inferiority. "Improving" the masculinist conception of objectivity by making it "truer" in its own terms will do nothing to alter the epistemology of which it is a part.

A second position is that of the feminist standpoint theorists discussed above. Writers such as Hartsock and Rose argue that women, because of their unique position, are capable of constructing a theory of objectivity that will end the domination of men. Like the feminist empiricists these theorists do not want to relinquish the goal of objectivity that they see as central to science. But unlike the feminist empiricists, they want significantly to redefine objectivity so that it avoids the pitfalls of masculinist science. Like the social scientists who criticized the application of positivism in the social sciences, these theorists espouse an antipositivist concept of objectivity. The problems with this approach have already been discussed. The feminist standpoint theorists' aim is to construct a successor science that replaces the masculinist definition of objectivity with a feminist conception. This move fails to displace the universalism and absolutism of the epistemology they claim to be replacing.

The third position that emerges from this literature also calls for a redefinition of objectivity. But the theorists in this group, unlike the feminist standpoint theorists, do not presuppose a unique women's perspective. Nor do they argue that feminists should develop a successor science to replace masculinist science. Unlike the feminist standpoint theorists they identify the Enlightenment's universalism and absolutism as the principal obstacle to the formulation of a feminist science. What is unique about this position is that its exponents fail to take their critique to its logical conclusion. While calling for a wholesale rejection of masculinist science and the Enlightenment epistemology that informs it, they explicitly reject the postmodern position, claiming that the position they espouse entails neither the anarchism nor relativism that they identify with postmodernism. They define their position as an attempt to redefine objectivity in the context of a critique of the absolutism of Enlightenment science while at the same time avoiding the "pitfall" of relativism. Donna Haraway's work is one of the best examples of this position. In "A manifesto for cyborgs" (1985) Haraway presents a radical critique of masculinist science and an innovative approach to the formulation of a feminist science. In this and other works she claims that a feminist science is not about having a special route to the truth but, rather, about changing possibilities (1986: 81). But she nevertheless is very concerned that the outright rejection of objectivity will result in nihilism (1981: 277). She notes:

> Feminists want some theory of representation to avoid the problem of epistemological anarchism. An epistemology that justifies not taking a stand on the nature of things is of little use to women trying to build a shared politics. (1981: 480)

In a footnote Haraway specifically separates her position from the postmodernism of Foucault, claiming that Foucault's work makes the "grand circulation of domination invisible." Much the same pattern defines the work of Evelyn Keller (1982; 1983a; 1983b; 1985). While Keller challenges the root of the masculinist conception of science and, particularly in her work on Barbara McClintock, offers a radical feminist alternative to that conception, she nevertheless wants to retain the notion of objectivity and, consequently, rejects postmodernism. She argues:

> By rejecting objectivity as a masculine ideal, it [postmodernism] simulta- neously lends its voice to an enemy chorus and dooms women to residing outside the realpolitik modern culture; it exacerbates the very problem it wishes to solve. (1982: 593)

Several of the theorists in this group, however, have somewhat tentatively moved beyond Haraway and Keller to challenge the notion of objectivity itself. Although this challenge owes much to postmodernism, the debt is rarely acknowledged. The argument employed in these discussions involves an attack on the objectivity/subjectivity dichotomy. Ruth Hubbard, for example, seems to be arguing for a reconceptualization of objectivity in science in some of her works. In a discussion of biology she claims that the task of feminism in biology is to point out that there is no objective, value-free science, but, rather, that all science is a part of its era's politics, economics and sociology (1981: 218). Although she does not draw out the implications of this statement her attack on the norm of objectivity constitutes one of the most radical challenges to the Enlightenment model of science that is found in the feminist literature. Elizabeth Fee continues this line of argument in a more explicitly postmodern direction. The problem with those who reject scientific authority, she argues, is that they assume that it must be either accepted or rejected: either we have objectivity or we do not. In order to argue for a position that avoids these two extremes, she claims, we must attack the objectivity that is a part of the "mythology" of science. To do so we must re-admit the human subject into the production of scientific knowledge (1981: 383–9).

These comments by Hubbard and Fee are so similar to the postmodern critique of science as it has been expressed by philosophers such as Hesse that it is tempting to identify it as a fourth, postmodern, position on objectivity. But this would be misleading. No major feminist critic of science has explicitly embraced postmodernism. Although many of the feminist positions owe much to postmodern conceptions, postmodernism does not constitute an identifiable position among the feminist critiques of science. The absence of a postmodern feminist critique of science testifies to the tenacity of the Enlightenment conception of science and, particularly, its claim to objectivity. Although feminists are willing to reject most aspects of masculinist science, they cling to objectivity because it constitutes the achievement of true knowledge that they find so hard to relinquish. Further, the absence of a postmodern position indicates the misunderstanding of postmodernism prevalant among the feminist critics of science. Nearly all assume that postmodernism entails anarchy, nihilism and relativism. What they fail to see is that their critique has much in common with postmodernism and that the epistemological eclecticism that their position entails is untenable. The feminist critique of masculinist science, if it is to be successful, must abandon objectivity along with the other trappings of Enlightenment science. It is significant that twentieth-century science has shown a marked tendency to abandon the certainty implicit in Enlightenment conceptions such as Newtonian physics. That feminists have been unwilling to acknowledge the significance of this reveals the limitation of their critique.

One of the elements of the attempt to construct a feminist science is the effort to define a model for a new kind of scientific enterprise. Feminists have argued that if the Enlightenment model is inherently sexist then we must find another model which can serve as the basis for scientific investigation. Both Merchant and Keller attempt to define such a model in their writings. It is interesting that both authors discuss the possibility of using a model of scientific investigation that was the precursor of modern science: the alchemical system. Both argue that alchemy embraces the androgenous equality of male and female principles that is denied by masculinist science. The alchemical system also espouses intercourse with nature rather than its domination, a principle in keeping with basic feminist values. This is a strange argument and a potentially reactionary one. Although the alchemical system rejects some of the elements of Enlightenment thought, it retains the basic duality between male and female that structures the scientific enterprise. Furthermore, scholars have noted that the alchemists did not regard the male and female principles as equal. Rather, they valued the male creative principle over the female (Tuana, 1986: 21). That the alchemical model is a poor choice for a model for feminist science seems clear even without these liabilities. To hark back to a prescientific model merely reinforces the charges that feminist science is "irrational" and "illogical." The goal of a feminist science should not be reaction, but, rather, a deconstruction of the dominant paradigm.

A more promising model for a feminist science is that presented by Keller in the context of her analysis of the biologist, Barbara McClintock. In her book, *A Feeling for the Organism* (1983a) and in a later article (1985) Keller describes

McClintock's approach to science as an alternative to the masculinist model. In presenting this model, she is careful to note that McClintock's approach to science did not arise from a feminist consciousness. Nor did it imply the addition of a feminist vision to the masculinist vision of science. McClintock's goal, rather, was to transform the creative vision of science itself (1985: 175). The element of McClintock's approach that Keller finds most useful in defining a non-sexist science is her style. Rejecting the rational model of masculinist science and the division between subject and object on which it rests, McClintock sought instead to gain an intimate knowledge of the plants she studied, what she called a "feeling for the organism." While scientists usually pride themselves on their ability to distance themselves from their subjects, McClintock instead sought a merging of subject and object in which the "I" disappears (1983a: 118). She challenged the norm of scientific detachment by arguing that good science requires a deep emotional investment on the part of the scientist, not the value-freedom that masculinist science espouses. She felt that reason alone could not embrace the mystery of the world but that something beyond reason was required (1983a: 198–9). McClintock defined that something beyond reason as a reliance on intuition rather than a strictly rational approach, a belief that led her to an interest in Tibetan Buddhism. Finally, McClintock sought to define a different relationship with nature that challenged the relationship of domination that governs masculinist science. She defined the goal of science not as prediction but as understanding and thus sought what Keller calls "empowerment." Rejecting the goal of manipulation, McClintock aimed for the kind of power that understands the world but also affirms our connection to that world (1985: 166).

Keller's description of McClintock's style offers a radical alternative to the dominant conception of scientific method. McClintock's rejection of the goals of scientific detachment, the domination of nature, and the achievement of value-freedom represent significant departures from masculinist science. In describing McClintock's approach, Keller avoids the error of defining a feminist science in terms of the addition of the feminine perspective to that of the masculine or even of substituting the feminine for the masculine (1985: 178). But there is also an element of Keller's analysis that is disturbing: her advocacy of what amounts to an intuitive approach to science. Although intuition can be seen as an important counter to the rationalist approach, an advocacy of intuition as opposed to rationality does not constitute an answer to the question of an alternative scientific method. Intuition, like irrationality, has been defined as a uniquely feminine quality, the opposite of the masculine quality of rationality. To appeal to intuition as opposed to reason thus entails not a displacement of this gender-based dichotomy, but an attempt to move from one side of the hierarchy to its opposite, to privilege the previously disprivileged side. The advocacy of intuition involves reifying the distinction between reason and emotion, rationality and irrationality that is central to Enlightenment epistemology. What is needed is not a reliance on intuition to the exclusion of reason but a means of breaking down the distinction between the two modes of thought.[5]

The critiques of masculinist science from a feminist perspective and the attempts to formulate a feminist science present a radical challenge to the received conception of science. The principal goal of the feminist critiques is to reveal the sexist bias at the root of western science and, in the case of the more radical critiques, to link that bias to the dualistic Enlightenment thought that informs western epistemology in general. This radical feminist critique of science both complements and expands the postmodern critique of Enlightenment thought. They share a fundamental rejection of Enlightenment dichotomies and the domination, manipulation and repression entailed by that epistemology. Many of the feminist critics have espoused an alternative science that is hermeneutic, pluralistic and non-hierarchical, qualities that are also prominent in the postmodern critique. Flax expresses this affinity very aptly with her argument that feminism and postmodernism share an "uncertainty" about grounding and that, although feminists may be tempted by the certainties of Enlightenment thought, ultimately the feminist movement belongs to the postmodern world (1986a). She argues that

> Feminist theorists, like other forms of postmodernism, should encourage us
> to tolerate and interpret ambivalence, ambiguity, and multiplicity as well as
> to expose the roots of our needs for imposing order and structure no matter
> how arbitrary and oppressive these needs may be. (1987a: 643)

Flax's understanding of the relationship between postmodernism and feminism, however, is not widely shared among feminist theorists.[6] Despite the similarity between the feminist and postmodern critiques, postmodernism has not posed an attractive alternative for most feminists. The most common objection to the postmodern position among feminists is its "relativism." Feminist standpoint theorists in particular object to postmodernism because it precludes the possibility of formulating one, true "women's perspective." The theorist who has taken the postmodern critique most seriously and has made the most sustained attempt to assess its relationship to feminism is Sandra Harding. In her book, *The Science Question in Feminism* (1986b) and a recent article (1986a) she analyzes what she sees to be the strengths and weaknesses of postmodern thought. On the plus side she sees postmodernism as revealing some of the errors of the feminist standpoint theorists. She argues that the postmodern critique allows us to see, first, that the critique of science advanced by the feminist standpoint theorists is not sufficiently radical. Unlike the postmoderns, feminist standpoint theorists do not challenge the fundamental aims of western science in their formulation of an alternative scientific method. Second, Harding argues that postmodernism also reveals the error of the assumption of one, true, feminine perspective. Employing postmodern arguments, Harding asserts that there is not one feminist standpoint but many; the perspectives of middle-class, black, and lesbian women cannot be subsumed under a single viewpoint (1986b: 141–63).

Despite these arguments that rely on a postmodern perspective, however, Harding ultimately rejects the position as an unsatisfactory one for feminism. Her first argument against postmodernism is her objection to its "absolute relativism" (1986b: 148). She claims that the relationship between nonfeminist postmodernism and feminist postmodernism is necessarily an "uneasy" one because of the need for a committed political stance in feminism (1986a: 656). In discussing the relativism of postmodern feminism, she asks whether we can afford to give up on the "one, true, feminist story of reality" (1986b: 28). She condemns the postmodern's inability to provide this conception of reality as evidence of their inability to provide a grounding for feminist theory. Her second argument against postmodernism is a broader one, involving an argument against all the epistemologies that claim to provide a basis for feminist thought. She asserts that none of the candidates for the foundation of feminist thought – liberal, radical, Marxist, or postmodern – are adequate. Looking to any of these perspectives to provide the analytic categories of feminism is a mistake, she argues, because feminist categories *should* be unstable (1986b: 243; 1986a: 648). Rather than attempting to resolve the contradictions and instabilities in feminist theory, she argues that we should accept them as a necessary aspect of the evolution of feminist thought.

Although Harding's attempt to assess the postmodern position is more serious than that of most feminists, it nevertheless falls short of a persuasive rejection of the position. Harding's first argument rests on a misunderstanding of the postmodern perspective and a fundamental contradiction in her own thought. If, as Harding herself argues, we must reject the dualism of Enlightenment thought, then we must reject the absolute/relative dualism as well. Her claim that postmodernism is relativistic rests on a dichotomized assumption concerning knowledge: that all knowledge is either absolute or relative. Even though Harding claims to be rejecting the dichotomies of Enlightenment thought, she is unable to conceptualize knowledge in terms that displace this dichotomy. Furthermore, as she continues her argument to assert that postmodernism fails to provide a true feminist story of reality, another contradiction arises. Harding condemns the feminist standpoint theorists for attempting to express a single women's perspective. But if no single women's perspective exists, as Harding herself insists, then it also follows that neither is there one, true feminist story of reality. A postmodern approach suggests that it is impossible to posit *either* a single women's perspective *or* a single, true feminist story of reality. Yet Harding wants to reject the former and espouse the latter. Harding's second argument, her assertion of the necessary instability of feminist categories is also suspect. What Harding is arguing for here is a kind of eclectic epistemology for feminism: it should pick and choose among the epistemological offerings of the various approaches that she mentions. But there is a serious problem with this suggestion. The other epistemologies that she mentions, liberal, Marxist and radical, are all Enlightenment epistemologies. They do not "mix" with postmodernism because the postmodern critique repudiates the basis of these epistemologies. Harding, like other theorists who have been discussed above, wants to combine the "good" aspects of Enlightenment epistemology with some useful elements of postmodernism. This eclecticism, however, is precluded by the radical nature of the postmodern critique.

Despite the rejection of postmodernism by Harding and many feminist critics of science, however, it is nevertheless the case that the postmodern position has a strong affinity with many of the arguments offered by the feminist critics. The postmodern critique of science expressed in the work of Hesse as well as the relevant aspects of the work of Gadamer, Foucault and Derrida reinforce and expand the feminist critique of masculinist science. It emphasizes that a radical critique of science must reject the reputed value-freedom of scientific investigation and assert instead that science is a socially and politically conditioned activity. By rejecting the absolutism and universalism of modern science postmodernism argues for a pluralistic, historically informed approach. In making this argument, postmodernism does not espouse "relativism" as its critics claim. Rather, it calls for a redefinition of knowledge that displaces the relative/absolute dichotomy and identifies all knowledge as hermeneutic. It rejects the metanarrative of the rationalist conception of science while at the same time resisting the temptation to formulate another metanarrative. Finally, by challenging the association of nature with women the postmodern critique reinforces the feminists' challenge to the domination of both women and nature that characterizes modern science without reifying the "naturalness" of women. On all of these issues the postmodern critique converges with some aspects of the feminist critique and reveals the limitations of those elements of the feminist critique that fail to challenge radically masculinist science. Seen in this light postmodernism is an important contribution to the feminist critique of science, not a threat to that critique as some feminists contend. It offers a means of reconceptualizing scientific activity that challenges the exclusion of women from the realm of science by challenging the definition of science itself.

IV Woman's "Nature"

The question of whether woman has an essential "nature" employs this concept in a way that is distinct from the way it is employed in the nature/culture dichotomy; those who discuss the "nature" of women are using "nature" in the Aristotelian sense of universal essence. It would seem to follow that the question of woman's nature is distinct from the question of woman's relationship to the natural world. The two issues, however, have been closely related. The dichotomy between nature and culture as it has been articulated in western thought since Plato is defined by the masculine/feminine dichotomy and characterized by the assumption that woman has an essential nature that is linked in some special way to the natural world. Although it is theoretically possible to posit woman's "nature" in different terms, this has not been the case in western thought. Furthermore, the notion that woman does have a special nature and that this nature does and should define her social role, is, like the link between woman and nature, rooted in the origins of western thought. The discussion of women from the Greeks onward has focused on the effort to define the essential nature of women and thereby to determine her proper social role. This effort is an outgrowth of the foundational, essentialist impulse that has characterized western philosophy since its inception. The effort to definitively identify woman's "true" nature is part of the desire to ground knowledge, and hence social life, in the absolute and the indubitable.[7]

The focus of the postmodern critique of this tradition of western thought is the rejection of foundationalist, universalistic thinking. The perspective that postmodernism provides for the question of woman's "nature," thus, is clear: it rejects the essentialist, foundationalist impulse that is at the root of the attempt to define woman's nature. The postmodern critique emphasizes that historically specific discourses constitute our knowledge of the world, a position that applies as well to the constitution of our concepts of men and women. For the postmoderns the attempt to formulate a universal concept of woman or man is futile and evidence of the continuing influence of foundationalist thought. This postmodern perspective on the question of woman's nature has much to recommend it. The attempt to define woman's nature and thereby to relegate her to an inferior social position has been central to the oppression of women in western history. Furthermore, the association of women with the natural world has been at the root of the effort to subordinate women, to justify their domination by the man of culture. It would seem to follow from this that the postmodern position would be a popular one in contemporary discussions of woman's "nature."

But this is not the case. Although some feminists have espoused the anti-essentialism of the postmodern perspective, the position has not been widely accepted. Three factors dictate the unpopularity of the postmodern position on this issue. First, the tenacity of foundationalist thought results in the continued effort to define woman's nature. The universalistic, absolutist tendency of western thought is strongly entrenched and is influential in the feminist movement as well as in other aspects of contemporary thought. Second, the tie between women and the natural world is also deeply rooted. The popularity of the eco-feminist movement within feminism is evidence of the positive connotations of a link with the natural world that many women still retain. These women are not receptive to the postmodern call to abandon this association. Finally, the postmodern position is unpopular because many feminists argue that it entails "abandoning difference." Opponents of the postmodern perspective argue that their denial of an essential nature for women entails the inability to talk about any differences between men and women. One feminist claims that this move to erase difference is "the last ruse of phallocentrism" (Schor, 1987: 109). She argues:

Before tearing down the cultural ghetto where the feminine has been confined and demeaned, we need to map its boundaries and excavate its foundations in order to salvage the usable relics and refuse of patriarchy, for to do so is perhaps the only chance we have to construct a post-deconstructionist society which will not simply reduplicate our own. (1987: 110)

One of the curious aspects of the attempt by contemporary feminists to define women's nature is that it unites many otherwise radically opposed schools of feminism. Although the arguments concerning women's nature are varied, they revolve around two closely related themes: women's special ties to the natural world and/or the characteristics that flow from her biologically determined reproductive capacity. The most explicit arguments for both a link between women and nature and a kind of biological determinism that emphasizes women's reproductive capacity come from the radical feminists. Theorists such as Daly, Griffin and Rich argue that woman possesses an essential nature and, specifically, that it is her body and her natural reproductive capacity that determines her essence. There are a number of varieties of this argument. One of the earliest versions of the "biology is destiny" argument was advanced by a theorist who, although positing a link between woman and nature, comes to a very different conclusion than subsequent radical feminists. In *The Dialectic of Sex* (1979) Firestone argues that it is woman's connection to nature through her reproductive and childrearing functions that is the principal source of her oppression. She asserts that it is only by altering their biological role in reproduction through technological means that women can free themselves from their oppression. Firestone's turn to technology, however, has not been the basis of most radical feminists' arguments concerning women's nature. O'Brien (1981), who also argues that women's reproductive capacity has been the source of male supremacy, turns this argument in a different direction. She asserts that women's link with nature through reproduction has a liberatory potential. It is this variety of the argument from woman's link with nature that has informed most contemporary radical feminist thinking. The best example of this position is found in the work of Susan Griffin. In *Woman and Nature: the roaring inside her* (1978) Griffin argues that woman's connection to nature through her reproductive function puts her in a position to repudiate the rape of nature that has characterized modern man's interaction with the natural world. Thus while for Firestone nature is the source of woman's oppression, for Griffin woman's connection to nature becomes the source of her, and the world's, salvation. Griffin argues that it is woman's link to nature that will free the world of the evils perpetuated by the domination of men.

Eco-feminists have capitalized on the connection between women and nature to articulate a feminist philosophy of liberation. One of the themes of both the eco-feminist and radical feminist movements has been an emphasis on woman's body. The feminists who emphasize women's body posit an essential, universal experience of the feminine body. Theorists such as Rich (1976) appeal to woman's body as the source of her essence, arguing that women have not been aware of their bodies because men have caused them to define their bodies in alien ways. What is needed, Rich argues, is for women to listen to their bodies and to become aware of their erotic potential: "We must touch the unity and resonance of our physicality, our bond with the natural order, the corporeal ground of our intelligence" (1976: 11). Another radical feminist theorist puts this same point very clearly in her statement that "the pursuit of woman's deepest erotic knowledge – the kind of knowledge, for example, that springs from the mothering relation – should become the taproot of women's lives" (Trask, 1986: 94).[8]

The radical feminists and eco-feminists' argument that women's nature is linked in a positive way to the natural world through her biologically determined reproductive capacity has strong appeal among contemporary feminists. In recent years, however, another variant of this approach to the question of woman's nature has arisen. The feminists who advance this variant of the argument, however, draw conservative rather than radical conclusions from their position. One of the sharpest critics of this position, Judith Stacey, has labeled the position "conservative pro-family feminism" (1983; 1986); other theorists have categorized it as "maternal thinking" after Sarah Ruddick's influential articles (1980; 1983; 1984; 1987). This movement is a product of what Friedan (1981) describes as the "second wave" of feminism. It emphasizes the differences between men and women, woman's link to nature through her reproductive function, and her moral superiority to men. Despite the fact that this is a distinctly contemporary movement, the themes espoused by these feminists are not new; they are themes that were central to the nineteenth-century feminist movement. Like the nineteenth-century suffragists, the conservative pro-family feminists argue for the moral superiority of women and identify that superiority as rooted in woman's role as childbearer and childrearer. Although few of the feminists in this group acknowledge this link to nineteenth-century feminism, there is an marked similarity between the two positions.

One of the first statements of this position is an article by Rossi published in 1977. In a bold and, at times, somewhat apologetic manner, Rossi argues that there is a significant biological difference between men and women that must be taken into account in assessing the family and men's and women's roles in it (1977: 2). She argues that the female's attachment to her children is biological, whereas the male's is social. From this it follows that mating and parenting are more closely linked for women than for men and that the "most important relationship in human society" is the mother–child bond (1977: 24). Rossi concludes her article by arguing that her position does not represent a defense of the status quo, asserting only that it entails that we must establish a "more natural environment for parenting" (1977: 25). The feminist community has been quick to define the conservative implications of Rossi's argument. Far from rejecting that argument, however, a number of other feminists have echoed Rossi's sentiments. Another expression of the pro-family position came several years later from a well-known feminist, Betty Friedan. In *The Second Stage* (1981) Friedan argues that the first stage of feminism erroneously emphasized "masculine" traits to the exclusion of "feminine" ones, thus alienating many women from the movement. In the second stage of the feminist movement, she argues, we must emphasize the feminine values that were submerged in the first stage. She defines these feminine values specifically in terms of the family and claims that by devaluing the family we have broken a cycle that is basic to life (1981: 36). Her thesis is that to achieve true freedom women today must not deny their "need as women to love or to have children" (1981: 72). Decrying the "sexual politics" that diverted the women's movement in the first stage, she calls for a new style of political leadership that has been "largely associated with women" (1981: 242).

The call for a new political style rooted in distinctively feminine values is also the theme of Sarah Ruddick's influential work on "maternal thinking." Ruddick's aim is to construct an "image of maternal power that is benign, accurate, sturdy and sane" (1980: 345). Women, she claims, possess cultures and traditions that, if brought into the public world, could transform politics and war. These traditions are a product of the maternal experience, qualities that flow from women's unique situation. Ruddick specifically identifies the qualities of maternal thinking with peace. She argues that out of maternal practice and the "preservative love" characteristic of women's experience a distinctive kind of thinking arises that is incompatible with military strategy and the eroticization of war but consistent with a pacifist commitment to non-violence (1983; 1984: 233). She claims that although maternal practice must first be transformed by feminist politics, a "critical feminist consciousness," it can serve as the basis for a new political ideal: "The real basis of female pacifism lies in the complicated social activity of preservation love" (1987: 479; 1984: 236).

Ruddick's argument that maternal thinking can serve as the basis for a feminist politics is strongly reinforced by a feminist who, as a political theorist, places this argument in a specifically political context. In her influential *Public Man, Private Woman* (1981), Jean Bethke Elshtain chronicles the exclusion of women from the public realm throughout the history of western political thought. She argues that this history is the history of men; women, whose domain has been the private world of the family, have not been allowed to participate in the public world of politics. The liberal feminist argument against this exclusion is that women should be allowed to join the public world as men's political equals. But Elshtain makes a different argument. She asserts that the values of woman's private sphere must be brought into the male public world. Her argument is that women should not adapt themselves to the male values of the public world, but, rather, should transform that world through the feminine values of the private sphere. In later articles she reinforces this argument and links it explicitly to the concept of maternal thinking. The liberal goal, and the goal of the first wave of feminism, was to integrate women into the public sphere. Elshtain opposes such integration, however, because it results in loss of identity: distinctively feminine values are obliterated (1982a: 46). The aim of a feminist politics today must be different. Elshtain argues that we must define a feminist commitment to a mode of public discourse embedded in maternal thinking. Maternal thinking has the advantage of affirming fragile human existence without adhering to sentimental "mothering values." Like Ruddick, Elshtain claims that maternal thinking must be transformed by feminist consciousness (1982a: 59). So transformed, however, feminine values have the reconstructive potential to restructure political discourse (1982c: 621).

In a recent article (1986b) Elshtain advances a position that adds complexity to her advocacy of maternal thinking and makes it clear where she stands relative to other feminist theorists. The subject of the article is a discussion of three ways in which feminists have discussed the understanding of sex roles in society. The first, which she labels "sex neutrality," is the position that the sexes are completely neutral and are totally constituted by culture. Elshtain criticizes this position on the grounds that it aims at transcending gender, even in the realm of procreation, a tactic she declares to be counterproductive for both women and men (1986b: 11). Second, she argues against a position she labels "sex polarity." The argument that women are "purer" than men, she asserts, creates a "closed" narrative in which the sexes are separate species (1986b: 13). Against both of these positions she argues for an approach she labels "sex complementarity." This position, like that of sex polarity, acknowledges sex differences, but, unlike that position, offers no privileged standpoint. She claims that it allows us to see female power and authority without positing the absolute superiority of the female standpoint (1986b: 16–19).

Elshtain's advocacy of "sex complementarity" is central to her defense of maternal thinking. In this and other articles she distances herself from the extreme social constructivist position (sex neutrality) as well as both radical and conservative feminists who want to posit the essentially female. Two themes dominate her discussion of these issues. First, she emphasizes that to deny differences between the sexes is to deny what she calls "embodiment." Her argument is that the sexes are different; they have different bodies in which they necessarily lead different lives as sexed individuals. What the extreme social constructivists fail to provide, she claims, is a "rich and robust picture" of human life (1984: 57). They want to create neutral, disembodied beings completely determined by social forces. Her position also entails preserving the family. Sexed bodies, she claims, have needs for intimacy and security that can only be met within a family (1982b: 444). She is careful to assert, however, that the argument for sexual difference need not entail social inequality. Rather, she claims, we can have both social justice and sexual difference (1984: 77). Her second theme also involves an attack on the social constructivist position. Elshtain wants to preserve a notion of human beings as agents, individuals who are not determined wholly by the social forces of the society in which they live (1984: 57). Rather, she wants to present a "self-constituting embodied subject" that, like Alcoff's agent, establishes an identity through a dialogue of inner and outer selves (1987: 149–50).

While Elshtain and Ruddick argue for a political program based in maternal thinking, Nel Noddings makes a similar argument for an ethical system based on distinctively feminine or maternal values. In *Caring* (1984) Noddings argues that ethics as it has been discussed in western thought has been cast in the language of the father; it has been a language of abstraction, of principles and of rules. The mother's view, on the other hand, has been silenced. The feminine view, in contrast to the masculine, is rooted in receptivity, relatedness and responsiveness (1984: 1–2). In her book, Noddings attempts to end the silence of women by articulating a "characteristically and essentially feminine" ethic built on caring. She claims that such an ethic of care is one that arises out of our experience as women. Like Gilligan, Noddings strongly objects to the characterization of woman's moral development as stunted. Rather she argues that "a powerful and coherent ethic and, indeed, a different sort of world may be built on the natural caring so familiar to women" (1984: 46). Finally, she argues against Chodorow that the mothering that is the root of the caring ethic is a natural rather than a social role; mothers learn how to care naturally. This natural caring of the mother is the basis for the feminine ethic that she advances.[9]

Two key aspects of the argument for maternal thinking emerge from these authors' discussions: the assumption of innate sex differences and the argument for a politics and ethics grounded in "feminine values." Both of these elements of the position have been attacked by other feminist theorists. In her indictment of conservative pro-family feminism, Stacey argues that these theorists forget the central tenet of the feminist movement, that sexual oppression is caused by the *social* construction of woman (1983; 1986). She argues that by positing innate differences between men and women, these theorists overlook the social source of woman's oppression. The central argument that Stacey advances is her claim that these theorists' call for a feminist politics rooted in maternal thinking is woefully inadequate in a political sense. She argues that the logical outcome of the reliance on traditional feminine values and the rejection of what Friedan calls "sexual politics" is the denial of the radical potential of feminism. Stacey even goes so far as to argue that the result of conservative pro-family feminism is the reinforcement of classical patriarchy (1986: 225). Elshtain's most recent work might be an attempt to counter arguments such as Stacey's. Elshtain is very aware of the social causes of women's oppression, but argues nevertheless that it is possible to have both sexual difference and social justice.

The theme of the political inadequacy of maternal thinking has been the subject of several other attacks by contemporary feminists (Fraser, 1986: 427; Dietz, 1985). But although this is a serious indictment of the position, it is not the most significant. Although the conservative pro-family feminists distinguish their position from that of the radicals, they share a key assumption with them: a belief in innate differences between men and women. This assumption entails serious problems. Most importantly, it reifies the dichotomy between the sexes that is at the root of the oppression of women; far from displacing it, they reinforce it. The history of dichotomous thinking in the west has shown that dichotomies always imply hierarchies. Western epistemology, particularly since the Enlightenment, reveals that the "separate but equal" status Elshtain strives for is an unrealizable ideal; oppositions always entail privileging. As one commentator puts it, "Differences become deficiences to those who peer through the bifocals of gender differentiation" (Nails, 1983: 643). By continuing the opposition discourse of masculine and feminine values, the maternal thinking theorists are also perpetuating the privileging inherent in that discourse.

Other problems are implicit in Elshtain's attack on the social constructivist position. Her principal argument is that social constructivism entails a denial of embodiment. Yet she fails to take account of the fact that Foucault, who must, by her standards, be considered an extreme constructivist, centers his theory in the description of how embodiment is accomplished in discursive formations. His description of various ways in which discourses both create and subjugate subjects focuses on bodies and his analysis of how sexuality is constructed through such discourses is central to his work. What his research suggests for feminism is, first, that gender is a social construction that we can analyze to expose the mechanisms that produce it, and, second, that displacing the dichotomized discourse of gender would allow us to talk about sexuality in a way that avoids the privileging that characterizes out present discourse. Elshtain's argument, in contrast, is that unless we continue to discuss gender in the old, dichotomized discourse of polarities we will not be able to discuss it at all. Foucault's work disproves this assumption. Foucault offers us a way to both analyze embodiment and discuss sexuality in terms of plurality and multiplicity rather than polarity.

The final problem with the proponents of maternal thinking is that they are dependent on yet another dichotomy: nature versus nurture. Elshtain in particular subscribes to this variant of the nature/culture dichotomy. She believes that we must choose between one of two poles: either the sexes are innately different (nature) or they are automatons determined by social forces (nurture). This belief prompts Elshtain to insist that we retain a notion of agentic subjectivity. But, once more, this assumption is wrong-headed. It is not necessary to think in terms of sex *or* gender, biology *or* social construction. Rather, we can think in terms of biological sex as something that we understand *through* social categories. Cixous, for example, argues that our bodies are themselves social constructions. Biological sex and socially constructed gender are not separate or opposed, but, rather, form an integral part of what we are as individuals. The appeal to nature, even as carefully circumscribed as the appeal is in Elshtain, is always a-historical and universalistic. The burgeoning feminist literature concerned with women of color continually points out that there is no one experience of being a woman, there is even no one experience of biological sex. We are, of course, sexed beings, but that biological fact is always understood socially and culturally. It can be understood in no other way.

Despite the popularity of the radical feminist position and maternal thinking, contemporary feminism has also seen a movement against the essentialism implicit in these positions. Several of those who argue against the essentialist feminists see the essentialists' argument in historical and philosophical terms, arguing that a move to essentialism entails repeating the errors of the western philosophical tradition. Thus, for example, Lloyd argues that glorifying the female as different may doom us to "repeat some of the sadder subplots of the history of western thought" (1984: 105). Even more directly Star argues:

> It is difficult to resist the urge to ask, "But what, *underneath it all*, really *are* the differences between men and women?" *What we must begin to give voice to as scientists and feminists is that there is no such thing, or place as underneath it all.* (1979: 116)

The theme that unites the attack on the search for an essential female nature is the emphasis on the social rather than the natural construction of "woman." The classic statement of this position is still de Beauvoir's assertion that women are made, not born. It is interesting to note that in later years de Beauvoir consistently maintained this position despite the surge of interest in "woman's nature" among what she called the "new feminists." In a 1979 interview she asserted that she was against the exalting of an essential difference in women "because it means falling once more into the masculine trap of wishing to enclose ourselves in our differences" (Simons and Benjamin, 1979: 342). She reinforced this position in a later interview:

> The "eternal feminine" is a lie because nature plays only a tiny part in the development of a human being. We are social beings. Furthermore, just as I do not believe that women are inferior to men by nature, nor do I believe that they are naturally superior either. (Schwarzer, 1984: 79)

The argument that "woman" is a social rather than a natural construct has often focused on questions of woman's biological nature. Some of these arguments follow de Beauvoir in their straightforward assertion that women are entirely socially constructed. Thus Eichler argues against what she calls the "biological fallacy": trying to explain social facts through biological facts. Eichler argues that biological facts derive their meaning from culture, not vice versa (1980: 11). Some of these arguments, however, move beyond this to question the fundamental dichotomy implicit in both conservative and radical biological arguments: nature versus nurture. Several feminists are beginning to question the validity of this variant of the nature/culture dichotomy (Birke, 1986; Holstrom 1982). Code argues that "Human beings are creatures of a sort whose nature is, in large measure, *structured* by nurture" (1983: 546). In an argument that explicitly appeals to postmodernism, Eichler asserts that the nature/culture distinction is itself a product of Cartesian dualisms (1980: 11). Grimshaw echoes these sentiments in

her argument that biology is not a substratum on which we can build a conception
of essential human nature because it is impossible to identify a completely non-
social sense of biology. She argues that woman's "second nature," her cultural
self, is so deeply rooted that it literally constitutes her personhood (1986: 130–6).

Perhaps the strongest arguments against an essential female nature in the
contemporary feminist literature come from the field of anthropology. In a number of recent collections, the question of the relationship between nature and
culture in the definition of sex roles has been examined (MacCormack and
Strathern, 1980; Ortner and Whitehead, 1981; Rosaldo and Lamphere 1974;
Reiter, 1975). The nearly unanimous conclusion of these researches is that
although the masculine/feminine dichotomy appears to be universal, the traits
associated with masculinity and femininity are not consistent across cultures.[10] The
conclusion drawn by these writers is that gender is entirely a social construct
constituted by cultures and the symbolic systems they deploy. The most powerful
and well-known statement of this thesis is Gayle Rubin's discussion in "The
traffic in women" (1975). Rubin posits the existence of what she calls the
"sex–gender system." She defines this as a set of arrangements by which a society
transforms biological sexuality into products of human activity in which these
transformed sexual needs are satisfied (1975: 159). Rubin's thesis ties in with de
Beauvoir's position in that it attempts to answer the question of how little girls
become women. Rubin's analysis of the sex–gender system characterizes the
central thrust of contemporary feminist anthropology: "Gender is a socially
imposed division of the sexes. It is a product of the social relations of sexuality"
(1975: 179).

It is difficult to assess the impact of these debates over woman's "nature."
While it is clear that the essentialist movement in feminism has some very vocal
detractors, the question is far from being resolved. The desire to define an essential
female nature is still very strong, particularly in the social sciences. The social
sciences, since their inception, have tried to formulate universalistic theories about
social structure; anti-essentialist arguments frustrate this urge. But this discussion
involves not simply a question of who will "win" the debate; there is also a
difficulty with the terms of the debate itself. Most of the arguments against
essentialism are still cast in terms of the dichotomies of Enlightenment thought:
either women are socially constructed or they are biologically determined. Most of
the participants in the debate believe that we must choose between an absolute or a
relative conception of human nature. What is missing in this debate, however, is
the argument that the issue is not choosing one side of the dichotomy or the other
but, rather, displacing the dichotomy itself. What Foucault and other postmodern
philosophers have argued is that we do not have to choose between the absolute or
the natural on one hand, the cultural or the relative on the other. Rather, they are
attempting to displace these Enlightenment dichotomies, to conceive of knowledge in a different way.

The feminist writers who have made the greatest contribution toward displacing these Enlightenment dichotomies and altering the terms of the debate are the French feminists. Like the postmodern philosophers, Cixous, Irigaray and Kristeva challenge the epistemological assumptions of the Enlightenment and attempt to address the question of "woman" in ways that avoid Enlightenment dichotomies. Many of their critics have noted, however, that the positions of these writers on the question of woman's nature are decidedly ambiguous. On one hand all of them argue at some points that the feminine is an ideological construct constituted by social and historical forces. In other contexts, however, all of them appeal to some seemingly essentialistic element, particularly the female body, as a quasi-universal source of self-knowledge for women. This ambiguity in their positions is difficult to interpret. It may represent a contradiction or simply a capitulation to the desire to define the essentially female. A more defensible explanation, however, is that this seeming confusion stems from their attempt to articulate a new discourse on women and the feminine, a discourse that does not depend on the nature/culture dichotomy.

The writings of Helene Cixous exhibit both the clearest example of the seeming contradiction between essentialist and anti-essentialist arguments and the strongest evidence of an attempt to overcome the dichotomy between them. On one hand Cixous is very forceful in her denunciation of the dichotomies of philosophical thought and particularly of the attempt to define an essential masculine or feminine nature. Her attack on the dualities of western thought that was discussed above reveals that she sees these oppositions as disprivileging women. In *The Newly Born Woman* Cixous specifically attacks the nature/culture dualism, arguing that the association of woman with nature links women with magic and mystery and explains why the sorceress and the hysteric are always women (Cixous and Clement, 1986: 8). Her attack on dualities is a preface to an attack on the essences they claim to represent. She explicitly rejects the notion that there is a "general woman" or a single feminine sexuality (1976: 876). She also rejects the association of the feminine with woman, the masculine with man. She asserts that there is no essence to masculinity or femininity, but, rather, that "everything is language" and that even the body is always a written, not a "natural" body (Cixous in Conley, 1984: 57). Furthermore, she identifies the effort to define essences, to ask "What is it?" as a distinctly masculine form of interrogation (1981: 45). In her clearest statement of an anti-essentialist position, she asserts:

> There is "destiny" no more than there is "nature" or "essence" as such. Rather, there are living structures that are caught and sometimes rigidly set within historico-cultural limits so mixed up with the scene of History that for a long time it has been impossible (and it is still very difficult) to think or even imagine an "elsewhere" . . . (Cixous and Clement, 1986: 83)

In her discussion of "writing the body," however, Cixous seems to be leaning toward an essentialist position and, hence, a departure from this anti-essentialist stance. In statements like "woman must write her body" and "woman is body more than man is . . . more body, hence more writing" Cixous seems to be appealing to an essential conception of feminine anatomy. Furthermore, her appeal to "*jouissance*" as a specifically feminine "libidinal economy" seems to entail an almost Freudian conception of a distinctively feminine ego (Cixous and Clement, 1986: 92). But although these passages have essentialist overtones, to conclude from this that Cixous is an essentialist is false for at least two reasons. First, as a number of commentators have argued, an appeal to the body need not entail essentialism because the body, like gender, can be interpreted as a social, not a natural construct (Hite, 1988: 123; DuPlessis, 1985: 273; Gilbert, 1986: xvi). This interpretation of the body as a social construct explains Cixous' seemingly essentialist moves. For Cixous, woman's body is an entity that has been defined by the masculinist symbolic, and, furthermore, has been excluded from the realm of the symbolic; woman is a lack because she lacks a relationship to the phallus (1981: 46). Woman, she asserts, has not been allowed to live in her own house, her body. Rather, women's bodies have been colonized (Cixous and Clement, 1986: 68). Writing the body is thus an attempt to inaugurate a discourse about the body that refutes this colonized status, not an appeal to some essentialist natural entity (1981: 54). Second, Cixous' reason for appealing to the body and feminine writing is to displace the symbolic, not to establish a new essentialism. She describes her appeal to the body as a subversive move (1976: 888): *jouissance*, she claims, has simultaneously sexual, political and economic overtones; it is a means of overcoming cultural repression (Cixous and Clement, 1986: 165–8). In a move that is reminiscent of Foucault, Cixous is looking to the silences of symbolic discourse as a way of deconstructing that discourse.

That Cixous is ambiguous and confusing in these passages is undeniable. Despite her ambiguity, however, there is strong evidence that the point of these discussions is an attempt to formulate a new way of talking about sexual difference rather than an appeal to woman's essential nature. She is very clear in her assertion that what we must avoid above all is falling into Freud's error of assuming a natural anatomical determination of sexual difference in terms of oppositions. She claims that it is impossible at this point in time to predict what will become of sexual difference in the future. But she nevertheless argues that we can see the broad outlines of the future of difference. We can imagine a change in the oppositional structures that now define the discussion of the masculine and the feminine, a different way of inscribing difference: "Difference would be a bunch of new differences" (Cixous and Clement, 1986: 81–3). Like the postmodern philosophers, what Cixous is attempting in her work is the articulation of a discourse on masculinity, femininity, the body and sexuality that displaces the masculinist discourse and relegates women to silence. Cixous' discourse attempts a discussion of difference that does not rest on oppositions, but, rather, defines difference as plural and fluid. The seeming contradictions in her work stem from the difficulty of her task. The discourse she is articulating violates all the rules and assumptions of these she rejects. The critics who conclude that her work is essentialist are overlooking this revolutionary nature of her discourse (Moi, 1985b: 110; Stanton, 1986: 170).

Although most critics will concede that Cixous' work is at least ambivalent on the issue of essentialism, this is not true of the work of Irigaray. There is nearly unanimous agreement that what Irigaray is attempting to do is to establish a definition of feminine sexuality rooted in a primordial conception of the female body (Weedon, 1987: 63; Stanton, 1986: 160; Plaza, 1978; Sayers, 1986: 42; Brown and Adams, 1979: 38). It is difficult to assess the accuracy of this charge because Irigaray is even less interested than Cixous in defining a "theory." In fact, one of the themes of Irigaray's work is to call into question the whole notion of theory and orthodoxy, defining them as masculinist and, hence, to be avoided. A good example of the difficulty that confronts an interpretation of Irigaray's work is the title of her influential book, *This Sex Which is Not One*. Does this title entail, as many of her critics contend, an attempt to define a true feminine sexuality or does it connote, rather, an attempt to deconstruct the unitary masculinist conception of sexuality and replace it with a plural, non-unitary conception? Irigaray gives her readers little assistance in answering questions such as these and, thus, compounds the difficulty of resolving the seeming contradictions in her work.

The case for an essentialist reading of Irigaray has been made by her many critics. They claim that she is establishing a fixed, unitary conception of feminine sexuality that is rooted in biology. These critics can quote passages in which Irigaray seems to be asserting precisely this. It is possible, however, to make just as plausible a case for interpreting Irigaray in non-essentialist terms. The first item in her defense is that she was a student of Lacan and, following him, defines the self in constructed rather than essentialist terms. Lacan's view of the self is very evident in Irigaray's treatment of women. Like Lacan, she rejects the search for the universal that characterizes masculinist views of the self. She is very explicit in her assertion that she is not attempting simply to reverse the values of phallogocentrism. She rejects the attempt to privilege the feminine over the masculine, dismissing it as a "studied gynocentrism" (1985b: 162). Second, unlike many essentialists, Irigaray rejects the maternal role as definitive of an essential femininity. She insists that women cannot remain in society in the position of "obscure nurturers" (1987: 13). The principal theme of her discussion of women is their plurality, a plurality that challenges unitary masculinist sexuality. If the female imaginary were to deploy itself, she insists, it would not be in a unitary form; it is, rather, both plural and fluid. She identifies the attempt to define women as essentially maternal as tantamount to attempting to define her as unitary and, thus, rejects the move. The result, she claims, would be a "phallic maternal" (1985b: 30,79).

One of Irigaray's more sympathetic critics argues that her writing is difficult because it lacks content; it simply deconstructs phallocentric thought (Burke, 1981: 296). This interpretation comes closer to describing the tenor of Irigaray's work than the many charges of essentialism. What Irigaray, like Cixous, is attempting to do is to articulate a discourse on women that displaces masculinist discourse. This is difficult because, in masculinist discourse, woman is defined as a lack. Irigaray remarks:

> So for woman it is not a matter of installing herself within this lack, this negative, even by denouncing it, nor of reversing the economy of sameness by turning the feminine into *the standard for "sexual difference;"* it is rather a matter of trying to practice that difference. (1985b: 159)

The effort to "practice the difference" is a theme that unites Irigaray's discussions of women, sexuality and the feminine. Her question is how we can talk about sexual difference in non-dualistic terms. "Sexual difference," she claims, "is probably the issue in our own age which could be our salvation on an intellectual level." For the work of sexual difference to take place, however, a revolution is necessary, a revolution in thought, ethics and discourse. The female subject cannot be discussed because the subject has always been male (1987: 118–28). When Irigaray appeals to the body and feminine sexuality in her work she is not attempting to define the "essence" of feminine sexuality. Rather, she is using feminine sexuality as an analogy to inaugurate a new discourse rooted in a non-oppositional notion of difference. Thus when she asserts that feminine sexuality is plural, that women are "strangers to dichotomy" (1987: 128), she is not attempting to define an essence, but, rather, to talk about sexual difference in a new way (1985b: 24). Like Cixous, she is attempting to open up the masculinist discourse of the symbolic, a discourse that excludes women. The means she devises to accomplish this goal is an appeal to women's sexuality as both metaphor and analogy, not essence.

The work of Kristeva presents a strange paradox. On one hand she is widely acknowledged to be the least essentialist of the three writers. She is adamant in her insistence that there is no essence to the subject itself, either masculine or feminine. Her explicit reliance on Lacan's constructed subject leads her to reject the whole notion of identity. The thesis that unites the many aspects of her work is that subjects are constituted by discourse and have no essence or identity apart from that discourse. This thesis informs Kristeva's discussion of women and their identity in two ways. First, it rules out the possibility of the essentially feminine; no essences exist, only discourses. Second, Kristeva's analysis of how the subject has been constituted in the various discourses she discusses reveals that it has only been constituted as masculine. Thus when Kristeva declares that woman and the feminine do not "exist" there is a double meaning to her statement: no essences exist and, hence, no essential woman exists; the only subject that has been constituted is masculine and, hence, no feminine subject exists. Kristeva's thesis of the constructed self, furthermore, does not end with the discussion of the consti-tuted subject; she extends this thesis to include the body and sexuality as well. She insists that the body, like the subject, is not fixed, but in process, it has no unity outside the signifying practice that articulates it (1984: 101). Similarly, she argues that the analysis of sex cannot be separated from that of language. She defines sexuality as a complex pattern of responses and meanings between linguistic systems (1987: 46).

Kristeva's rejection of essences and identity, her insistence that the masculine, the feminine, the body and even sexuality are all products of discourse, seems to absolve her of any charge of essentialism. There is another aspect to Kristeva's thought, however, an aspect frequently overlooked by those who are searching for the feminine essence, that exhibits clear signs of essentialism: her discussion of the semiotic and the symbolic. The problem in her discussion is not that she identifies the semiotic as essentially feminine and the symbolic as essentially masculine. Kristeva is careful to argue that the semiotic is simply that element that has been constituted as the feminine in discourses since Plato's "semiotic chora." The problem with Kristeva's formulation is, rather, that she defines the symbolic and the semiotic as essential elements in the constitution of the subject. They are not themselves products of discourse but, rather, the elements out of which every discourse on the subject is constituted. Kristeva argues that although subjects have been constituted differently in different discourses, these two essential elements always supply the necessary elements of the discourse. The subject that emerges from the discourses is a product of the interaction of these two necessary, primordial elements. The combination of this essentialist thesis and the radical anti-essentialism of Kristeva's theory of identity produces some strange results in her work. For instance, even though Kristeva denies that *jouissance* is an element of the essentially feminine, she nevertheless defines it as an essential element in its own right. For her it is an integral part of the semiotic that, through art, flows into languages (1984: 79). Similarly, even though the semiotic itself is not essentially feminine, Kristeva argues that it is a necessary element of the constitution of the subject. This also explains the revolutionary character of the semiotic. Because of the way in which the subject has been constituted since the Enlightenment, the semiotic today functions as a means of transgressing the (masculine) symbolic.

The fact that Kristeva refuses to abandon a notion of the primordial, essential elements of the subject does not, strictly speaking, represent a contradiction in her work. She can consistently maintain that while the subject has no fixed identity, the identities that it acquires in discourses are constituted from fixed elements. Furthermore, it is not difficult to understand why Kristeva makes this essentialist move. She wants to retain a notion of what the subject "really" is, in order to avoid a totally "relative" conception of the subject. Like Cixous and Irigaray, she is attempting to construct a new discourse about the subject, the feminine and women. But unlike them she wants to ground this discourse in some fixed entities. Because of the essentialism implicit in her theory of the semiotic and the symbolic, her discourse is less successful than that of Cixous' and Irigaray's. The discourse she formulates, however, is not without its advantages. Her insistence that neither the masculine nor the feminine has any essential identity makes her very aware of the mechanisms by which the "feminine" is embedded in cultural stereotypes. Because she defines the subject as constructed through discourse she is sensitive to the technology of that construction and its deployment. Most importantly, she sees what is constituted as the "feminine" within our present discourse of the subject as a subversive force with revolutionary potential. She argues that woman's *jouissance* breaks out of the symbolic chain as it is presently constituted (1986a: 154). Her definition of the feminine as revolutionary and subversive is the most valuable aspect of her theory. Like the positions of Cixous and Irigaray, it allows us to define the feminine not as a primordial essence but as a means of displacing the masculinist symbolic.

Despite the differences among them and the ambiguities internal to each position, the work of Cixous, Irigaray and Kristeva offers a significant contribution to the feminist discussion of women and nature. They provide an important antidote to those who assert an essentialist concept of woman and/or a fundamental association between women and nature. Their attempt to formulate a new discourse about women, sexuality and the body is a crucial step toward the articulation of sexual difference that is non-oppositional and non-hierarchical. Their attack on the dichotomous discourse of sexual difference is an effort to break the hold that this discourse has exerted over the lives and status of women. It is not an effort to eliminate difference, but to lessen the power of the privileged concept of difference that until now has been hegemonic. The articulation of this new discourse has been strongly influenced by postmodern philosophy and exhibits many similarities to that approach. The emphasis on language and discourse and the way in which they constitute subjects and their sexuality is a dominant theme of these three writers as well as the work of Foucault. Like Foucault these writers stress that the discourses that structure and define social reality are historically variable. Foucault's position emphasizes that there is not a biological or "natural" grounding for our conceptions, but, rather, that they must be defined in social and historical rather than universalist terms. Although these writers may appear at times to be appealing to biology, a careful analysis of the positions that they articulate reveals that they have more in common with Foucault than the position that biology is destiny.

The attack on essentialism, although it is not always linked to postmodern philosophy, is an important component of contemporary feminist theory. The argument that feminists should not employ essentialistic, universalistic concepts has been used not only to argue against a single definition of "woman" but also against the universalistic definition of concepts such as patriarchy, male domination and gender (Young, 1984; Ferguson 1984:154; Cornell and Thurschwell, 1985; Smith, 1983; Nicholson 1986; Lerner, 1986). The theme of these theorists' arguments is that to understand the phenomenon of woman's oppression we must understand it in historically, culturally, and socially specific terms. Employing universalistic concepts or appealing to an essential feminine nature will only lead feminism back to Enlightenment epistemology. The only means of displacing that epistemology lies in the formulation of a discourse that articulates women and sexuality in radically different terms. Cixous, Irigaray and Kristeva have begun to indicate the form that discourse might take, what the "future of difference" might be. Postmodern philosophy can be useful in this attempt to frame that discourse. It provides a means of displacing the sterile dichotomies of Enlightenment thought, dichotomies that have excluded woman from the realm of science and devalued her by identifying her with the forces of nature.

Notes

1 For a further discussion of these issues see Hekman (1986: 44–5) and Weinsheimer (1985).

2 An interesting corollary of the sociobiological thesis can be found in Ivan Illich's *Gender* (1982). Although Illich is discussing sexual roles from a social rather than biological point of view and although he claims to be attacking the inferiority of women in the modern world, his theory nevertheless shares the essentialist assumptions of sociobiologists. Illich's argument amounts to the assertion that women and men are essentially different and that this difference is properly manifest in what he calls the regime of "gender." In societies ruled by gender men and women have separate, clearly defined roles that reflect their essences. In the regime of sex, however, these essential divisions and roles are lost. He states:

> The paradigm of *Homo oeconomicus* does not square with what men and women actually are. Perhaps they cannot be reduced to humans, to economic neuters of either male or female sex. Economic existence and gender might be literally incompatible. (1982: 66)

Illich's concept of gender, which assumes two human natures, places women in a permanently inferior position that is similar to sociobiology's conclusions. For a feminist critique of Illich see Bowles et al. (1983).

3 For more illustrations of this attitude see Roberts (1976), Eichler (1980: 119), many of the articles in Hubbard and Lowe (1979), and Hubbard, Henefin and Fried (1979).

4 For a critique of feminist standpoint theorists see Harding (1986b: 141, 192). Although Harding's critique is consistent with the postmodern perspective she later rejects the postmodernist stance.

5 In her discussion of a feminist science, Arditti also advocates an intuitive approach (1980: 366).

6 For other discussions of the relationship between postmodernism and feminism see chap. 2. n. 12.

7 See Stern (1965) for a contemporary example of the effort to define woman's nature and draw conclusions from it for the way women should live.

8 In her critique of the effort to define an essential female nature and experience Clavir labels these theorists "metaphysical feminists" (1979: 404).

9 For a critique of the ethic of care see Tronto (1987a; 1987b).

10 This same question is taken up in a more biological context in Lowe and Hubbard (1983).

5

The Possibilities of a Postmodern Feminism

I The Feminist Case Against Postmodernism

Contemporary feminism is, by any standard, a diverse movement. It is impossible to define a single "feminism," much less a political program that unites all feminists. It is difficult, therefore, to characterize in general terms the relationship between postmodernism and feminism. Some feminists are sympathetic to and even supportive of the postmodern position and many feminist positions are consistent with the postmodern critique. Despite this, however, most feminists regard postmodernism with attitudes that range from skepticism to hostility, attitudes that are a product of the modernist roots of contemporary feminism. Several of the principal objections that feminists have raised against the postmodern position are derivative of the general criticisms advanced by modernists; others are unique to the feminist movement. Even the standard criticisms of postmodernism, however, have assumed a special prominence in the feminist movement. Because feminism is challenging not only particular social arrangements but the very foundations of western thought and social structure, it demands a political and philosophical approach that is equal to this task. This, many feminists contend, is where postmodernism fails.

The first theme of both the feminist and the modernist critique of postmodernism is the charge of relativism.[1] The opposition of postmodernism and modernism on the issue of relativism, however, is not a debate in the strict sense because the two sides do not share a common definition of relativism. For the modernist relativism is an evil to be avoided at all costs. Espousing relativism is tantamount to giving up on notions of truth and falsity, rationality and irrationality. Modernists rarely feel a need to defend their objections to relativism. Once they have identified a position as relativistic they assume that the argument has been resolved in their favor. Against this position the postmoderns do not attempt to espouse the relativism that the modernists reject. Rather, the postmodern argument involves rejecting Enlightenment epistemology that defines knowledge as either absolute or relative. Although the postmoderns argue that the modernists' search for absolute grounding is misconceived, they do not attempt simply to reverse the dichotomy by advocating a relative as opposed to an absolute knowledge. Rather they argue that all knowledge is contextual and historical, thus rendering the opposition between absolute and relative obsolete. Thus the "debate" between modernists and postmodernists on this issue cannot be resolved. Both sides see their opponents' position as misconceived because they disagree on the fundamental character of knowledge.

Closely related to the charge of relativism is the claim that postmodernism is nihilistic. From the modernist perspective there is a clear distinction between relativism and nihilism: the relativist accepts some standards of truth and falsity, albeit not absolute ones, while the nihilist rejects any standards at all. Critics of postmodernism point to the fact that many postmodern philosophers link their position to that of Nietzsche, the philosopher who is most closely connected to nihilism. Nietzsche's nihilism involved more than a questioning of old truths and values; rather, it involved the claim that it is futile to attempt to discover a basis for truth. In one of the most thorough discussions of Nietzsche's nihilism, Tracy Strong argues that his position entails the attempt to reach a state that is known to be impossible; it is a realization that there is no truth but that we should nevertheless continue to strive for it (1975: 17; 1984: 102). This definition of nihilism reveals the presuppositions of the modernist position. The definition of nihilism, like that of relativism, is parasitic on the assumption of the necessity for a foundation for knowledge. If we assume, as the postmoderns do, that knowledge is not in need of absolute foundations, then the charge of nihilism, like that of relativism, becomes irrelevant. In fact, from the postmodern perspective, there is little difference between the two concepts; both are derivative of the same epistemological assumptions concerning knowledge. Nietzsche, despite his postmodern inclinations, reveals his modernist assumptions in his attitude toward nihilism. He assumes, along with those he criticizes, that anything other than absolutely grounded knowledge is questionable. The postmoderns who follow him, in contrast, have displaced the epistemological assumptions that Nietzsche had begun to challenge by rejecting the notion of grounding altogether.

Most feminist criticisms of postmodernism focus on these epistemological themes of relativism and nihilism. Although they may not explicitly acknowledge it, most feminists cling to modernist assumptions about knowledge. Both liberal and socialist feminism are rooted in the modernist presuppositions of the creeds that define them. Likewise, radical feminists who attempt to provide an absolute grounding for knowledge in a feminist rather than a masculinist epistemology are also following the foundationalist principles of modernist thought. The epistemological objections to postmodernism among feminists, however, are overshadowed by a related issue: the alleged political inadequacy of postmodernism. Feminists, even more than the other critics of postmodernism, are concerned that postmodernism precludes the possibility of liberating political action. The defenders of modernism have argued that postmodernism abandons the central values of Enlightenment thought: autonomy, individualism, rights, etc. This charge, which has been most effectively argued by Habermas and other critical theorists, centers around the claim that postmodernism obviates the possibility of committed political action and, most particularly, action that is guided by the Enlightenment's goal of emancipation. At its worst, Habermas argues, postmodernism leads to a form of conservative reaction; at its best it maintains the status quo and thus serves to perpetuate the injustices of the existing system. The charge that postmodernism is politically bankrupt is particularly relevant to the concerns of feminism. From the outset feminism has been an explicitly political movement and as such demands a coherent political program. More importantly, however, feminism, unlike other political movements, is challenging not just one aspect of the status quo but the basis of the social structure itself: male privilege. Thus the charge that postmodernism ultimately supports the status quo is one that feminists cannot dismiss lightly (White, 1986).

Most feminists who discuss postmodernism dismiss it without extensive analysis by relying on one of these general criticisms of the movement. But the particular needs of the feminist movement have also produced some critiques of postmodernism that are unique to feminism. A good example of these criticisms can be found in the work of Nancy Hartsock. In *Money, Sex and Power* (1983b) Hartsock does not explicitly discuss postmodernism, but she makes a statement that sets the tone for her rejection of the position in her subsequent work:

> The real issues are the extent to which feminists can borrow from phallocratic ideologies without their own analyses suffering in consequence, and the extent to which feminist theory can take place without being relocated onto the ground provided by a specifically feminist epistemology. (1983b: 295)

This statement can be interpreted in two different ways. A postmodernist might argue, with Derrida, that feminism must displace the logocentric and, hence, phallocratic epistemology of the metaphysics of presence. But the interpretation that is closer to Hartsock's intent is a quite different one. She has argued consistently that feminists must reject all epistemologies that are formulated by male theorists and adopt an epistemology that privileges the female standpoint. Like Audre Lorde she is arguing that "the master's tools can never dismantle the master's house" (Lorde, 1981: 99). Both of these demands entail that Hartsock reject postmodernism as an inadequate basis for feminist theory. Not only is postmodernism primarily a product of male theorists, but, more importantly, it rejects the whole notion of a privileged standpoint, either masculine or feminine.

In a subsequent article (1987) Hartsock attacks the postmodern position more explicitly. The theme of her analysis revolves around the argument that women, like colonized people, have been what she calls "marginalized." Like colonized people women have always been defined as at the periphery rather than as at the center. Following theorists who consider the problems of marginalization,

Hartsock argues that in order to transcend this inferior status women must constitute themselves in a way that overcomes their marginalization: "But to the extent that we have been constituted as Other, it is important to insist as well on a vision of the world in which we are at the center rather than at the periphery" (1987: 201) Using the perspective of the problem of marginalization, Hartsock claims that postmodernism would hinder rather than help feminists in their effort to achieve the goal of overcoming marginalization because it rejects the epistemology of subjects and objects. Women cannot constitute themselves as subjects in a postmodern world because postmodernism denies the transcendental subject of the modern episteme. Postmodernism rejects any epistemology that is defined in terms of center and periphery and would thus reject a woman-centered epistemology as much as a man-centered one. Hartsock's argument here is very similar to that of Alcoff. The thrust of her argument is that just as women are realizing the possibility of overcoming their marginalization, postmodernism is denying them their day in the sun.

Hartsock's critique of postmodernism does not end with this epistemological point. Her second objection is that postmodernism offers women no help in their project of political change. She claims that Foucault's strategy of resistance to power and Rorty's tactic of rejecting modernism in favor of "conversation" are inadequate to the political needs of feminism. Finally, she claims that postmodernism is deficient for failing to provide an epistemology that offers the possibility of the creation of knowledge. Although both of these arguments are derivative of the modernist critique of postmodernism, Hartsock argues that they are particularly important for feminism.

Hartsock's arguments are important for two reasons. First, they are representative of many of the feminist critiques of postmodernism. Although they are not the only objections to postmodernism that feminists have voiced, they are the most central. Second, her critique reveals that, for most feminists, there are two major obstacles standing in the way of the formulation of a postmodern feminism. The first obstacle is postmodernism's rejection of epistemology. Hartsock claims that postmodernism denies the possibility of both the subject and knowledge and that, as a consequence, it is deficient on epistemological grounds. The second obstacle is political. She claims that postmodernism obviates the possibility of committed political action and, thus, must be rejected. Although these two arguments are connected, they are best dealt with separately. Derrida's work offers the best defense of the rejection of epistemology that Hartsock attacks. Foucault, on the other hand, specifically addresses the question of the possibilities of political action that are entailed by his position. An examination of each of their positions offers refutations of Hartsock's critiques. It also provides the outlines of a postmodern feminism.

Although the strongest case for a postmodern feminism can be made through the examination of the work of Derrida and Foucault, Gadamer's perspective is not irrelevant to this task. As several feminists have pointed out, Gadamer's perspective can be very useful for a feminist analysis (Bowles, 1984; Buker, 1985). His understanding of the hermeneutic circle can be used to show how the dichotomies of Enlightenment thought entail a disprivileged status for women. Furthermore, although Gadamer's perspective is rooted in an emphasis on tradition, his position nevertheless provides the basis for a critique of existing political arrangements. Although Gadamer's critics claim that his position entails political acquiescence, he explicitly denies this. He asserts that hermeneutics always involves the critique of tradition, not a blind acceptance of its prejudices:

> It is a grave misunderstanding to assume that emphasis on the essential factor of tradition which enters into all understanding implies an uncritical acceptance of tradition and sociopolitical conservatism. In truth the confrontation of our historic tradition is always a critical challenge of this tradition. (1979: 108)[2]

In recent years there has been a great deal of interest in the question of the relationship between feminism and postmodernism among feminist theorists. The literature dealing with this question, however, is very mixed. It ranges from theorists, like Hartsock, who reject postmodernism outright to those who advocate a positive relationship between feminism and postmodernism. In between these two poles are the majority of commentators, theorists who argue that the relationship between feminism and postmodernism is necessarily ambivalent. Many of the theorists taking the in-between position argue that while postmodernism can be useful for feminism it can be dangerous as well. De Lauretis, for example, while using some of Foucault's positions, cautions that his view leads to a kind of "paradoxical conservatism" (1984: 94) and an inadequate view of sexuality (1987: 14). Likewise, Meese argues that deconstruction has something to offer feminism but that feminists must beware of "this other trespasser" (1986: 14). And both Rabine (1988) and Poovey (1988) assert that feminism can use deconstruction, but that the relationship between the two must always be somewhat adversarial.

Another common characteristic of the literature on postmodernism and feminism is listing the difference and similarities between the two approaches. Vickers (1982), Du Plessis (1985) and Gross (1986a) all discuss the similarities between postmodernism and feminism but stop short of advocating the wholesale adoption of postmodernism. The thesis that emerges out of these and related articles is that postmodernism can be useful to feminism, but only if it is rewritten for the unique needs of the feminist project (Weedon, 1987). The two best statements of this thesis are Fraser and Nicholson (1988) and Diamond and Quinby (1988b). Fraser and Nicholson advocate an integration between postmodernism and feminism but assert that postmodernism must be politicized to meet the needs of feminism. On the other hand, however, they assert that postmodernism can be used to refute the essentialism implicit in many feminist theorists. Diamond and Quinby focus on the methodological usefulness of the postmodernism of Foucault. They argue that Foucault's emphasis on the body, power, discourse and the subject can be used to facilitate feminist research and aid in the understanding of the technologies of gender. They argue for a relationship between postmodernism and feminism that entails a "friendship grounded in political and ethical commitment," a friendship which, they claim, will not be without tensions (1988b: ix). The essays they have collected in their edited volume echo these sentiments.

Using postmodern philosophy to meet the unique needs of feminism is a theme that characterizes nearly all of the feminist theorists who discuss postmodernism. One of the variants of this theme is represented in the work of Young (1985; 1986a; 1986b) and Jardine (1985). Young's rejection of what she calls "humanist feminism" owes an explicit debt to postmodernism. Similarly, her questioning of the essentialism implicit in "gynocentric feminism" has postmodern roots. Despite its essentialism, however, Young applauds the gynocentric movement as a necessary corrective to Enlightenment/humanist epistemology (1985: 181–2). An even stronger endorsement of a gynocentric feminism mixed with postmodern elements is found in the work of Jardine. In Jardine's highly complex argument, she approaches the question of the proper relationship between feminism and modernity. She argues that because of feminism's roots in humanism/modernism, it would seem to have little in common with the postmodern creed. But, employing a postmodern argument, Jardine claims that the epistemological legacy of modernism does not allow us to investigate what constitutes sexual difference (1985: 40). This creates a dilemma for feminism: we must undermine the conceptual systems on which man's "truth" is founded, but these conceptual systems are at the same time the basis of feminist thinking (1985: 153). Jardine's solution to this dilemma is to attempt to describe a movement that she claims characterizes French feminism today: the putting into discourse of "woman" or the "feminine." She defines this phenomenon as "gynesis" and describes it as an attempt to deconstruct phallocratic discourse and to replace the privilege of the Father with another privileged discourse: the feminine. Jardine, unlike the French feminists she claims to be describing, argues for a move toward an essentialist feminism. She advocates the creation of the female subject that must be injected into and replace phallocratic discourse. She claims that we need a new theory and practice of the speaking subject, a theory that can accommodate the female subject (1985: 44). "The demise of the Subject, of the Dialectic, and of Truth has left modernity with a void that it is vaguely aware must be spoken differently and strongly: as a woman, through gynesis" (1985: 154).

The movement of Jardine and Young from modernism through postmodernism to an essentialist gynocentrism does not offer a workable model for the integration of postmodernism and feminism because it violates the postmodernist rejection of essentialism. The only contemporary feminist theorist who speaks almost unreservedly for the marriage of postmodernism and feminism that is consistent with postmodern principles is Jane Flax (1986a; 1986b; 1987a;

1987b). Arguing that feminist theory is quite literally a variant of postmodern philosophy, Flax forsees a fruitful interaction between the two movements. Although she claims that feminism's relationship to deconstruction is necessarily ambivalent, this is a minor quibble (1986a: 196). Overall, her thesis is that feminists can contribute gender sensitivity to postmodern philosophy and postmodernism can correct the essentialist tendencies of some feminist thought. "If we do our work well," Flax concludes, "'reality' will appear even more unstable, complex and disorderly than it does now" (1986a: 213). Flax's position is the most positive statement of the relationship between postmodernism and feminism in the literature today. But her position needs more substantiation than she offers in these articles. She does not answer the objections of those theorists who advocate a tentative relationship between postmodernism and feminism. Nor does she specifically refute the charges of relativism, nihilism and political inadequacy. A careful examination of the work of Derrida and Foucault from a feminist perspective, however, can provide refutations of the objections of postmodernism's feminist critics. It also reveals that the conversation between feminism and postmodernism begun by these critics can and should be continued, but in a more positive tone.

II Other Critiques

The critique of phallocratic (masculinist) epistemology is not unique to feminist positions informed by postmodernism. Several other schools of contemporary feminism have launched critiques of masculinist epistemology which, although they fall short of the radical postmodern critique, nevertheless call into question the sexism and hierarchical dualisms of Enlightenment epistemology. Each of these critiques, however, remains caught in the masculinist epistemology that it claims to transcend and thus is less successful than the postmodern critique.

The first of these critiques is found in the work of those who advocate androgyny. Feminists who espouse the concept of androgyny are, like the postmoderns, critical of the masculinist epistemology that divides human characteristics into exclusively masculine and feminine categories. They attempt to overcome this dualism by arguing that human beings are essentially androgynous and that, as feminists, we should seek to restore that fundamental androgyny. The argument for androgyny has been cast in a number of different guises. Carolyn Heilbrun argues that androgyny is a fundamental human trait that has been lost in our contemporary civilization. In *Toward a Recognition of Androgyny* (1973) she documents androgynous themes in the western tradition from the Greeks to the present. Jane Singer (1976) takes a similarly fundamentalist stance. She argues that androgyny is "an intrinsic principle of human life" (1976: viii), a primordial image in Jung's sense. Like Heilbrun, she traces the existence of androgyny in history and argues that it has been expunged from the Judeo-Christian tradition.

In our culture, she asserts, androgyny has been replaced by male dominance (1976: 22). Singer's work is instructive because of the explicitness with which she states one of the central tenets of androgyny: the fundamental and essential difference between the masculine and feminine natures. For Singer, the aim of androgyny is "to recognize the inner oscillation between Masculine and Feminine modalities of being and to hear with the inner ear the music of their interplay" (1976: 323). Singer argues that the interplay between these two modalities should be heard within every individual; it is erroneous to assign the masculine exclusively to men and the feminine to women. But for Singer the two principles always remain separate. Her point is that androgyny combines but does not confuse the essential differences between masculine and feminine.

The fundamentalism of Heilbrun and Singer does not, however, characterize all theories of androgyny. Both Trebilcot (1982) and Elshtain (1987) argue that "masculine" and "feminine" are socially constructed. The empirical works on androgyny, furthermore, although they avoid the question of the social or natural roots of the masculine and feminine principles, tend to emphasize social factors (Kaplan and Sedney, 1980; Kaplan and Bean 1976; Bem 1976). Kaplan and Sedney, for example, define androgyny as the "combined presence of socially valued, stereotypic, feminine and masculine characteristics" (1980: 6). They emphasize that androgyny overcomes the pervasive dualism of both eastern and western cultures and replaces it with a concept of unity and totality (1980: 57). The theme of these empirical studies on androgyny is that androgynous individuals are psychologically healthier than those who exhibit predominantly masculine or feminine characteristics. Most of the authors of these studies argue that we should attempt to overcome the stereotypical masculine and feminine roles that our society assigns us and move instead in the direction of an androgynous personality for all individuals.

Although this goal is certainly laudable, it disguises the serious problems with the argument for androgyny. First, as a number of commentators have pointed out, androgyny claims to value the masculine and feminine principles equally while in actuality privileging the masculine. Those who argue for androgyny do not question the commonly accepted definitions of masculine and feminine qualities: the masculine is rational, active, autonomous and objective; the feminine is passive, emotional, irrational and dependent. Those who advocate androgyny argue that the devaluing of the feminine characteristics is unjustified and that in an androgynous world the feminine qualities would be regarded as equal to the masculine. The fact that these writers do not challenge the established definitions of masculine and feminine, however, entails that their conception retains the disprivileging of the feminine that has characterized these definitions for millenia. Perhaps the most telling argument against androgyny is the fact that the androgynous personality presupposes the feminized male, not the masculinized female (Raymond, 1981; Secor, 1974). Harris (1974) points out that alchemists, who claimed to be androgynous, actually envisioned their work from a masculine perspective. A second issue raises a more serious objection to the androgynous ideal. At the root of androgyny is the assumption that there are distinct male and female characteristics, whether innate or acquired, that are united in the androgynous personality. Those who advocate androgyny do not question these polarities but, rather, presuppose them; they form the basis of the androgynous unity. It follows that androgyny perpetuates the dualities that constitute the inferior status of women. Instead of attempting to displace these dualities androgyny grounds its ideal personality in them. Androgyny thus remains firmly rooted in the masculinist epistemology that created the polarities in the first place.

A second critique of masculinist epistemology is embodied in the call for a feminist epistemology. Those who advocate a feminist epistemology usually rely on an appeal to the uniqueness of women's experience or perspective, arguing that this uniqueness provides women with a privileged epistemological standpoint *vis-à-vis* the masculine. Arguments against this position have been advanced above. A particular variant of the call for a feminist epistemology, however is worthy of special note. In her works *Gyn/Ecology* (1978), *Pure Lust* (1984) and *Webster's First New Intergalactic Wickedary of the English Language* (1987), Mary Daly, like the French feminists, argues that women have been unable to express themselves in the masculine language that has dominated western thought. Daly's strategy against this domination is to advance a critique of the "dis-passion" that prevails in patriarchy, a critique that strives for the "cosmic har-mony" of women who choose to escape patriarchy. This goal is to be accom-plished by breaking the power of masculine-dominated language. By releasing words, she claims, we can release ourselves (1984: 2–4). What Daly attempts to do, particularly in the last two works, is to redefine the derogatory words that have been assigned to women. Her style, syntax and definitions defy the accepted rules of writing which is, of course, precisely her purpose. A good example of her "releasing" of language comes from the end of *Pure Lust*:

> This call of the Wild, this Summons to hear the Word of the Wierd, is Siren's song. It guides us on paths of Be-Longing, of living in harmony with Spheres. It teaches the lore of Be-Friending, of sharing magnificent treasures. It inspires to the risk of Be-Witching, of joining the whirling world of Wonderlust. (1984: 417)

What Daly is attempting to do in these works is to redefine masculinist words and create what she calls "New Words" (1984: 262). "New Words" allow us to see the world in a new light and to experience ourselves as women in ways that are impossible using masculine language. Daly's project raises a number of difficult questions. Can only women use these "New Words" or can men use them as well? Is the, presumably feminist, epistemology she is creating superior to masculinist epistemology? Daly does not answer any of these questions directly. It seems clear, however, that her intent is to reject the old masculinist vocabulary by substituting a new feminist vocabulary. Such a move, however, is ultimately ineffectual. It is futile to attempt to replace one set of concepts with another set because the new set will simply assume the privileged status of the set it replaces. If, as Daly advocates, we replace our dualistic, hierarchical epistemology with another one that is also based on the privileging of a particular set of concepts, in this case, the feminine, the result will be, once more, dualism and hierarchy. Daly seems to be headed in this direction with her "New Words." What she has failed to accomplish, however, is the displacing of the polarities that structure masculinist epistemology.

A third critique of masculinist epistemology that has interested a number of feminists is that of critical theory. A strong argument for the application of critical theory to feminism is presented by Mills (1987). Arguing that critical theory is "the most advanced philosophy of our time," Mills asserts that it can be used to advance the cause of the women's movement (1987: xi). Specifically, she argues that critical theory's concern with the domination of nature is useful in combating the domination of women (1987: xii). Love (1987) is likewise optimistic about the possibilities of a feminist critical theory. Other feminists, however, are more restrained in their praise of critical theory. Both Fraser and Benhabib are sympathetic to Habermas' approach and have attempted to use critical theory to formulate a feminist critique of Enlightenment epistemology. But both are also critical of elements of critical theory's approach. Benhabib, in an article defending Habermas against Lyotard's postmodernism, finds Habermas' structural analysis to be superior to Lyotard's "neo-liberal interest group pluralism" (1984: 123). But she faults Habermas for failing to recognize what she calls the "lack of metanarratives and foundational guarantees" (1984: 126). Similarly, Fraser argues that although Habermas wants to be critical of male dominance, he fails to provide categories that are sufficient to the task (1985b: 128–30).

Habermas, like Foucault, Derrida and Gadamer, is critical of the instrumental reason of Enlightenment thought and the power structures it has created in the modern world. He is also sympathetic to the hermeneutic approach of Gadamer and a critic of the dualisms of Enlightenment thought, particularly as they regard rationality. At least in his early work, however, Habermas espouses what is essentially a foundationalist position. In his well-known dispute with Gadamer, Habermas' principal thesis was that Gadamer, in rejecting the Enlightenment, had thrown the baby out with the bath water.[3] Against Gadamer, Habermas argued that the Enlightenment contains both good and bad elements. He asserts that the good elements, notably the emancipatory impulse, should not be discarded along with the bad, a position that leads him to reject postmodernism's more sweeping critique of Enlightenment thought (1983: 196–7).

In his more recent work, however, Habermas has significantly qualified his foundationalist stance. In *The Theory of Communicative Action* (1984) he straddles the fence on the foundationalism issue, arguing that, while foundations are required, they are historically defined. He claims that "I have said goodbye to the emphatic philosophical claim to truth,'' an elitist conception of truth, he asserts, that is a "last remaining piece of myth" (1986: 129). Habermas argues that he does not condemn post-structuralism and even notes, as have other commentators, the similarity between Adorno's critique of the Enlightenment and that of the postmoderns (1986: 157; Nagele, 1986: 108–9).

Elsewhere, however, Habermas makes it clear that his qualified rejection of foundationalism does not entail a move to postmodernism. We live in the world of modernity, he claims, not some postmodern sequel to it (1986: 212). In his most extended discussion of modernity and postmodernity, *The Philosophical Discourse of Modernity* (1987), Habermas traces the path of the critique of modernity in modern philosophical thought. His thesis throughout is that we cannot "leap out of the discourse of modernity" but, rather, must confront it. For Habermas, modernity is in crisis, but not ended (Dews, 1986: 33). His critique of postmodernism, particularly the work of Derrida and Foucault, centers around two themes. First, he claims that their attempts to transcend modernity have failed. Both, he claims, remain caught in the discourse of modernity, particularly the philosophy of the subject (1987: 179, 274). Second, he argues that Foucault's position ends in an "unholy subjectivism" that precludes the possibility of resistance to oppression. Foucault, he claims, gives us no reason to oppose repression, only an analysis of it (1987: 276–94). In a similar discussion of the postmodern era, Bauman makes a statement that nicely summarizes the position that Habermas presents in his book:

> The age of modernity (that is, the age marked by the presence of the dual values of personal autonomy and societal rationality) cannot end; it can only be consummated. It has not yet been. It remains the function of intellectuals to bring the project of humanity toward its fulfillment. (1987: 192)

It is interesting that, in one of his few discussions of feminism, Habermas identifies the feminist movement as a social movement that is part of the liberating tradition of the Enlightenment and examines it in terms of the categories of the epistemology of emancipation (1981b: 34). This discussion reveals that, despite his critique of foundationalism, Habermas is, as he himself admits, a modernist and committed to the fulfillment of the modernist program. Without arguing the philosophical merits of this position, it is sufficient to note that the modernist program is exclusive of women. Although modernists like Habermas seem eager to "liberate" women, they want to do so by turning women into the modernist version of man: rational, autonomous and objective. The modernist project for women as it has been articulated by Habermas incurs three problems: first, it assumes that there is some essential realm of freedom, sexual or otherwise, that we can be liberated *to*; second, it assumes that if we can rid ourselves of oppression we can also rid ourselves of power (Fay, 1987: 214); and, third, it assumes that women can and should adopt the persona of the modernist man.

The problem that unites these three critiques of masculinist epistemology is that they fail to displace the dualistic epistemology that is at the heart of Enlightenment thought. Both those who advocate androgyny and those who espouse a feminist epistemology, ground their theories in the basic dualism that informs all the polarities that constitute Enlightenment thought: masculine/feminine. The third alternative – Habermas' critical theory – is even less distanced from Enlightenment epistemology. His concept of emancipating women, like that of the liberals, involves bringing them into the realm of subjectivity and rationality, that is, the realm of the masculine. Feminists have frequently attacked dualistic epistemology as detrimental to the status of women. They have argued that it implies hierarchy and defines women as inferior (Cixous, 1980: 90–1). In a thorough critique of dualism from a feminist perspective, Whitbeck argues that dual organization is always sexual organization (1984: 67). Yet many feminists' attempts to overcome dualistic epistemology, like those discussed above, have succeeded only in perpetuating it. It is their success in overcoming dualistic epistemology and the sexism inherent in it, however, that makes postmodernism so important for the feminist project. Both Derrida and Foucault attack the dualistic discourses of modernity and provide a way of discussing sexual difference that avoids the masculine/feminine polarity that continues to characterize much of contemporary feminist theory.

III Derrida: Supplementary Logic

The difficulties confronting the task of constructing an argument for the relevance of Derrida's work for contemporary feminism are significant. Derrida's abstract speculations seem totally removed from the real world not only of politics but also of the mechanisms of male domination. Furthermore, the accusations of relativism and nihilism that have been leveled at postmodernism in general seem particularly relevant in the case of Derrida. The charge that his position fails to provide a basis for political action is rarely made, precisely because of what appears to be the obvious irrelevance of his work for politics. Despite this, however, Derrida's rejection of epistemology and his attack on the metaphysics of presence are positions that should be taken seriously by feminists. His displacement of epistemology can be useful to contemporary feminist theory because it provides a way of a reconceptualizing the feminine in non-dualistic terms. Although Derrida is, undoubtedly, both abstract and obscure, it does not follow that his position is irrelevant to feminist theory.

One of the themes of the critics who attack Derrida, both feminist and non-feminist, is that deconstruction entails a purely negative attitude, that "every reading is a misreading" necessarily means that there is no truth. Derrida's reply to this charge is to question the definition of truth employed by his critics. If they assume that there is only one truth and that it must be absolutely grounded, then the critics are correct: deconstruction destroys the notion of truth; it entails a negative stance. But if one assumes that there is not one truth, but, rather, "truths," that is, that truth is multiple rather than unitary, then deconstruction can lead to "true" interpretations; it is positive rather than negative. Even if the question of whether deconstruction is negative can be answered satisfactorily, however, it leads to a further question that is particularly important for feminists: is it neutral? A neutral stance is especially deadly for feminism because it serves to perpetuate the status quo of male domination. Derrida's critics argue that deconstruction, by advancing multiple readings, cannot effect a change in the dominant, accepted interpretation.

Derrida refutes this criticism very directly. Deconstruction, he states, is not neutral because it is a strategy that centers on intervention (1981b: 43). Derrida's definition of deconstruction as intervention establishes three important theses that refute the argument that deconstruction is either negative or neutral. First, it defines deconstruction as a radical activity. Far from being neutral or conservative it is radical in the literal sense: it attacks the root of the problem, the classical oppositions of the metaphysics of presence. Second, it defines deconstruction as a practice that overturns these classical oppositions and *displaces* the system that they create. This is absolutely essential to a feminist reading of Derrida. Since the beginning of western thought the opposition between masculine and feminine has informed all of the polarities of western epistemology and defined the disprivileging of women. What Derrida sees very clearly is that we must deconstruct these polarities if that epistemology is to be overturned. He defines this project as exceeding the "logocentric closure" that these oppositions create (1981b: 36). The third important aspect of this definition is Derrida's reference to a "field of non-discursive forces" (1982: 329). Although the reference is brief it is nevertheless significant. It indicates that Derrida recognizes that the epistemological polarities of logocentric thought are reflected in non-discursive formations, that is, social structure. The intervention that he calls for is thus not "just" a linguistic intervention but a social one as well. In another passage Derrida reinforces this point by asserting that deconstruction is not a discursive or theoretical affair, but a practico-political one (1987: 508).

Derrida's project of deconstruction has been identified by many of his critics as a-historical. Although his writings are highly abstract and frequently impenetrable, a close analysis of the project of deconstruction reveals it to be anything but a-historical. At the center of the project of deconstruction is a concern with the historically constituted polarities of western thought. At one point Derrida defines deconstruction as simply a question of "being alert to the implications of the historical sedimentation of the language which we use" (1970: 271). But although deconstruction is a method that is rooted in the historical, it does not rely on historical conventions to establish its truth, a point particularly germane to feminist interests. Culler emphasizes this point in his discussion of the difference between deconstruction and pragmatism (1982: 153–4). While the pragmatist conception of truth involves an appeal to convention, deconstruction does the opposite. Convention always involves exclusion, the "logocentric closure" that Derrida rejects. The point of deconstruction is to violate this exclusion by intervening in that closure. Deconstruction, unlike pragmatism, rejects the complacency of the historical given by seeking to displace it.

Establishing Derrida's attitude toward deconstruction is important for a feminist reading of his work. It refutes the charges that deconstruction is negative or neutral and that it is "merely" linguistic. These arguments indicate the usefulness of Derrida's work for feminist thought. But there are also elements of his work that bear directly on feminist issues. The first of these is Derrida's use of feminine metaphors to replace the masculine metaphors that dominate the metaphysics of presence. Commenting on this tendency in Derrida, Spivak states that he constructs a "hymenal fable" in "what may be construed as a feminist gesture" (1976: lxvi). (In a Derridean move, Spivak crosses out the word "feminist" in this passage.) Although Derrida's use of feminine metaphors is significant, it is important to note the particular way in which he employs these metaphors. Derrida is not trying to replace one set of privileged concepts and associations, the masculine, with another privileged set, the feminine. In fact, Derrida claims that he is not really employing feminine metaphors at all because to do so would presuppose knowledge of woman's essence (1985: 31). Derrida clearly rejects such essentialism and the privileging that it produces. In employing feminine metaphors to break the binary opposition of phallocratic thought, he is not attempting to move from one binary concept to another but from the binary to the multiple.

The most extended use of this "hymenal fable" is found in *Dissemination* (1981a), although references to it are also found in other works (1979a; 1980a; 1981b). In these passages Derrida explains how feminine metaphors in general and the hymen in particular deconstruct binary logic. Derrida argues that because the hymen is a sign of fusion it abolishes opposition and difference. In the hymen there is no difference between desire and satisfaction, between exterior and interior, between difference and non-difference. Because the hymen is a fusion it succeeds in displacing the whole series of oppositions that are at the center of binary logic. It produces what Derrida calls a "medium," an element that envelops both terms of an opposition. Derrida defines a medium as that which stands between opposites by revealing the confusion of those opposites (1981a: 212). The hymen stands between the inside and the outside of a woman, hence between desire and fulfillment; it is both love and murder. There is no "phenomenology of the hymen," Derrida concludes "because the center in which it folds back, as little in order to conceal itself as in order to denude itself, is also an abyss." As a multiple that is self-inscribing it cannot be described in phallocratic terms (1981a: 265).

Derrida discusses other terms that perform a similar function to that of the hymen: pharmakon, supplement, *différance*, invagination (1981a: 221; 1979a: 97, 1980b: 217). But in all his discussions of these terms his point is the same. He is utilizing them because they break open the binary oppositions at the root of western epistemology. That one of the central terms that he employs, hymen, is from the feminine body does not entail the construction of a feminist epistemology. Nor does it follow Hegelian dialectic by constituting a third term that is a synthesis of opposites. Derrida's approach, rather, is a "paradoxical logic" that is never formalized (1980b: 221). The terms he employs destroy the opposition between the two terms between which they are located by revealing the confusion of the opposition they supposedly represent. The demand for truth itself, he claims, is "recounted and swept along" in the process he describes (1979a: 98). These terms reveal that the linear, unitary, phallocratic "will to truth" cannot be sustained.

One of the themes of the feminist critique of rationality is the connection between phallocentrism and logocentrism, that is, the masculine definition of the will to truth that defines the western philosophical tradition. It is significant that Derrida explicitly makes this connection. In "The purveyor of truth" (1975) Derrida accuses Lacan of "phallogocentrism," a composite of phallo-centrism and logocentrism. Commenting on Derrida's use of this word Gallop remarks:

> The composite word declares the inextricable collusion of phallocentrism with logocentrism . . . and unites feminism and deconstructive, "grammatological" philosophy in their opposition to a common enemy. (1976: 30)

One of the most important statements of the connection between phallocentrism and logocentrism is Irigaray's description of Plato's cave. Derrida also offers a description of Plato's cave that, like that of Irigaray, defines Plato's allegory as central to the statement of logocentrism. Although Derrida does not explicitly make the link between the logocentric and the phallocentric in this context, like Irigaray he attacks the logocentric as the search for one truth built on the opposition of polarities. The masculine, particularly masculine sexuality, is unitary, based on the absolute polarity of masculine and feminine. Against this Derrida proposes not the elevation of the female but the replacement of the unitary with the multiple:

> Imagine Plato's cave not simply overthrown by some philosophical movement but transformed in its entirety into a circumscribed area contained within another – an absolutely other – structure, an incommensurably, upredictably more complicated machine. (1981a: 324)

This "absolute other" as Derrida conceives it is not a feminist epistemology, but, rather, a structure that has been feminized in a metaphorical sense through the replacement of oppositions with multiplicity.

Derrida offers an explicit discussion of women and feminism in three contexts.

The first text is a discussion in *Spurs* (1979b) of Nietzsche's position on women. It is particularly appropriate that Derrida should approach this aspect of Nietzsche's writing. Nietzsche's famous discussion of truth and women is central to his challenge to the "will to truth" of Western philosophy, a challenge that Derrida continues in his attack on the metaphysics of presence. Derrida's discussion of Nietzsche on women is also significant because of the ambiguity in Nietzsche's discussion of women. Although Nietzsche despises the will to truth that he defines as the opposite of the feminine, he is equally negative toward the feminine itself. Despite his rejection of logocentric thought, Nietzsche is incapable of embracing its opposite, that is, the multiplicity and ambiguity that he sees to be characteristic of the feminine. There is a sense in which, in his analysis of women, Nietzsche experienced a failure of nerve, that is, a failure to make the leap to anti-essentialism and antifoundationalism. The same, however, cannot be said of Derrida. In his discussion of Nietzsche's commentary on women, Derrida makes it clear that, in turning away from logocentrism and the metaphysics of presence, he is explicitly embracing what the feminine has represented in that epistemology. He is not, however, espousing a feminine "essence." Indeed, he specifically rejects the notion that any such essence exists. But, unlike Nietzsche, he espouses what logocentric thought has labeled the "feminine" qualities of multiplicity and ambiguity.

Derrida begins his discussion with some sweeping generalizations about women. In assessing these generalizations it is important to note that he is discussing qualities that have been attributed to women by the epistemology of logocentrism, not the "essentially feminine." His first point is that woman is connected with distance; she seduces from a distance. It is thus necessary to keep one's distance from women: "a distance from distance must be maintained" (1979b: 49). Derrida's point in discussing distance in this context is to emphasize the contrast between women and distance on one hand and logocentrism's focus on presence and immediacy on the other. A second respect in which the feminine represents a contrast to logocentrism is the fact that women have no determinable identity: "There is no such thing as the essence of woman because woman averts, she is averted of herself." This averting also applies to truth. There is no "truth" of woman because "woman is but one name for that untruth of truth" (1979b: 51)

The relationship between woman and truth is the dominant theme of Derrida's discussion. His analysis focuses on those who attempt to find "truth" in woman, to replace the masculine truth of logocentrism/phallocentrism with a feminine truth. Against this position, one that is taken by many radical feminists, Derrida argues:

> Because, indeed, if woman *is* truth, *she* at least knows that there is no truth, that truth has no place here and that no one has a place for truth. And she is woman precisely because she herself does not believe in truth itself, because she does not believe in what she is, in what she is believed to be, in what she thus is not. (1979b: 53)

In this passage Derrida is rejecting the notion that "woman" represents any essence, whether of woman, truth or untruth. What he is arguing is that women *represent* not untruth, but the opposition to the will to truth. Derrida is interested in what "woman" represents because he sees it to be consistent with his effort to deconstruct the will to truth. In the ensuing discussion he explores various aspects of this representation. Women, unlike men, do not believe in truth; they do not seek truth in a linear fashion but, rather, engage in play (1979b: 61–2). Women are connected with writing, style with men (1979b: 57). Women are too clever to believe in the opposition of castration/anti-castration because either one would trap them in phallocentrism (1979b: 61).

Nietzsche's discussion of women and truth contained an explicit attack on the feminism of his day. He argued that these feminists attempted to follow the masculine will to truth and thus to become men. Like Nietzsche, Derrida also has no sympathy for feminists who want to turn women into men. His reasons for rejecting this position, however, are clearer than Nietzsche's. The woman who believes in truth, he asserts, is merely mimicking the errors of logocentrism: "And in order to resemble the masculine dogmatic philosopher this woman lays claim – just as much claim as he – to truth, science and objectivity in all their castrated delusions of virility" (1979b: 65). In another context Derrida echoes this sentiment with the claim that all "metaphysical desire" is masculine, even when it is manifest in a woman (1978a: 320). In conclusion he concurs with Nietzsche that there is no such thing as truth *or* woman: truth, like woman, is plural (1979b: 103). Significantly, it also follows from this that there is no such thing as *the* sexual difference (1979b: 139). For Derrida, as for the French feminists, the feminine is a disruptive force, a means of displacing the edifice of phallogocentrism. Sarah Kofman expresses Derrida's attitude toward women and truth very clearly in her commentary:

> The voice of truth is always that of the law of God, of the father. The metaphysical logos has an essential virility. Writing, that form of disruption of presence, is, like the woman, always put down and reduced to the lowest rung. Like the feminine genitalia, it is troubling, petrifying – it has a Medusa effect. (Quoted by Mahony in Derrida, 1985: 97)

In the second text in which Derrida deals explicitly with the issue of feminism he reiterates several of the themes of *Spurs* but also, in a surprising move, turns to the question of the role of feminist politics. In an interview with Christie MacDonald published in *Diacritics* (Derrida and MacDonald 1982) Derrida repeats his central theme with regard to feminism: the rejection of a single, unitary essence of the female. In this context he not only rejects this notion, he also claims that it is antifeminist. He once more explicitly identifies the logocentrism and rationality of western thought with phallocentrism. But he then goes on to draw a unique conclusion from this connection. Rather than identifying femininity as an object of knowledge, the phallocentrism of western thought "should rather permit the invention of another inscription, one very old and very new, a displacement of bodies and places that is quite different" (1982: 70). This is consistent with the theme of Derrida's project of deconstruction, cast here in terms of the attempt to displace phallocentrism and invent "another inscription." But Derrida then introduces a significant qualification of this statement that appears to contradict deconstruction itself. He asserts that although feminists should be looking not for another truth but for "another inscription," the "real conditions of woman's struggle" call for an intermediate strategy. He defines this strategy as the preservation of "metaphysical presuppositions" because "they belong to the dominant system that one is deconstructing on a *practical level*" (1982: 70).

Taken at face value this statement is astounding. Here the arch-enemy of metaphysics is calling for the preservation of metaphysical presuppositions in the name of practicality. As the interview proceeds, however, Derrida clarifies his meaning in this statement and links it with his project of deconstruction. In her next question, MacDonald outlines what she identifies as the two phases of deconstructing the masculine/feminine polarity at the root of female oppression. The first phase involves simply reversing the opposition: woman is privileged over man. The second phase, however, involves the forging of a "new" concept. Derrida concurs with this analysis, but cautions that feminists should not think of the second phase as a "new" concept because the elevation of a "new" concept will lead to hierarchies and polarities, precisely the problem that feminism is attempting to overcome. Phase two, he claims, must have a different structure than phase one, a structure that involves a transformation or general deformation of logic. If sexual difference is defined as the opposition between masculine and feminine, he claims, then the masculine will always win (1982: 72). The goal of feminism must be a way of speaking about sexuality that is not oppositional or a-sexual, but

> would be sexual otherwise: beyond the binary difference that governs the decorum of all codes, beyond the opposition feminine/masculine, beyond bisexuality as well, beyond homosexuality and heterosexuality which comes to the same thing. (1982: 76)

The goal is, in short, that of a multiplicity of sexual voices.

These passages reveal Derrida's position more clearly. Although he concurs with the need to exalt female difference within the terms defined by the metaphysics of presence, he insists that this should only be a temporary phase in the movement. The theme that dominates his discussion, however, is one that is consistent with his larger project of deconstruction: the privileging of the essentially feminine merely perpetuates the dualities that must be overcome. Although he concedes that the privileging of the feminine may be a temporary practical necessity of feminist politics, he insists that it cannot be its goal because in any opposition the masculine will always win. Derrida's further point, that feminists must not seek to constitute a third term, a new concept, is also crucial. He emphasizes that feminism should not seek to replace one truth with another but, rather, to inscribe a new structure of multiple truths, multiple voices of sexuality. He rejects the oppositional politics implicit in the privileging of the feminine, first, because it will fail, and, second, because it will lead to a new regime of privilege rather than its displacement.

These themes are reiterated in the third context in which Derrida discusses feminism and politics. In a wide-ranging interview on "Deconstruction in America" (Derrida et al., 1985), Derrida not only discusses feminism, but also an issue particularly relevant to the feminist critique of his work: the political nature of the project of deconstruction. Derrida begins by repeating the themes established in the 1982 interview. In discussing these themes, however, he employs a definition of "feminism" that can be misunderstood (Russo, 1986: 225). He defines feminism as a position that attempts to replace the unitary masculinist epistemology with an equally unitary feminist epistemology. He thus declares that deconstruction is not feminist and, further, defines feminism as a form of phallogocentrism (Derrida et al., 1985: 30). It is important to note, however, that in these passages Derrida is not attacking what is commonly understood as "feminism." Rather, he is attacking a particular form of feminism, a form that he sees to be "immobilizing." This form of feminism, he claims, reproduces what we must be fighting against, logocentric closure. In this context he once more admits that this form of feminism may be a tactical necessity in the present. But he also asserts that it cannot be a desirable goal for women in the long term (Derrida et al., 1985: 30). After this attack on a particular understanding of feminism, however, Derrida nevertheless claims that deconstruction is relevant to women. Deconstruction, he asserts, "naturally presupposes a radical deconstruction of phallogocentrism and a new interest in women's questions"; it entails a certain thinking of women (Derrida et al., 1985: 30). Here Derrida is reiterating a theme that has appeared repeatedly in his writings, the revolutionary character of deconstructive practice, particularly as it relates to the question of women. His position on this issue is two-sided. First, deconstruction is relevant to women because it displaces the phallogocentrism that defines their inferior status. Second, within the project of deconstruction "woman" is a disruptive force. Like writing, it provides a means of breaking apart the binary logic of the metaphysics of presence. It follows that deconstruction is relevant to feminism, more broadly defined, and to its politics. At one point in the interview Derrida remarks that "If deconstruction *really* consisted in saying that everything happens in books it wouldn't deserve *five* minutes of anybody's attention" (Derrida et al., 1985: 15). In the course of the interview he presents a strong case that deconstruction is worthy of the attention even of feminists.

In these interviews Derrida calls for a "new inscription" of truths as a way of displacing phallogocentrism. In these discussions, however, he does not specify how this inscription is effected. In other contexts he takes up this issue in some detail. His clearest discussion of it is his description of what he calls a "supplementary logic," a logic that breaks the binary oppositions of logocentrism. This discussion is particularly relevant to a feminist reading of his work. Although Derrida has defined his whole program of deconstruction as an approach that intervenes in a field of oppositions, it is only with his notion of supplementary logic that he specifies precisely how this intervention takes place. His most comprehensive discussion of the issue is found in *Positions* (1981b). In a discussion that is typically dense and enigmatic, Derrida tries to locate the notion of a supplement in relation to other approaches to the binary oppositions of the western episteme. One approach, like that of many feminists, is to invert the hierarchy implicit in these binary oppositions. Another, employed in the Hegelian dialectic, is to constitute a third term that synthesizes the two terms of the opposition. Against both of these alternatives Derrida wants to adopt an approach that marks an "interval" between these two approaches. To mark this interval, he states, it is necessary to analyze

> within the text of the history of philosophy . . . certain marks, shall we say
> (I mentioned certain ones just now, there are many others) that *by analogy* (I
> underline) I have called undecidables, that is, unities of simulacrum, "false"
> verbal properties (nominal or semantic) that can no longer be included
> within philosophical (binary) opposition, but which, however, inhabit
> philosophical opposition, resisting and disorganizing it, *without ever*
> constituting a third term, without ever leaving room for a solution in the
> form of speculative dialectics . . . the *supplement* is neither a plus nor a
> minus, neither an outside nor the complement of an inside, neither accident
> nor essence, etc . . . .(1981b: 42–3)

This passage, although far from clear, contains the central elements of Derrida's position. Derrida insists that the supplement, that which destroys the binary oppositions of western epistemology, is not in itself a theory; nor does it constitute a new concept – a third term. Rather its function is to undo the closure of logocentric oppositions. The notion of the supplement is related to other terms that Derrida employs: pharmakon, hymen, *différance*, writing, spacing, trace. These terms are all supplements in that they break through binary oppositions; he describes them as "brisures" or "hinge-words" (Young, 1981: 18). Binary oppositions that are at the root of conceptuality itself are erupted by the supplement. What Derrida has accomplished with his notion of the supplement is even more radical than disrupting these foundational binary oppositions. He goes further to reveal that the binary oppositions of western thought are not, in fact, opposites at all. The oppositions he analyzes reveal themselves not as polarities but as two confused elements that inhabit each other. In his notion of the supplement Derrida quite literally deconstructs the basis of western logic. As one of his critics has noted, supplementarity is a dangerous concept because it reveals a deep structural contradition within western epistemology (Llewelyn, 1986: 99).

In his discussion of the second phase of the feminist movement, Derrida is appealing to this notion of the supplement. His point is quite clear: the way to destroy the masculine/feminine opposition is not to invert it but to deconstruct it. Creating a third term that would only constitute its own set of hierarchies and oppositions is just as futile as the tactic of inversion. Derrida's thesis is that the solution lies in a new inscription, an interval between these two other approaches. This is reminiscent of Foucault's statement that new ways of thinking always arise from the spaces *between* the concepts of the old episteme; it always involves the filling of an empty space that was not conceptualized in the old structure. What Derrida is saying here about feminism is similar. He asserts that what is needed is a new, non-polarized way of thinking about sexuality that rests on multiplicity rather than opposition.

Derrida's comments about feminism and deconstructive feminist practice are not widely read and discussed by feminist theorists. Most feminists who discuss his work at all dismiss it on the grounds that it is relativistic and nihilistic. Even among feminist writers who are sympathetic to deconstruction, few have endorsed Derrida's position as a useful one for feminism. In a discussion of the political implications of the "French Derrideans," Nancy Fraser argues that feminism must ultimately move beyond the discourse of deconstruction because it cannot help us answer the questions that feminism necessarily raises (1984: 152). Likewise, Meese, who argues that feminism can learn from deconstruction, argues that deconstruction cannot bridge the gap between the theoretical and the political that is so necessary for feminism. Although Meese calls for a definition of sexual difference in non-oppositional terms, she does not feel that deconstruction supplies this definition (1986: 80–4). Alice Jardine advances another criticism. Although she lauds Derrida's use of feminine discourse, she questions whether his tactic is simply a "new use of reason." She suggests that perhaps Derrida is attempting to usurp feminist discourse, to seduce it away from the feminists themselves (1985: 207). Similarly, Spivak claims that Derrida is attempting a *male* appropriation of the female voice (1983: 190).

Explicit feminist defenses of Derrida's position are very scarce. Several feminists have pointed approvingly to his connection between phallocentrism and logocentrism (Burke, 1981), but this is an insight that is not unique to Derrida; many feminists have made this connection without the aid of deconstruction. The most enthusiastic defense of Derrida's position from a feminist perspective can be found in the work of Nancy Holland (1985; 1986). Holland argues that a feminist reading of Derrida's attack on metaphysics entails the position that metaphysics is a realm from which women are excluded (1985: 225). She suggests that we can interpret Derrida's use of feminine metaphors in two ways: either as the creation of a metaphysics of the feminine or as the assertion of the exclusion of women from the realm of metaphysics. The first option would result in replacing phallocentrism with vaginocentrism, an option that neither she nor Derrida advocates. The second option, however, is more promising. We can use Derrida, Holland suggests, by inserting the concept "woman" into all of his discussions of the disprivileged side of the polarities of western thought. The most useful of these is the concept of writing. Woman, like writing, has been disprivileged in western discourse. Derrida's critique of the philosophical tradition, she asserts, can be read as a critique of both the role of the written word *and* the role of women. She argues that for Derrida neither writing nor women are "other" in the tradition of philosophy but, rather, are excluded from the philosophical tradition itself (1986: 2–14).

Holland's remarks suggest that deconstruction can be seen as a revolutionary force, and, specifically, one that can further the revolutionary aims of feminism. It provides a way of displacing the polarities of the metaphysics of presence and, with them, the inferior status of women. Holland's position, however, is unusual. Few feminist writers see deconstruction as revolutionary and most explicitly reject it as an inappropriate vehicle for feminist politics. One of the few exceptions to this is Nancy Fraser. Although Fraser rejects deconstruction as a viable basis for feminism, she concedes that *"différance"* can be interpreted as a means of resistance to Terror. She argues that deconstruction implies a politics of resistance and/or revolution (1984: 133). Another writer who identifies at least the possibility of a politics of resistance in Derrida's thought is Michael Ryan (1982). In his analysis of the links between Marxism and deconstruction, Ryan argues that if Marxists were to carry the critique of capitalism into bourgeois philosophy the result would be something like a politicized deconstruction (1982: 46). Working around this thesis, Ryan is cautious regarding the political implications of deconstruction. In a discussion of Derrida's work he states: "The undecidability or structural incompleteness that opens the possibility of infinite extension can lead to epistemological nihilism and a nonpolitics of abdication" (1982: 40). In another passage, however, he is more optimistic about the political possibilities of deconstruction: "To affirm the abyss deconstruction opens in the domain of knowledge is politically to affirm the permanent possibility of social change" (1982: 8).

Derrida himself has little to say about politics; there is, as he would acknowledge, no political program to be gleaned from his work.[4] His goal is to break up the binary oppositions of the metaphysics of presence, not to outline political practice. Despite his silence on politics, however, he makes it clear that he is aware of the social and political effects of his efforts. He asserts that his attack on the metaphysics of presence is inseparably linked to a social and political structure, what Foucault calls a discursive formation. The similarities between the work of Derrida and Foucault suggest that the kind of political resistance that Foucault advocates is compatible with Derrida's approach. Foucault's program of "local resistance" is the political expression of Derrida's rejection of absolutes and essences. The anti-essentialism of both Foucault and Derrida entails the rejection of the notion of a politics grounded in an appeal to absolute moral principles or absolute knowledge and truth. When discussing the necessity of emancipating ourselves from the language of western philosophy in *Writing and Difference*, Derrida advocates a strategy of resistance in the discursive realm that parallels Foucault's call for resistance in the political realm (1978b: 28).

This is not to say that there is a political program, for feminism or any other political movement, in the work of Derrida. One must look to Foucault's work for such a program. Derrida's contribution to feminism lies in the discursive, not the non-discursive realm, but within that realm his contribution is significant. Derrida does not offer a program of political revolution, but he defines "woman" as a revolutionary force. For Derrida "woman," along with "writing," serve as the means by which the binary logic of western thought can be displaced. Along with Irigaray, Cixous and Kristeva, Derrida identifies the feminine as a disruptive force that displaces the will to truth that defines the western metaphysical tradition. In his discussion of supplementary logic he explains how this disruption takes place. The terms he employs – woman, writing, trace, hymen – explode opposites, they reveal the confusion of the alleged polarities.[5] By describing in detail the mechanisms of this disruption, Derrida adds an important element to feminist discussions of the role of "woman" in contemporary discourse.

Derrida's discussion of woman as a supplement is tied to another contribution of his approach. One of the key questions in contemporary feminism is how feminists are to deal with the question of sexual difference. The first possible option is to ignore difference, that is, to treat women and men as equals. That this option is not a viable one is now widely acknowledged by feminists. It was tried by liberal feminists who attempted to fit women into the masculine mold. It results in treating women as if they were men because men set the standard for what a "person" is. The second option is to emphasize the difference between men and women. The problems with this option are becoming clear despite its current popularity. It courts essentialism because it necessarily stresses what women "really are," thus obscuring the important social and historical differences among different women's situations. It also creates an oppositional politics of masculine versus feminine that perpetuates the polarity between the sexes. It continues the hierarchies and the privileging characteristic of masculinist epistemology. Finally, it risks perpetuating the perception of women as inferior. No matter how much feminists may try to revalorize "the feminine," the disprivileging of the feminine sphere is so deeply rooted in western culture that it is unlikely to be dislodged by their efforts.

A third option is suggested by the work of Derrida. His position suggests not abandoning difference but conceptualizing it in a new way, creating "another inscription" of the sexual. Derrida's approach conceptualizes difference not in terms of polarities but in terms of multiplicities and pluralities and thus provides a radically new way of talking about the feminine, the masculine and sexuality. His efforts to displace the binary logic of western thought, a logic that he identifies as rooted in the masculine/feminine opposition, reveals that what we have defined as opposites invade and inhabit each other. Masculine and feminine are not opposites, but elements that represent multiple differences, pluralities of characteristics that cross and recross the alleged boundary between the two. An number of feminists have accused Derrida and/or deconstruction of attempting to erase difference. Meese claims that by problematizing difference, deconstruction prevents its reinscription (1986: 88). Di Stefano asserts that deconstruction denies the feminine, that it leads to "the incredible shrinking woman" (1987). This is a misreading of Derrida's concept of difference. His aim is not to erase difference but to inscribe it in non-oppositional terms, to displace the polarity of difference by revealing the multiplicity of differences.

Derrida's contribution to feminism, then, lies in his displacement of binary logic and his new inscription of difference. The binary logic of western thought is displaced through a supplementary logic that uses the concept "woman" to overthrow the polarities of the metaphysics of presence. Feminist deconstruction entails a radical restructuring of western thought and practice, a fact that Derrida both acknowledges and explicates in his work. Furthermore, his inscription of difference, an inscription that, while not denying difference, rejects polarities, opens up a new discourse on women and sexuality. This discourse speaks in a multiplicity of sexual voices; it is a discourse which has no center, neither masculine nor feminine, yet does not erase either the masculine or the feminine. It is a discourse that can and should be central to feminists' attempts to reconceptualize sexual difference.

IV Foucault and Political Action: A Feminist Perspective

The charges of relativism, nihilism and political inadequacy that have been leveled at the postmodern approach have particular significance as critiques of Foucault's position. Although these charges have also been made against Derrida and other postmodern writers, they carry more weight when advanced against Foucault's position because Foucault, unlike the other theorists, has consciously placed himself in the political arena and identified his position as a politics of resistance. Whereas Derrida's critics might conclude that his conceptual nihilism, although misconceived, is relatively harmless, Foucault does not get off so easily. Because of the political nature of Foucault's subject matter and his personal political involvement, his alleged relativism and nihilism have assumed a specifically political dimension. His critics charge that no program of political action flows from his position and, specifically, that it precludes the possibility of any coherent resistance to repressive political regimes.

The argument over the political implications of Foucault's position has divided his commentators into two opposing camps. Foucault's critics take the position that his approach definitively precludes principled political action because the logic of his analysis denies the possibility of anything but a relative conception of truth.

Most of these critics concede that Foucault's intention is both moral and political, but they argue that this intention contradicts the logic of his analysis and renders it inconsistent. Most of Foucault's defenders also argue that Foucault's position has a moral intent, but assert that this intent is not inconsistent with what his critics have identified as his "relativistic" stance. These defenders of Foucault argue that his program of local resistance is both a coherent political stance and consistent with his rejection of absolute truth. These two positions and their variants have structured the debate over the political implications of Foucault's position and, by extension, his relevance to feminism.

The critics who charge that Foucault's position precludes principled political action rest their case on an analysis of his position on the status of truth. One of the principal themes of Foucault's work is his attack on the "will to truth" that has characterized western philosophy since Plato. Truth, he claims, is not something otherwordly, but, rather, is a product of individual regimes of truth and, thus, inseparable from power. He defines truth as "the totality of rules according to which the true is distinguished from the false and the concrete effects of power are attached to what is true" (1981; 306). Foucault's critics object to this formulation on two grounds. First, they argue that Foucault's conception of truth is "relativistic;" it precludes the possibility of judging one regime of truth to be superior to another. Second, they object to Foucault's connection between truth and power. For these critics, truth is a liberatory concept; truth is not, by definition, linked to institutions of power, but, rather, frees us from power. Although they concede that Foucault appeals to resistance to repression, they argue that Foucault's rejection of a liberating concept of truth precludes the possibility of resistance. As they see it, Foucault's analysis of truth leads to the conclusion that we cannot escape from the truth/power nexus that necessarily dominates all societies; although we can change the complexion of that domination we cannot avoid it altogether. They assert that on Foucault's definition of truth and power, emancipation is not a coherent goal for political theory.

One of the best representatives of this line of criticism is an article written by Charles Taylor (1984). Taylor advances four arguments against Foucault's position. First, he claims, Foucault obviates the possibility that any good can come of his analyses. If we can only move from one truth/power regime to another, then, for Taylor, there seems to be little point in the exercise of political analysis. Second, Taylor questions what he identifies as Foucault's "subject-less" approach to history. How, he asks, can we talk about political action when Foucault has deprived us of a political actor? Third, Taylor claims that Foucault is inconsistent because, logically, his discussion of masks or falsehoods make no sense without the corresponding notion of a truth that transcends specific regimes of power. Fourth, he argues that, ultimately, Foucault can only advocate local resistances to regimes of power; no comprehensive program is entailed by his position.

Taylor's critique of Foucault is subject to what Bove has called "hermeneutic blinders" (1988: xvii). Taylor attempts to fit Foucault's program into the traditional categories of political theory, and, when Foucault fails to fit into these categories, Taylor rejects his position as nihilistic. Taylor's failure lies in his inability to see that it is precisely Foucault's intent to deconstruct the traditional categories of political theory. Other critics of Foucault, however, although still accusing him of inconsistency, have been more sympathetic toward Foucault's rejection of orthodoxy and more willing to concede that Foucault's moral intent counts for something. Fraser (1981b: 282) Philip (1983: 42) and Major-Poetz (1983: 42) all argue that Foucault's work is inconsistent, but they also assert that this inconsistency saves him from the charge of nihilism. This is a strange defense; it makes sense only if incoherence is preferable to nihilism. There are several variations on this more muted criticism of Foucault. Horowitz criticizes Foucault's anti-essentialism because it does not allow him to distinguish between forms of power that merely construct subjectivity and those that construct dominated subjectivity (1987: 61). If Foucault were able to make this distinction, Horowitz suggests, he could distinguish between good and bad regimes without abandoning his thesis with regard to truth and power. Foucault's anti-essentialism also comes under attack by Balbus (1982). In an argument specifically directed to feminism, Balbus asserts that because Foucault refuses to privilege any discourse above any other he "deprives [women] of the conceptual weapons with which they can understand and begin to overcome their universal subordination" (1982: 476).

These criticisms of Foucault's relativism and nihilism are countered by those who seek to defend his position. One line of defense that has been adopted by Foucault's supporters is the claim that it is not Foucault's intent to offer a theory of truth, much less a political program founded in such a theory, and, thus, that he should not be faulted for failing to provide one. Rorty (1986) states this thesis strongly with his claim that Foucault, in rejecting both positivism and historicism, wants to abandon the search for "Truth" altogether. Hacking (1986) echoes this in his argument that Foucault is not defending an irrationalist theory of truth but merely studying the empirical conditions under which scientific statements come to be counted as true or false. That Foucault should be judged as a historian rather than a philosopher is also the theme of Hoy's discussion (1986). Hoy argues that historians, unlike philosophers, are not required to tell us how we should lead our lives, only how we do lead them.

Although these arguments come closer to understanding Foucault's position, they have a serious liability: they relieve Foucault of the charge of inconsistency by denying to his work any moral or political relevance. Although it is true that Foucault argues that the intent of his work is not to offer an alternative, to formulate a metacritique of existing relationships of domination that appeals to an absolute truth, it does not follow that his work is a-political. Foucault's argument here is a complex one. He rejects the Enlightenment's concept of the legislating intellectual who dictates "Truth" in the political sphere in favor of what he defines as the "specific intellectual." The specific intellectual is one whose aim is to "question over and over again what is postulated as self-evident, to disturb people's mental habits . . . to dissipate what is familiar and accepted . . ." (1988a: 265). This is a role that rejects the Enlightenment's Archimedean point, but is nevertheless far from a-political. There are a number of Foucault's defenders who emphasize this undeniably moral tone that pervades all of his writings. They defend Foucault by asking how we can accuse him of nihilism when the moral thrust of his work is so self-evident. Lemert and Gillan, for example, claim that although Foucault does not offer an alternative political program he advocates the "forging of a revolutionary link between power and knowledge," a link that would create a "nomadic joy" (1982: 91). Foucault's decentering of man, Lemert asserts, does not necessarily entail the dehumanizing of moral life (1979: 230–1). Another strong defense of Foucault comes from Michael Shapiro. Shapiro states that Foucault advocates a "radical partisanship" model of political interpretation and practice. Although Foucault does not offer a specific political program, Shapiro claims that he provides us with criteria by which we can select a less repressive interpretive scheme (1980: 24). He also argues that, implicit in Foucault's understanding of the self and subjectivity, is a theory of resistance (1987: 4–5). Along the same lines Davidson (1986) argues that Foucault accurately defines his most recent work as an "ethics," a task that involves the study of the self's relationship to itself.

Another central theme of Foucault's defenders is an examination of his relationship to the humanist tradition. Although Foucault's decentering of man and his attack on man's "doubles" in *The Order of Things* seems to entail an outright rejection of the humanist tradition, many of his defenders, like Lemert, want to qualify this rejection. For these writers Foucault's rejection of humanism entails rejecting the values that have, since the beginning of modern politics, defined the difference between repressive and nonrepressive regimes. Thus these defenders of Foucault have attempted to argue that he does not entirely repudiate humanism. Hooke, for example, argues that Foucault can subscribe to humanist values without himself being a humanist (1987: 40). Keenan makes much the same argument when he claims that Foucault talks of individuals as citizens having rights and obligations in a way very reminiscent of the humanist tradition he claims to reject (1987: 21). Hiley (1985) argues that although Foucault rejects humanism he does not reject the Enlightenment and its goal of liberation. In the most spirited defense of Foucault's "humanism," Fraser argues that Foucault's work is compatible with the modern humanist values of autonomy, reciprocity, mutual recognition and human dignity (1981a: 4). She claims that "Foucault's deconstruction of metaphysical humanism does not entail the delegitimation of the normative ideals of moral humanism" (1981a: 36) and that we "can and should combine postmodern antifoundationalism and anti-transcendentalism with substantive modern normative humanism" (1981a: 38). She also challenges Habermas' claim that Foucault is a "young conservative." Along with Hiley she claims that Foucault is attacking not the Enlightenment, but only certain aspects of humanism (1985a: 166). She finds the emancipatory force that characterizes humanism to be a prime motivating factor in Foucault's work (1985a: 171).

Although these arguments are persuasive in a narrow sense, they fail to take account of the larger perspective of Foucault's work. The attempt to define Foucault's project in terms of humanism and the Enlightenment is a backward-looking project; it is an attempt to fit his work into the epistemological categories that he is rejecting. This attempt denies the radical nature of Foucault's work. It also denies two principal theses that Foucault has sought to establish: that we can discuss resistance to repression without formulating a metacritique of power; that we can discuss subjects and action without reference to a Cartesian constituting subject. What these defenders fail to see is that Foucault's work encourages us to look ahead rather than behind, to look to the silences of the old epistemological order and to abandon the effort to resuscitate the old categories. The attempt to define Foucault's work in new rather than old categories characterizes two major interpretations of his work. Poster (1984) and Rajchman (1985) both argue, although in different ways, that Foucault's work is not classifiable in terms of the old categories of social theory. Poster's principal thesis is that Foucault is best interpreted as continuing in the Marxist tradition of resistance to oppression and domination, but by "other means" (1984: 40). Poster claims that although Foucault rejects the intellectual edifice of critical theory he remains within the problematic that it has defined. Foucault rejects Marxism and the traditional epistemological premises of the movement because it calls for a "totalizing history." In opposition to this totalizing history Foucault proposes a "new history" that espouses "truths," not one truth. What Foucault accomplishes, Poster argues, is the achievement of a task similar to that of Marx without his metaphysical baggage (1984: 164). Rajchman's analysis of Foucault posits that what Foucault is engaged in is a permanent questioning, a skepticism that does not have a particular end (1985: 4). Rajchman's thesis is that Foucault's concern with freedom is one that rejects the universalist narrative of abstract freedom in favor of an emphasis on concrete freedom. Rajchman argues that Foucault's freedom is not equal to liberation, but, rather that "It is the motor and principle of skepticism: the endless questioning of constituted experiences" (1985: 7). What Foucault is trying to do, Rajchman argues, is free us from the rationality and subjectivity of modern philosophy. Instead he proposes a philosophy that is "neither prescriptive nor descriptive. It is occasion, spark, challenge. It is risk; it is not guaranteed, backed up, or assured: it always remains without an end" (1985: 123).

Both Foucault's critics and his defenders would concede that the relationship between Foucault's historical analyses and his political stance is a complex one. They would, however, agree on one central point: Foucault rejects any absolute grounding for truth or knowledge that could serve as a basis for political action. The overall theme of Foucault's works is his rejection of the absolutes and dichotomies of Enlightenment thought. If it is assumed that any coherent program of political action must be grounded in absolute truth and knowledge then the unavoidable conclusion of the analyses of both Foucault's critics and his defenders is that he does not offer the possibility of such a program. It would seem to follow from this that those who accuse Foucault of political inadequacy must be declared correct. Such a conclusion, however, is premature. The assumption that political action, to be valid, must be founded in absolute values is precisely the assumption that Foucault is challenging. If the answer to the question of whether Foucault provides an absolute grounding for political action is a firm "no" then perhaps the problem lies with the question rather than the answer. A better question is what basis for political action *does* emanate from Foucault's position because, quite clearly, his work has a political intent.

In his historical and genealogical studies Foucault presents what he calls the history of the relations between thought and truth (1988a: 257). He does not ignore the question of truth, but, rather, presents it in a way that displaces the Enlightenment's search for absolute truth, rejecting the metanarratives and absolutes that characterize the Enlightenment's will to truth. The political program that flows from this approach to truth likewise rejects absolutes and the metacritiques on which Enlightenment political theory is founded. It is a politics that aims to disrupt the familiar, to explode the accepted categories. If Foucault's work is examined in the light of these factors the nature of his political program can be interpreted in an entirely different way. The first aspect of Foucault's work that is relevant to his formulation of a political program is his discussion of how the knowledge/power regime that characterizes modernity might be supplanted in favor of one which is less repressive. In *The Order of Things* Foucault seems to be suggesting that the "man-centered" epistemology of the modern episteme is being replaced by another regime of truth. Since much of Foucault's work is designed to show that the truth/power relationship of modernity and, specifically, of humanism, is particularly oppressive, his suggestion that it might be undergoing a change is significant. He states, for example, that in our society "the relationship between power, right and truth is organized in a highly specific fashion" (1980: 93). Although he is careful to specify that we cannot separate truth from power, he nevertheless argues that we should work to detach "the power of truth from the forms of hegemony, social, economic and cultural within which it operates at the present time" (1980: 133). The specific task of the intellectual, he argues, is to explore whether it is possible to constitute a "new politics of truth" (1981: 306). Intellectuals cannot "emancipate" truth from power, but they can and should be involved in a struggle over the status of truth and the economic and political role that it plays (1980; 133).

What Foucault seems to be suggesting in these passages is that it may be possible for us, because we find ourselves at the time of an epistemological rupture, to construct a new truth/power relationship that is less repressive than our present one. In a much-quoted passage from *The History of Sexuality* he refers to a "different economy of bodies and pleasures" (1978a: 137) that may characterize this new regime. He speculates that it is impossible to tell what man might achieve "as a living being," as the set of forces that resist (1978a: 144). In another context he refers to a "new economy of power relations" (1982: 210) that may be emerging in our time. Foucault never specifies precisely what he means in these passages nor does he offer any more than these enigmatic hints about what this "new economy" entails. Many of his critics have faulted him for this lack of specificity. But there is a very particular reason for his vagueness when discussing an alternative to the present truth/power nexus: it is not his aim to lay out an alternative vision of a new society, but, rather, to examine critically the existing structure. As he puts it, "Nothing, you see, would be more foreign to me than the quest for a sovereign, unique and constraining form" (1978b: 10). Foucault wants to suggest that a new regime may be emerging, not to promote that new form as a superior ideology. He states

> I am not looking for an alternative . . . What I want to do is not the history of solutions and that's the reason I don't accept the word *alternative*. I would like to do the genealogy of problems, of *problematiques*. My point is not that everything is bad, but that everything is dangerous. (1984: 343)

He defines his role not as a superman leading society to a new vision of the future, a legislating intellectual, but as a "specific intellectual" who calls the present into question:

> I dream of the intellectual who destroys evidence and generalities, the one who, in the inertias and constraints of the present time, locates and marks the weak points, the openings, the lines of force, who is incessantly on the move, doesn't know exactly where he is heading nor what he will think tomorrow for he is too attentive to the present . . . (1988a: 124)

Aside from the few passages refering to the "new economy," Foucault's books contain little discussion of the political intent of his position. His interviews, however, tell a different story. It is tempting to dismiss Foucault's interviews as peripheral to the "serious" work found in his books. But this would be counter to Foucault's intent. Foucault regards his interviews as an integral part of his work, an opportunity to express the political relevance of his position in a way that is not appropriate in the context of his historical studies (Deleuze, 1988: 15). These interviews reveal a strongly committed political thinker. Because so many of Foucault's critics are concerned with his political stance interviewers frequently focus on political questions in their discussions, and Foucault has responded to these questions in a forceful way. A good example of the Foucault that emerges in these interviews is found in a discussion with Noam Chomsky in which the two theorists discuss the topic of justice. Although Foucault makes it clear that he rejects any notion of ideal justice, an ideal society, or an absolute human nature, it is significant that he does not rule out a political program that appeals to justice.

Justice, he argues, functions within a society of classes as a claim made by the oppressed classes and as a justification for that oppression (Chomsky and Foucault, 1974: 184–5). This definition of justice entails a political task: "we should indicate and show up, even where they are hidden, all the relationships of political power which actually control the social body and oppress or repress it." Even more specifically he argues that we must criticize the workings of institutions that appear to be neutral and independent. We must unmask the political violence that has been exercised through them in obscure ways so that we can fight it (1974: 171).

Much the same theme is found in an interview published in 1982–3. Again, Foucault rejects any absolutes by insisting that a society without restrictions is inconceivable (1982–3: 17). The important question, he asserts, is not whether a society without restraints is possible or desirable, but whether the system of constraints in which a society functions leaves individuals the liberty to transform the system. He argues, "But a system of constraints becomes truly intolerable when the individuals who are affected by it don't have the means of modifying it" (1982–3: 16). Earlier in the interview, when Foucault is discussing the question of freedom of sexual choice, he is even more adamant on the subject of political opposition. With regard to this freedom, he states, "one has to be absolutely intransigent" (1982–3: 12). What emerges from these discussions is a clear theme: relinquishing absolutes does not entail relinquishing judgment or critique. Foucault asserts that we cannot appeal to absolutes to ground our judgments, nor can we establish our critiques as metacritiques. But this does not entail nihilism. That we must seek the truth without appealing to an absolute "Truth" is the message that unites these discussions. In another context he states this very succinctly: "Nothing is more inconsistent than a political regime that is indifferent to truth; but nothing is more dangerous than a political system that claims to lay down the truth . . . (1988a: 267).

What these passages establish, in no uncertain terms, is that, for Foucault, a program of political action *does* flow from his work. Far from advocating political quiescence, Foucault claims that "the analysis, elaboration, and bringing into question of power relations . . . is a permanent political task inherent in all social existence" (1982: 222). Foucault is quite aware of the political charges against him and responds to them very strongly. "How," he asks, "can anyone imagine that I think change is impossible since what I have analyzed was always related to political action?" (1988b: 14) Foucault asserts that his "ethic" is to be an "anti-strategist," that is, one who is "respectful when something singular arises, to be intransigent when power offends against the universal" (1981: 9). The political program that emerges from these interviews is one of resistance, but a resistance that is locally, not universally grounded. Foucault argues that we can and must resist regimes that fail to allow us the means of modifying them. We must seek to disturb, disrupt and explode the categories of knowledge/power that oppress us. These tasks, however, do not entail recourse to an absolute sense of justice or truth but "merely" to a historically and socially specific definitions.

Foucault supplies a theoretical justification for his political position in an article in which he discusses his attitude toward the Enlightenment and humanism. He states his position with regard to these two events very clearly: he rejects humanism but not the Enlightenment itself. Foucault defines the opposition between the Enlightenment and humanism in terms of the Enlightenment's call to critique as opposed to humanism's universalizing and hence subjugating tendencies. Against the background of this opposition Foucault argues for historical investigations that are genealogical without being transcendental. The theme of his discussion is his assertion that instead of looking for universalizing, totalizing answers to political and moral problems, we should pursue contextual, historical, or what he calls "local" solutions. He answers what his critics see to be the dangers of "local inquiries" by replying that we can always begin again when we reach our limits (1984: 46–7). Finally, in a passage that best expresses his attitude toward political programs, he states:

> The critical ontology of ourselves has to be considered not, certainly, as a theory, a doctrine, or even as a permanent body of knowledge that is accumulating; it has to be conceived as an attitude, an ethos, a philosophical life in which the critique of what we are is at one and the same time the historical analysis of the limits that are imposed on us and an experiment with the possibility of going beyond them. (1984: 50)

What Foucault is advocating here, a "critical ontology of ourselves," is a critique that acknowledges the historical rootedness of all critiques. As stated here this notion of historically rooted critique is very similar to Gadamer's claim that all analysis of prejudice involves critique. Like Gadamer, Foucault is arguing that, in the context of understanding ourselves as historical beings, we can and do critique ourselves; we understand our limits while at the same time going beyond them. He is arguing, furthermore, that this critique will not involve the formation of a new doctrine, a new metanarrative. Rather, it involves critique as a way of life, an endless questioning of power and the mechanisms of repression.

What Foucault is arguing in these and related passages amounts to a forceful answer to his critics' charge that any coherent political program must be grounded in an absolute, universal conception of truth and justice. His program of "local resistance" centers around the argument that, as contextual, historical beings, launching local resistance efforts against specific regimes is more appropriate and more effective than trying to formulate universal theories to justify acts of resistance. He offers a number of specific arguments to support his advocacy of local resistance. First, he claims that there is only a "very tenuous link" between universal philosophical conceptions and the political attitudes of someone who claims to subscribe to them and, thus, that in practice the formulation of these conceptions is not relevant to the immediate political struggle (1984: 374).

Second, he suggests that those who attempt to ground political programs in absolute truths may actually be shirking their political responsibility, that is, the necessity of analyzing and opposing specific historical regimes. In a particularly revealing interview Foucault raises an issue that many of his critics presuppose without question: is a "progressive" politics necessarily linked to totalizing themes, "themes that quarantee to history the inexhaustible presence of the Logos"? His answer is that such a politics has a negative rather than a positive effect. It takes refuge in "a global history of totalities" rather than in the necessary and difficult task of analyzing specific historical regimes and organizing resistance to them (1978b: 19–20).

In these passages Foucault does more than merely claim against his critics that he does indeed have a coherent political program. Rather, he claims that the "local resistance" that he advocates is superior to the totalizing theories that his critics claim are a necessary grounding for political action. The argument that Foucault is making here, furthermore, is a direct consequence of his position on the nature of knowledge and truth. In his attack on Enlightenment epistemology he insists that absolute groundings are unnecessary and misconceived. Here he is making the same claim for political knowledge. Since the beginning of political philosophy, but particularly in the modern era, there has been an insistence on absolute truths to ground political programs. Foucault counters this with the argument that such grounding is unnecessary, misconceived, and even counterproductive. In his argument against Foucault, Taylor finds this position unacceptable. Taylor argues that "mere" local resistance is inadequate; what is called for is a principled program of political action grounded in absolute truth. Against Taylor, Foucault's position is that, since moral and ethical standards are themselves historical and contextual, the critique of regimes that violate those standards are likewise contextual rather than universal. Appealing to universal values to ground resistance, Foucault argues, is not only irrelevant but also ineffectual in the sense that is diverts attention from the real and immediate task of resistance. In arguing against a very similar set of objections, Richard Rorty articulates a position that is consistent with Foucault's approach. A belief can regulate action, Rorty claims, and can even be worth dying for, even if those who hold it are aware that this belief is both historical and contingent (1989: 189).

Foucault does not discuss how his program of local resistance might be applied to a feminist politics or, for that matter, any political program at all. But Foucault's advocacy of a local, contextual and historical approach is directly relevant to several key issues in contemporary feminist theory. The first is the issue of the use of universal concepts in the analysis of the oppression of women. There is a strong tendency among contemporary feminist theorists to appeal to universal concepts to ground their critiques of masculine domination. Appeals to female nature, patriarchy and male dominance as universals of human life are common in feminist discussions. Foucault's position offers a means of counteracting this tendency. His position encourages us to eschew universal concepts, to explore the specific, local mechanisms of the oppression of women rather than to sketch the outlines of the universal phenomenon of male dominance. His position suggests that instead of appealing to an essential female nature we should attempt to understand how femininity is socially constructed in particular societies; instead of deploring the universality of patriarchy we should analyze the historical evolution of patriarchal structures; instead of proclaiming universal male dominance we should examine the specific instances of that phenomenon.

Second, the program of local resistance that arises from Foucault's contextual approach to knowledge, truth and power generates a politics that is germane to the problem of formulating a specifically feminist political practice. Foucault's position entails that the analysis of male dominance must be local and contextual and that the resistance to that domination must be equally specific. Feminists cannot resist patriarchy as a universal phenomenon. But they can resist specific instances of patriarchy, they can oppose specific patriarchal structures. A feminist politics that is consistent with Foucault's program is one that would seek to understand, analyze, and oppose the patterns of male dominance and female oppression that characterize a particular society in a specific historical context. This opposition, furthermore, need not appeal to universal values of human dignity, autonomy or freedom. In many instances of oppression these western humanist values are irrelevant. And even in cases where these values are relevant they are appropriate not because of their universality but because they are a product of that particular society's value structure. What Foucault is asserting in all cases, however, is that the specific instance of oppression will generate a specific resistance to that oppression. The oppression produces the resistance, no other grounding is required.

Although many feminists remain skeptical of a Foucaultian-inspired feminist politics, a number of feminist theorists are beginning to assert the relevance of Foucault for feminist analysis.[6] The recent anthology, *Foucault and Feminism* is a good example of the nature of the current interest in Foucault among feminist theorists as well as the limits of that interest. In their introduction to the volume Diamond and Quinby argue for, if not a marriage of Foucault and feminism, at least a "friendship grounded in political and ethical commitment" (1988b: ix). Many of the authors in the volume echo Sawicki's observation that Foucault's advantage for feminism lies in the historical dimension of his position and his rejection of absolutes (1988: 189). Many of the analyses in the volume use Foucault's perspective to examine the social construction of gender in various aspects of society. But many of these authors also reiterate the criticism of Foucault that has characterized the reception of postmodernism among feminist theorists. Despite her praise of Foucault, Sawicki argues that Foucault's "pluralism" implies a pessimism that obviates "the possibility of an answer" (1988: 189). Martin reinforces this criticism by arguing that Foucault's position denies women's "need to construct the category woman and to search for truths, authenticity and universals" (1988: 13).

These criticisms indicate that despite an increased interest in Foucault's perspective, even sympathetic feminists are skeptical about the viability of a Foucaultian politics. These criticisms also indicate the tenacity of the Enlightenment/humanist epistemology for feminist thought. The belief that coherent political action must be grounded in absolutes is deeply rooted in feminist as well as modernist thought. Foucault's attack on that belief involves a radical reconceptualization of knowledge, truth, power and politics. The resistance to a full acceptance of Foucault's politics testifies to the radical nature of Foucault's position. And, in the case of feminist theory, it also stems from a fundamental tension in feminist thought. On one hand feminists want to deconstruct the phallocentrism of Enlightenment thought, a project that has much in common with postmodernism. But, on the other hand, they want to articulate a distinctively feminine voice that can oppose masculinist discourse (Ferguson, 1988: 1). The obstacle standing in the way of an acceptance of Foucault's perspective is that all but a few feminists believe that the articulation of a feminine voice must be grounded in absolutes: a notion of identity rooted in the constituting Cartesian subject and an articulation of values rooted in universal ethical claims. Foucault, by deconstructing these Enlightenment beliefs, posits the possibility of a different kind of politics, a politics that fosters resistance without reference to a constituting subject or absolute values. It is a resistance that relies on the articulation of a discourse that displaces and explodes the masculine discourse of domination.

One of the aspects of Foucault's perspective on knowledge and power is that power is not localized in one social sphere, whether economic or political, but, rather, is diffused throughout the multitude of institutions that constitute society. Foucault's critics have attacked him for this position, arguing that if, as he asserts, power is everywhere, then it is nowhere and, thus, cannot be opposed. Foucault's point, however, is a very different one: power, being everywhere, must be opposed everywhere. This is a thesis that is particularly relevant to the formulation of a feminist politics. The discourses that constitute women as subordinate are not localized in a single institution, but permeate every aspect of society; they are an element of every institution. The subordination of women thus cannot be eradicated by reforming the political and/or economic structures alone because elements of that subordination are constituted by the plurality of discursive regimes that structure all aspects of society, not just these two structures. Thus female subordination will not be eliminated by giving woman the vote or equal pay. A Foucaultian politics speaks to this peculiarity of the subordination of women. It suggests that we must oppose those knowledge/power discourses that subordinate women everywhere throughout society. The result of such a strategy is not, as Foucault's critics claim, political acquiescence, but, rather, a broadly based political resistance.

In *The Postmodern Condition* (1984) Lyotard argues that knowledge in the postmodern era has lost the universally legitimating discourse that characterizes the epistemology of modernity. This is a position that is reiterated in the work of a number of prominent contemporary writers (Walzer, 1983; 1987; Bauman, 1987; MacIntyre, 1981; 1988). Foucault's politics as well as his theory of knowledge addresses this postmodern condition. His argument is two-fold. First, he asserts, like these writers, that the universalizing discourse of the Enlightenment has been displaced; it can no longer perform the function of legitimating knowledge in all realms. His position is that knowledge in our era is undergoing an epistemological rupture, a transition to a new epistemological configuration. Second, Foucault argues that the Enlightenment's universalizing conception of knowledge was, from its inception, misconceived. Like any other knowledge/power discourse, Enlightenment discourse is historical and contextual and, hence, its claim of universality was, from the outset, fraudulent. It follows that it is futile, as some contemporary theorists claim, to attempt to reconstitute that discourse, to reformulate the Enlightenment project. The Enlightenment project, Foucault argues, has been justifiably laid to rest.

Our present situation is one in which, in the absence of a transcendent metanarrative, different discourses compete for ascendency. This is a situation that necessitates a different approach to politics. Since political action cannot appeal to the legitimating norms of a metanarrative, political opposition must be guided by a different conception of knowledge that generates a different means of opposition to the subjugation imposed by the discourses that structure societal relations. It is Foucault's position that opposition is effected by formulating discourses that oppose repressive, subjugating discourses, a theory of opposition that is informed by a discursive conception of knowledge/power. He argues that opposition to repression operates by appealing to a different discursive configuration of knowledge/power that constitutes a different truth. Such a new discursive formation cannot claim the status of a metanarrative. Nor can it claim to eradicate power. It can, however, claim to alleviate the oppression of the discourse it opposes. Foucault's postmodern theory of political opposition is a position that is directly applicable to the challenge of formulating feminist political practice. What feminism has been about since its inception is a critique of the discourses of male domination that constitute women as inferior. That critique has three aspects. First, it involves understanding how the feminine has been constituted as inferior, what Foucault calls a "critical ontology of ourselves." This critical ontology involves re-evaluating and disrupting the rules, familiarities and accepted categories that define the feminine. Second, it involves both exploring the limits of those discourses and what lies beyond them. Discourses, even hegemonic discourses, are not closed systems. The silences and ambiguities of discourse provide the possibility of refashioning them, the discovery of other conceptualizations, the revision of accepted truths. These refashionings and revisions lead to the third aspect: the formulation of a feminist discourse that constitutes the feminine, the masculine and sexuality in a different way. In the postmodern era feminists cannot oppose the discourses of male domination by appealing to a metanarrative of universal justice and freedom. They can be opposed, however, by formulating a

feminist discourse that displaces and explodes the repressive discourses of patriarchal society. Foucault's position, and that of postmodernism more generally,
supplies a means of formulating such a discourse and articulating a feminist
political practice. It provides a strategy that deconstructs masculinist discourse/
power without attempting to resurrect the Enlightenment project of metanarratives and liberation. It is a strategy that feminists can and should employ in both
theory and practice.

V Conclusion

A fundamental ambiguity informs the feminist movement in the late twentieth
century. On one hand it offers a challenge to the received opinions of western
thought in both theory and practice. It questions the dualities and hierarchies that
have dominated western thought and institutions since their inception. What
began as a call for political equality for women has culminated in a radical challenge
to the very foundations of western thought and social structure. But on the other
hand the feminist movement is also a product of the evolution of western thought.
It is intimately tied to the emancipatory impulse of the Enlightenment and, both
historically and theoretically, has its roots in the liberal and Marxist traditions.

This ambiguity in the legacy of contemporary feminism is not easily resolved.
Feminism's ties to the politics and epistemology of liberalism and Marxism are
deep. But the realization of the sexism of Enlightenment epistemology and the
politics it spawns has undermined feminism's allegiance to that epistemology.
Liberalism and Marxism will allow women into the public space of politics, but
only if they renounce the "feminine" values that excluded them from this realm in
the first place. This is due to the fact that the Cartesian, constituting subject that is
the centerpiece of modernist epistemology is inherently masculine. The rational,
autonomous subject of modernity is not only constitutive of modernist
epistomology, it is also constitutive of the sexism that epistemology has fostered.
Feminism's understanding of the profound limitations of Enlightenment
epistemology has forced it to look elsewhere for an approach to both knowledge
and politics that avoids the sexism of the modern episteme.

While feminism's criticism of the modern episteme is, on the whole, still
tentative, postmodernism's critique of modernity is unambiguous.
Postmodernism rejects outright the modern episteme and the institutional structures that it has produced. It attacks the dualisms and hierarchies of Enlightenment
thought, defying the "will to truth" that has characterized western thought since
its inception. Against the absolutist, unitary conception of truth that defines the
modern episteme the postmoderns propose a plural understanding of truth. They
argue that all knowledge is historical and contextual, that it is a product of
particular discourses. They further argue that the discourses that create knowledge
create power as well, power that constitutes subjects and objects and the

mechanisms by which subjects are subjugated. The postmodern conception of the subject as a process, a constituted entity, is its most fundamental challenge to Enlightenment thought. Its rejection of the constituting Cartesian subject that creates knowledge through rational abstraction places postmodernism in fundamental opposition to Enlightenment assumptions.

This book is an attempt to trace the convergences between contemporary feminist thought and postmodernism. The two movements are by no means identical. They spring from different theoretical and political sources and, at present, regard each other with suspicion. The similarities between the two movements, however, are striking. Feminism and postmodernism are the only contemporary theories that present a truly radical critique of the Enlightenment legacy of modernism. No other approaches on the contemporary intellectual scene offer a means of displacing and transforming the masculinist epistemology of modernity. This fact alone creates a bond between the two approaches.

It is not the intent of the foregoing to advocate a marriage between postmodernism and feminism. The two movements are and will remain separate. They will continue to have differences, primarily due to the on-going political focus of the feminist movement. What I am arguing, however, is that both these approaches can benefit from a closer association. The discourse theory of knowledge advanced by postmodernism can serve as a means of correcting some of the essentialist tendencies of contemporary feminism. Further, the postmoderns' emphasis on the constitutive powers of discourse can continue to remind feminists that women are made, not born. On the other hand, a feminist perspective can contribute a needed gender sensitivity to postmodern thought. Feminists can use the discourse theory of postmodernism to increase our understanding of the constitution of gender in various societies. In short, I am arguing that the conversation between postmodernism and feminism that has begun in recent years is a fruitful one and should be continued.

One of the central arguments of this book is that the discourse theory of knowledge developed by postmodern thinkers demands a new way of conceptualizing both truth and political action that, far from being detrimental to the political needs of feminism, actually fosters them. This argument involves two related theses. First, because postmodernism rejects not only the Cartesian, constituting subject but also the dichotomy between the transcendental subject and the wholly constituted subject, it provides an understanding of the subject directly relevant to feminism. It presents the subject as an entity that is constituted by discourses but is also capable of resistance to that constitution. It is a subject that can resist its subjugation and attempt to fashion new modes of subjectivity. Second, postmodernism's discourse theory of knowledge presents an understanding of language as fluid and multiple. Languages are not closed systems. The gaps, silences and ambiguities of discourses provide the possibility for resistance, for a questioning of the dominant discourse, its revision and mutation. Within these silences and gaps new discourses can be formulated that challenge the dominant discourse. This theory of discourses and their mutability provides an accurate understanding of the task of feminism. Feminists have attempted to fashion new discourses about the feminine, discourses that resist the hegemony of male domination, that utilize the contradictions in these hegemonic discourses in order to effect their transformation. In this task the perspective of postmodernism is a help rather than a hindrance. Both postmodernism and feminism are counter discourses that challenge the modern episteme at its roots. This fundamental commonality suggests that an alliance between these two movements will further the aims of both.

Notes

1 For an interesting discussion of relativism and postmodern thinking see Margolis (1986).
2 I have defended Gadamer's critical stance elsewhere (1986: 109–17). See Wachterhauser (1986: 50) for a discussion of the relationship between postmodernism and hermeneutics.
3 See Hekman (1986: 129–39) for a discussion of this debate.
4 In an article on Foucault and Derrida, Keenan reports an incident in which Derrida acknowledges the difficulty of drawing direct political implications from his work (1987: 19).
5 See Spivak (1984: 1987a) for an elaboration of these themes. In his discussion of the oral tradition in the west, Ong suggests that the defeat of oralism in the academic world coincided with the advent of women into academia. The coincidence of women and writing he suggests parallels Derrida's thesis (1967: 252).
6 For an excellent illustration of a feminist use of Foucault's position see Kathy Ferguson (1984).

References

Acker, Joan et al. 1983. Objectivity and truth: problems in doing feminist research. *Women's Studies International Forum*, 6: 423–35.

Alcoff, Linda 1988. Cultural feminism versus post-structuralism: the identity crisis in feminist theory. *Signs*, 13 (3): 405–36.

Allen, Christine 1979. Nietzsche's ambivalence about women. In Laverne Clark and Lynda Lange (eds), *The Sexism of Social and Political Theory*, Toronto: University of Toronto Press, 117–33.

Allison, David 1973. Translator's introduction. In Jacques Derrida, *Speech and Phenomena*, Evanston: Northwestern University Press, xxxi–xiii.

Apel, Karl 1981. Social action and the concept of rationality. *Phenomenology and the Human Sciences*. Supplement to *Philosophical Topics*, 12: 9–35.

Arditti, Rita 1980. Feminism and science. In Rita Arditti, Pat Brennen and Steve Cavrak (eds), *Science and Liberation*, Boston: South End Press, 350–68.

Bacon, Francis 1964. *The Philosophy of Francis Bacon*, ed. B. Farrington. Liverpool: Liverpool University Press.

Balbus, Issac 1982. *Marxism and Domination*. Princeton: Princeton University Press.

—— 1985. Disciplining women: Michel Foucault and the power of feminist discourse. *Praxis International*, 5: 466–83.

Bartky, Sandra 1988. Foucault, femininity and the modernization of patriarchal power. In Irene Diamond and Lee Quinby (eds), *Feminism and Foucault: reflections on resistance*, Boston: Northeastern University Press, 61–86.

Bauman, Zygmunt 1987. *Legislators and Interpreters: on modernity, postmodernity and intellectuals*. Ithaca: Cornell University Press.

Beardsley, Elizabeth Lane 1976. Referential Genderization. In Carol Gould and Marx Wartofsky (eds), *Women and Philosophy*, New York: G. P. Putnam, 285–93.

Belenky, Mary et al. 1986. *Women's Ways of Knowing*. New York: Basic Books.

Bem, Sandra 1976. Probing the promise of androgyny. In Alexandra G. Kaplan and Joan P. Bean (eds), *Beyond Sex-Role Stereotypes*, Boston: Little Brown, 47–62.

Benhabib, Seyla 1984. Epistemologies of postmodernism: a rejoinder to Jean-François Lyotard. *New German Critique*, 33: 103–36.

—— 1986a. *Critique, Norm and Utopia: a study of the foundations of critical theory*. New York: Columbia University Press.

—— 1986b. The generalized and the concrete other: the Kohlberg – Gilligan controversy and feminist theory. *Praxis International*, 5: 402–24.

Birke, Lynda 1986. *Women, Feminism and Biology: the feminist challenge*. New York: Methuen.

Bleier, Ruth 1979. Social and political bias in science. In Ruth Hubbard and Marian Lowe (eds), *Genes and Gender II*, New York: Gordian Press, 49–69.

—— 1984. *Science and Gender: a critique of biology and its theories on women*. New York: Pergamon Press.

—— 1986. Introduction. In Ruth Bleier (ed.), *Feminist Approaches to Science*, New York: Pergamon Press, 1–17.

Bloch, Maurice and Jean Bloch 1980. Women and the dialectics of nature. In Carol MacCormack and Marilyn Strathern (eds), *Nature, Culture and Gender*, Cambridge: Cambridge University Press, 25–41.

Bordo, Susan 1986. The Cartesian masculinization of thought. *Signs*, 11: 439–56.

—— 1987. *The Flight to Objectivity*. Albany: State University of New York Press.

Bove, Paul 1988. Foreword: the Foucault phenomenon: the problematics of style. In Giles Deleuze, *Foucault*, Minneapolis: University of Minnesota Press, vii–xi.

Bowles, Gloria 1984. The uses of hermeneutics for feminist scholarship. *Women's Studies International Forum*, 7: 185–8.

—— et al. 1983. Beyond the blacklash: a feminist critique of Ivan Illich's theory of gender. *Feminist Issues*, 3: 3–43.

Braidotti, Rosi 1987. Envy: or with your brains and my looks. In Alice Jardine and Paul Smith (eds), *Men in Feminism*, New York: Methuen, 233–41.

Brennan, Teresa and Carole Pateman 1979. "Mere auxilliaries to the commonwealth": women and the origins of liberalism. *Political Studies*, 27 (2): 183–200.

Broughton, John 1983. Women's rationality and men's virtues. *Social Research*, 50 (3): 597–642.

Brown, Beverly and Parveen Adams 1979. The feminine body and feminist politics. *M/F*, 3: 35–50.

Brown, Wendy 1987. Where is the sex in political theory? *Women and Politics*, 7 (1): 3–23.

Buker, Eloise 1985. Hermeneutics: problems and promises for doing feminist theory. Unpublished paper.

Bunch, Charlotte 1981. Beyond either/or: feminist options. In Charlotte Bunch et al. (eds), *Building Feminist Theory*, New York: Longman, 44–56.

Burke, Carolyn 1981. Irigaray through the looking glass. *Feminist Studies*, 7: 288–306.

Chodorow, Nancy 1978. *The Reproduction of Mothering*. Berkeley: University of California Press.

Chomsky, Noam and Michel Foucault 1974. Human nature: justice vs power. In Fons Elder (ed.), *Reflexive Water*, London: Souvenier Press, 133–97.

Cixous, Helene 1976. The laugh of the Medusa. *Signs*, 1 (4): 875–93.

—— 1980. Sorties. In Elaine Marks and Isabelle de Courtivron (eds), *New French Feminism*, Amherst: University of Massachusetts Press, 90–8.

—— 1981. Castration or decapitation. *Signs*, 7: 41–55.

—— and Catherine Clement 1986. *The Newly Born Woman*, trans. Betsy Wing. Minneapolis: University of Minnesota Press.

Clavir, Judith 1979. Choosing either/or: a critique of metaphysical feminism. *Feminism Studies*, 5: 402–10.

Clement, Catherine 1983. *The Lives and Legends of Jacques Lacan*, trans. Authur Goldhammer. New York: Columbia.

Cocks, Joan 1984. Wordless emotions: some critical reflections on radical feminism. *Politics and Society*, 13: 27–57.

Code, Lorraine 1983. Responsibility and the epistemic community: woman's place. *Social Research*, 50 (3): 537–55.

Conley, Verena 1984. *Helene Cixous: writing the feminine*. Lincoln: University of Nebraska Press.

Cook, J. A. and M. M. Fonow 1986. Knowledge and women's interests – issues of epistemology and methodology in feminist sociological research. *Sociological Inquiry*, 56: 2–29.

Cornell, Drucilla and Adam Thurschwell 1985. Feminism, negativity, intersubjectivity. *Praxis International*, 5: 484–504.

Cott, Nancy 1986. Feminist theory and feminist movements: the past before us. In Juliet Mitchell and Ann Oakley (eds), *What is Feminism*, New York: Pantheon, 49–62.

Culler, Jonathan 1982. *On Deconstruction: theory and criticism after structuralism*. Ithaca: Cornell University Press.

Curran, Libby 1980. Science education: did she drop out or was she pushed? In Brighton Women and Science Group, *Alice Through the Microscope*, London: Virago, 22–41.

Daly, Mary 1973. *Beyond God the Father*. Boston: Beacon Press.

—— 1978. *Gyn/Ecology: the metaethics of radical feminism*. Boston: Beacon Press.

—— 1984. *Pure Lust: elemental feminist philosophy*. Boston: Beacon Press.

—— and Jane Caputi 1987. *Webster's First New Intergalactic Wickedary of the English Language*. Boston: Beacon Press.

Davidson, Arnold 1986. Archaelogy, genealogy, ethics. In David Couzens Hoy (ed.), *Foucault: a critical reader*, New York: Basil Blackwell, 221–33.

De Beauvoir, Simone 1948. *The Ethics of Ambiguity*. New York: Philosophical Library.

—— 1972. *The Second Sex*. Hammondsworth, England: Penguin Books.

De Lauretis, Teresa 1984. *Alice Doesn't: feminism, semiotics and cinema*. Bloomington: Indiana University Press.

—— 1987. *The Technologies of Gender*. Bloomington: Indiana University Press.

Deleuze, Giles 1988. *Foucault*. Trans. Sean Hand. Minneapolis: University of Minnesota Press.

Delphy, Christine 1984. *Close to Home*. Trans. Diana Leonard. Amherst: University of Massachusetts Press.

Derrida, Jacques 1969. The ends of man. *Philosophy and Phenomenological Research*, 30: 31–57.

—— 1970. Structure, sign and play in the discourse of the human sciences. In Richard Macksey and Eugenio Donato (eds), *The Structuralist Controversy*, Baltimore: Johns Hopkins University Press. 246–72.

—— 1973. *Speech and Phenomena*. Trans. David Allison. Evanston: Northwestern University Press.

—— 1975. The purveyor of truth. *Yale French Studies*, 52: 31–113.

—— 1976. *Of Grammatology*. Trans. Gayatri Spivak. Baltimore. The Johns Hopkins University Press.

—— 1977. The question of style. In *The New Nietzsche*, ed. David Allison, New York: Delta, 176–89.

—— 1978a. *Edmund Husserl's Origin of Geometry: an introduction*. Trans. John Leavey, Jr. Stony Brook, N.Y.: Nicholas Hays.

—— 1978b. *Writing and Difference*. Trans. Alan Bass. Chicago: University of Chicago Press.

—— 1979a. Living on: borderlines. In *Deconstruction and Criticism*, New York: Seabury Press.

—— 1979b. *Spurs/Eperons*. Chicago: University of Chicago Press.

—— 1980a. *The Archeology of the Frivolous*. Pittsburgh: Duquene University Press.

—— 1980b. The law of genre. *Glyph*, 7: 202–32.

—— 1981a. *Dissemination*. Chicago: University of Chicago Press.

—— 1981b. *Positions*. Trans. Alan Bass. Chicago: University of Chicago Press.

—— 1982. *Margins of Philosophy*. Trans. Alan Bass. Chicago: University of Chicago Press.

—— 1984. *Signepone/Signsponge*. Trans. Richard Rand. New York: Columbia University Press.

—— 1985. *The Ear of the Other*. Trans. Peggy Kamuf. New York: Schocken Books.

—— 1987. *The Post Card: from Socrates to Freud and beyond*. Chicago: University of Chicago Press.

—— and Christie MacDonald 1982. Choreographies. *Diacritics*, 12: 66–76.

—— et al. 1985. Deconstruction in America: an interview with Jacques Derrida. *Critical Exchange*, 17: 1–33.

Dews, Peter 1986. Editors's introduction. In Peter Dews (ed.), *Jurgen Habermas: autonomy and solidarity*, London: Verso, 1–34.

Diamond, Irene and Lee Quinby (eds) 1988a. *Feminism and Foucault: reflections on resistance*. Northeastern University Press.

—— 1988b. Introduction. In Irene Diamond and Lee Quinby (eds), *Feminism and Foucault: reflections on resistance*, Boston: Northeastern University Press, ix–xix.

Dietz, Mary 1985. Citizenship with a feminist face: the problem of maternal thinking. *Political Theory*, 13: 19–37.

Dinnerstein, Dorothy 1976. *The Mermaid and the Minotaur: sexual arrangements and the human malaise*. New York: Harper and Row.

Di Stefano, Christine 1987. Postmodernism/postfeminism?: the case of the incredible shrinking woman. Unpublished paper.

—— 1988. Dilemmas of difference: feminism, modernity and postmodernity. *Women and Politics*, 8 (3/4): 1–24.

Donovan, Joshephine 1986. *Feminist Theory*. New York: Ungar.

Duchen, Claire 1986. *Feminism in France: from May '68 to Mitterand*. Boston: Routledge and Kegan Paul.

Du Plessis, Rachael 1985. For the Etruscans. In Elaine Showalter (ed.), *The New Feminist Criticism*, New York: Pantheon, 271–91.

Easlea, Brian 1980. *Witch-Hunting, Magic and the New Philosophy: an introduction to debates of the scientific revolution 1450–1750*. Sussex: Harvester Press.

—— 1981. *Science and Sexual Oppression*. London: Weidenfeld and Nicolson.

Eichler, Margrit 1980. *The Double Standard: a feminist critique of feminist social science*. London: Croom Helm.

Eisenstein, Hester 1983. *Contemporary Feminist Thought*. Boston: G. K. Hall.

Eisenstein, Zillah 1981. *The Radical Future of Liberal Feminism*. New York: Longman.

Elshtain, Jean Bethke 1981. *Public Man, Private Woman*. Princeton, N.J.: Princeton University Press.

—— 1982a. Antigone's daughters. *Democracy*, 2: 46–59.

—— 1982b. Feminism, family and community. *Dissent*, 442–9.

—— 1982c. Feminist discourse and its discontents: language, power and meaning. *Signs*, 7: 603–21.

—— 1984. Symmetry and soporofics: a critique of feminist accounts of gender development. In B. Richards (ed.), *Capitalism and Infancy*, London: Free Association Books, 55–91.

—— 1986a. *Mediations on Modern Political Thought: masculine/feminine themes from Luther to Arendt*. New York: Praeger.

—— 1986b. The new feminist scholarship. *Salmagundi*, 71: 3–26.

—— 1987: Against androgeny. In Anne Phillips (ed.), *Feminism and Equality*, New York: New York University Press, 139–59.

Engels, Friedrich 1985. *The Origins of the Family, Private Property and the State*. Hammondsworth: Penquin Books.

Evans, Martha Noel 1987. *Masks of Tradition: women and the politics of writing in twentieth-century France*. Ithaca: Cornell University Press.

Farganis, Sondra 1986. Social theory and feminist theory: the need for dialogue. *Sociological Inquiry*, 56: 50–68.

Farrington, Benjamin 1964. Introduction. In B. Farrington (ed.), *The Philosophy of Francis Bacon*, Liverpool: Liverpool University Press, 9–55.

Faure, Christine 1981. The twilight of the goddesses, or the intellectual crisis of French feminism. *Signs*, 7: 81–6.

Fausto-Sterling, A. 1981. Women and science. *Women's Studies International Quarterly*, 4: 41–50.

—— 1985. *Myths of Gender*. New York: Basic Books.

Fawcett, Millicent 1971. Introduction. In John Stuart Mill, *On Liberty, Representative Government, and The Subjection of Women*, London: Oxford University Press, v–xviii.

Fay, Brian 1987. *Critical Social Science: liberation and its limits*. Ithaca: Cornell University Press.

Fee, Elizabeth 1981. Is feminism a threat to objectivity? *International Journal of Women's Studies*, 4: 378–92.

—— 1982. A feminist critique of scientific objectivity. *Science for the People*, 14: 30–3.

—— 1986. Critiques of modern science. In Ruth Bleier (ed.), *Feminist Approaches to Science*, New York: Pergamon Press, 42–56.

Feral, Josette 1978. Antigone or the irony of the tribe. *Diacritics*, 8 (3): 2–14.

Ferguson, Ann 1984. On conceiving motherhood and sexuality: a feminist materialist approach. In Joyce Tribilcot (ed.), *Mothering: essays in feminist theory*, Totowa, N.J.: Rowman and Allanheld, 153–82.

Ferguson, Kathy 1984. *The Feminist Case Against Bureaucracy*. Philadelphia: Temple University Press.

—— 1988. Interpretation and genealogy in feminism. Unpublished paper.

Finn, Geraldine 1982. On the oppression of women in philosophy – or whatever happened to objectivity? In Geraldine Finn and Angela Miles (eds), *Feminism in Canada*, Montreal: Black Rose Books, 145–73.

Firestone, Shulamith 1979. *The Dialectic of Sex: the case for feminist revolution*. London: Women's Press.

Fish, Stanley 1980. *Is There a Text in This Class?: the authority of interpretive communities*. Cambridge, Mass.: Harvard University Press.

Flanagan, Owen and Jonathan Adler 1983. Impartiality and particularity. *Social Research*, 50 (3): 576–96.

Flax, Jane 1980. Mother – daughter relationships: psychodynamics, politics and philosophy. In Hester Eisenstein and Alice Jardine (eds), *The Future of Difference*, Boston: G. K. Hall, 20–40.

—— 1986a. Gender as a social problem: in and for feminist theory. *American Studies/ Amerika Studien*, 193–213.

—— 1986b. Psycholanalysis as deconstruction and myth: on gender, narcissism and modernity's discontents. In Kurt Shell (ed.), *The Crisis of Modernity: recent theories of culture in the United States and West Germany*, Boulder, Col.: Westview Press, 320–51.

—— 1987a. Postmodernism and gender relations in feminist theory. *Signs*, 12 (4): 621–43.

—— 1987b. Re-membering the selves: is the repressed gendered? *Michigan Quarterly Review*, 26 (1): 992–110.

Foucault, Michel 1971. *The Order of Things: an archaeology of the human sciences*. New York: Random House.

—— 1972. *The Archaeology of Knowledge*. Trans. A. M. Sheridan Smith. New York: Random House.

—— 1973a. *The Birth of the Clinic*. New York: Pantheon.

—— 1973b. *Madness and Civilization*. New York: Vintage.

—— 1977. *Discipline and Punish*. Trans. Alan Sheridan. New York: Random House.

—— 1978a. *The History of Sexuality*, vol. 1. Trans. Robert Hurley. New York: Random House.

—— 1978b. Politics and the study of discourse. *Ideology and Consciousness*, 3: 7–26.

—— 1980. *Power/Knowledge*. New York: Pantheon Books.

—— 1981. Is it useless to revolt? *Philosophy and Social Criticism*, 8: 2–9.

—— 1982. The subject and power. In Hubert Dreyfus and Paul Rabinow, *Michel Foucault: beyond structuralism and hermeneutics*, Chicago: University of Chicago Press, 208–26.

—— 1982–3. Sexual choice, sexual act: an interview with James O'Higgins. *Salmagundi*, 10–24.

—— 1984. *The Foucault Reader*. Ed. Paul Rabinow. New York: Pantheon.

—— 1985. *The Use of Pleasure*. New York. Pantheon.

—— 1986. *The Care of the Self*. New York: Pantheon.

—— 1988a. *Michel Foucault: politics, philosophy, culture*. Ed. Lawrence Kritzman. New York: Routledge.

—— 1988b. Truth, power, self: an interview. In Luther Martin et al. (eds), *Technologies of the Self*, Amherst: University of Massachusetts Press, 9–15.

—— and Richard Sennett 1982. Sexuality and solitude. In David Rieff (ed.), *Humanities in Review I*, New York: Cambridge University Press, 3–21.

—— and Gerard Raulet 1983. Structuralism and poststructuralism: an interview with Michel Foucault. *Telos*, 55: 195–211.

Fraser, Nancy 1981a. Foucault and the problem of the normative foundations of postmodern social critique. Unpublished paper.

—— 1981b. Foucault on modern power: empirical insights and normative confusions. *Praxis International*, 1: 272–87.

—— 1984. The French Derrideans: politicizing deconstruction or deconstructing the political? *New German Critique*, 33: 127–54.

—— 1985a. Michel Foucault: a young conservative? *Ethics*, 96: 165–84.

—— 1985b. What's critical about critical theory?: the case of Habermas and gender. *New German Critique*, 35: 97–131.

—— 1986. Toward a discourse ethic of solidarity. *Praxis International*, 5: 425–9.

—— and Linda Nicholson 1988. Social criticism without philosophy: an encounter between feminism and postmodernism. In Avner Cohen and Marcelo Descal (eds), *The Institution of Philosophy: a discipline in crisis?*, Totowa, New Jersey: Rowman and Littlefield.

Freud, Sigmund 1971. Femininity. In James Strachey (ed.), *The Complete Introductory Lectures on Psychoanalysis*, London: Allen and Unwin, 576–99.

Fried, Barbara 1982. Boys will be boys will be boys: the language of sex and gender. In Ruth Hubbard, M. S. Henifin and B. Fried (eds), *Biological Woman: the convenient myth*, Cambridge, Mass.: Schenkman, 47–69.

Friedan, Betty 1981. *The Second Stage*. New York: Simon and Schuster.

Gadamer, Hans-Georg 1975. *Truth and Method*. New York: Continuum.

—— 1976. *Hegel's Dialectic: five hermeneutic studies*. Trans. P. Christopher Smith. New Haven: Yale University Press.

—— 1979. The problem of historical consciousness. In Paul Rabinow and William Sullivan (eds), *Interpretive Social Science*, Berkeley: University of California Press, 103–60.

—— 1985. *Philosophical Apprenticeships*. Trans. R. Sullivan. Cambridge, Mass.: MIT Press.

Gallop, Jane 1976. The ladies' man. *Diacritics*, 6: 28–34.

—— 1982. *The Daughter's Seduction: feminism and psychoanalysis*. Ithaca, New York: Cornell University Press.

—— 1985. *Reading Lacan*. Ithaca: Cornell University Press.

Gasche, Rodolphe 1986. *The Tain of the Mirror: Derrida and the philosophy of reflection*. Cambridge, Mass.: Harvard University Press.

Gatens, Moira 1986. Feminism, philosophy and riddles without answers. In Carole Pateman and Elizabeth Gross (eds), *Feminist Challenges*, Boston: Northeastern University Press, 13–29.

Gay, Peter 1988. *Freud: a life for our times*. New York: Norton.

Giddens, Anthony 1979. *Central Problems in Social Theory*. Berkeley: University of California Press.

1985. Jurgen Habermas. In Quentin Skinner (ed.), *The Return of Grand Theory in the Human Sciences*, Cambridge: Cambridge University Press, 122–39.

Gilbert, Sandra 1986. Introduction: a tarentella of theory. In Helene Cixous and Catherine Clement, *The Newly Born Woman*, Minneapolis: University of Minnesota Press, ix–xviii.

Gilligan, Carol 1982. *In a Different Voice*. Cambridge, Mass.: Harvard University Press.

—— 1987. Remapping development: the power of divergent data. In Christie Farnham (ed.), *The Impact of Feminist Research in the Academy*, Bloomingdale: University of Indiana Press, 77–94.

Gottlieb, Roger 1984. Mothering and the reproduction of power: Chodorow, Dinnerstein and social theory. *Socialist Review*, 14: 93–119.

Gould, Steven Jay 1986. Cardboard Darwinism. *New York Review of Books*, 33 (4): 47–54.

Granier, Jean 1977. Perspectivism and interpretation. In David Allison (ed.), *The New Nietzsche*, New York: Delta, 190–200.

Griffin, Susan 1978. *Woman and Nature: the roaring inside her*. New York: Harper and Row.

—— 1981. *Pornography and Silence*. New York: Harper and Row.

Grimshaw, Jean 1986. *Philosophy and Feminist Thinking*. Minneapolis: University of Minnesota Press.

Gross, Elizabeth 1986a. Conclusion: what is feminist theory? In Carole Pateman and Elizabeth Gross (eds), *Feminist Challenges*, Boston: Northeastern University Press, 190–204.

—— 1986b. Philosophy, subjectivity and the body: Kristeva and Irigaray. In Carole Patemen and Elizabeth Gross, *Feminist Challenges*, Boston: Northeastern University Press, 125–43.

Habermas, Jurgen 1981a. Modernity versus postmodernity. *New German Critique*, 22: 3–14.

—— 1981b. New social movements. *Telos*, 49: 33–7.

—— 1983. *Philosophical–Political Profiles*. Trans. Frederick G. Lawrence. Cambridge, Mass.: MIT Press.

—— 1984. *The Theory of Communicative Action*, vol. 1, Trans. Thomas McCarthy. Boston: Beacon Press.

—— 1986. *Jurgen Habermas: autonomy and solidarity*. Ed. Peter Dews. London: Verso.

—— 1987. *The Philosophical Discourse of Modernity*. Cambridge, Mass.: MIT Press.

Hacking, Ian 1986. The archaelogy of Foucault. In David Couzens Hoy (ed.), *Foucault: a critical reader*, New York: Basil Blackwell, 27–40.

Handelman, Susan 1982. *The Slayers of Moses*. Albany: SUNY Press.

Haraway, Donna 1978. Animal sociology and a natural economy of the body politic. Part I: a political psychology of dominance. *Signs*, 4: 21–36.

—— 1981. In the beginning was the word: the genesis of biological theory. *Signs*, 6: 469–81.

—— 1985. A manifesto for cyborgs: science, technology and socialist feminism in the 1980s. *Socialist Review*, 80: 65–107.

—— 1986. Primatology is politics by other means. In Ruth Bleier (ed.), *Feminist Approaches to Science*, New York: Pergamon Press, 77–118.

Harding, Sandra 1977. Does objectivity in social science require value-neutrality? *Soundings*, 60: 351–66.

—— 1980. The norms of social inquiry and masculine experience. *Philosophy of Science Association*, vol. 2, ed. P. D. Asquith and R. N. Gieve, East Lansing, Mich.: Philosophy of Science Association, 305–24.

—— 1981. Gender politics of infancy. *Quest*, 5 (3): 53–70.

—— 1983. Why has the sex/gender system become visible only now? In Sandra Harding and Merril Hintikka (eds), *Discovering Reality*, Boston: D. Reidel, 311–24.

—— 1984. Is gender a variable in conceptions of rationality: a survey of issues. In Carol Gould (ed.), *Beyond Domination*, Totowa. N.J.: Rowman and Allanheld, 43–63.

—— 1986a. The instability of the analytic categories of feminist theory. *Signs* 11: 645–64.

—— 1986b. *The Science Question in Feminism*. Ithaca: Cornell University Press.

—— 1987. The curious coincidence of feminine and African moralities. In Eva Kittay and Diana Meyers (eds), *Women and Moral Theory*, Totowa, N.J.: Rowman and Allenheld, 296–315.

Harris, Daniel 1974. Androgyny: the sexist myth in disguise. *Women's Studies*, 2: 171–84.

Hartmann, Heidi 1981. The unhappy marriage of Marxism and feminism: towards a more progressive union. In Lydia Sargent (ed.), *Women and Revolution*, Boston: South End Press, 1–41.

Hartsock, Nancy 1983a. The feminist standpoint: developing the ground for a specifically feminist historical materialism. In Sandra Harding and Merril Hintikka, *Discovering Reality*, Boston: D. Reidel, 283–310.

—— 1983b: *Money, Sex and Power*. New York: Longman.

—— 1987. Re-thinking modernism: minority vs. majority theories. *Cultural Critique*, 7: 187–206.

Heidegger, Martin 1977. *The Question Concerning Technology and Other Essays*. Trans. William Lovitt. New York: Harper and Row.

Heilbrun, Carolyn 1973. *Toward a Recognition of Androgyny*. New York: Alfred A. Knopf.

Hein, Hilde 1981. Women and science: fitting men to think about nature. *International Journal of Women's Studies*, 4: 369–77.

Hekman, Susan 1983. *Weber, the Ideal Type and Contemporary Social Theory*. Notre Dame: University of Notre Dame Press.

—— 1986. *Hermeneutics and the Sociology of Knowledge*. Notre Dame: Notre Dame University Press.

Held, Virginia 1987. Feminism and moral theory. In Eva Kittay and Diana Meyers (eds), *Women and Moral Theory*, Totowa, N.J.: Rowman and Littlefield, 111–38.

Hendler, Sheldon 1976. Introduction. In June Singer (ed.), *Androgyny: toward a new theory of sexuality*, Garden City, N.Y.: Doubleday, 1–12.

Hesse, Mary 1980. *Revolutions and Reconstructions in the Philosophy of Science*. Bloomington, Ind.: Indiana University Press.

Hiley, David 1985. Foucault and the question of Enlightenment. *Philosophy and Social Criticism*, Summer, 63–83.

Hillman, James 1972. *The Myth of Analysis*. Evanston: Northwestern University Press.

Hindess, Barry and Paul Hirst 1977. *Mode of Production and Social Formation*. London: Macmillan.

Hirsch, Eric 1967. *Validity in Interpretation*. New Haven, Conn.: Yale University Press.

Hite, Molly 1988. Writing – and reading – the body: female sexuality and recent feminist fiction. *Feminist Studies*, 14 (1): 121–42.

Hochschild, Arlie Russel 1975. The sociology of feeling and emotion: selected possibilities. In Marcia Millman and Rosabeth Kanter (eds), *Another Voice: feminist perspectives on social life and social science*, New York: Doubleday, 280–307.

Holland, Nancy 1985. Heidegger and Derrida redux. In Hugh Silverman and Don Ihde (eds), *Hermeneutics and Deconstruction*, Albany: SUNY Press, 219–26.

—— 1986. The treble clef/t: Jacques Derrida and the female voice. Unpublished paper.

Holstrom, Nancy 1982. Do women have a distinct nature? *Philosophical Forum*, 14: 25–42.

Hooke, Alexander 1987. The order of others: is Foucault's antihumanism against human action? *Political Theory*, 15: 38–60.

Hooyman, Nancy and Susan Johnson 1977. Sociology's portrayal of women: socio-political implications. *Soundings*, 60: 449–65.

Horowitz, Gad 1987. The Foucaultian impasse: no sex, no self, no revolution. *Political Theory*, 15: 61–80.

Hoy, David Couzens 1985. Jacques Derrida. In Quentin Skinner (ed.), *The Return of Grand Theory in the Human Sciences*, Cambridge: Cambridge University Press, 41–64.

—— 1986. Introduction. In David Couzens Hoy (ed.), *Foucault: a critical reader*, New York: Basil Blackwell, 1–25.

Hubbard, Ruth 1981. The emperor doesn't wear any clothes: the impact of feminism on biology. In Dale Spender (ed.), *Men's Studies Modified*, Oxford and New York: Pergamon Press, 213–35.

—— 1988. Science, facts and feminism. *Hypatia*, 3: 5–17.

—— and Mary Sue Henifin, and Barbara Fried (eds) 1979. *Women Look at Biology Looking at Women*. Cambridge, Mass.: Schenkman.

—— and Marian Lowe 1979. Conclusions. In Ruth Hubbard and Marian Lowe (eds), *Genes and Gender II*, New York: Gordian Press, 143–51.

Huyssen, Andreas 1981. The search for tradition: avant-garde and postmodernism in the 1970s. *New German Critique*, 22: 23–40.

Illich, Ivan 1982. *Gender*. New York. Pantheon Books.

Irigaray, Luce 1985a. *Speculum of the Other Woman*. Trans. Gillian C. Gill. Ithaca, New York: Cornell University Press.

—— 1985b. *This Sex Which is Not One*. Trans. Catherine Porter. Ithaca, New York: Cornell University Press.

—— 1987. Sexual difference. In Toril Moi (ed.), *French Feminist Thought*, New York: Basil Blackwell, 118–30.

Jaggar, Alison 1983. *Feminist Politics and Human Nature*. Totowa, N.J.: Rowman and Allanheld.

Jardine, Alice 1985. *Gynesis: configurations of woman and modernity*. Ithaca, New York: Cornell University Press.

Jay, Martin 1982. Should intellectual history take a linguistic turn: reflections on the Habermas – Gadamer debate. In Dominic LaCapra and Steven L. Kaplan (eds), *Modern European Intellectual History*, Ithaca: Cornell University Press, 86–110.

Johnson, Barbara 1981. Translator's introduction. In Jacques Derrida, *Dissemination*, Chicago: University of Chicago Press, vii–xxxiii.

Jones, Ann Rosalind 1981. Writing the body: toward an understanding of *L'Ecriture Feminine*. *Feminist Studies*, 7: 247–63.

Jones, Kathleen 1988. On authority: or why women are not entitled to speak. In Irene Diamond and Lee Quinby (eds), *Feminism and Foucault: reflections on resistance*, Boston: Northeastern University Press, 119–33.

Jordanova, L. 1980. Natural facts: a historical perspective on science and sexuality. In Carol MacCormack and Marilyn Strathern (eds) *Nature, Culture and Gender*, Cambridge: Cambridge University Press, 42–69.

Kahane, Claire 1985. Introduction: Part 2. In Charles Bernheimer and Claire Kahane (eds), *In Dora's Case: Freud, hysteria, feminism*, New York: Columbia University Press, 19–32.

Kaplan, Alexandra and John Bean 1976. *Beyond Sex-Role Stereotypes*. Boston: Little Brown.

Kaplan, Alexandra and Mary Anne Sedney 1980. *Psychology and Sex Roles: an androgynous perspective*. Boston: Little Brown.

Keenan, Tom 1987. The "paradox" of knowledge and power: reading Foucault on a bias. *Political Theory*, 15 (1): 5–37.

Keller, Evelyn Fox 1982. Feminism and science. In Nannerl Keohane, Michelle Rosaldo and Barbara Gelpi (eds), *Feminist Theory: a critique of ideology*, Chicago: University of Chicago Press, 113–26.

—— 1983a. *A Feeling for the Organism*. New York: W. H. Freeman.

—— 1983b. Gender and science. In Sandra Harding and Merrill Hintikka (eds), *Discovering Reality*, Boston: D. Reidel, 187–205.

—— 1985. *Reflections on Gender and Science*. New Haven, Conn.: Yale University Press.

—— and Christine Grontkowski 1983. The mind's eye. In Sandra Harding and Merrill Hintikka (eds), *Discovering Reality*, Boston: D. Reidel, 207–24.

Keohane, Nannerl 1981. Speaking from silence: women and the science of politics. In Elizabeth Langland and Walter Gove (eds), *A Feminist Perspective in the Academy*, Chicago: University of Chicago Press, 86–100.

Kerber, Linda et al. 1986. On *In a Different Voice*: an interdisciplinary forum. *Signs*, 11 (2): 304–33.

Kimball, Meredith 1981. Women and science: a critique of biological theories. *International Journal of Women's Studies*, 4: 318–38.

Kitcher, Philip 1985. *Vaulting Ambition*. Cambridge, Mas.: MIT Press.

Kittay, Eva and Diana Meyers (eds) 1987. *Women and Moral Theory*. Totowa, N.J.: Rowman and Littlefield.

Kohlberg, Lawrence 1982. A reply to Owen Flanagan and some comments on the Puka–Goodpaster exchange. *Ethics* 92 (3): 513–28.

Kramarae, Cheris 1981. *Women and Men Speaking: frameworks for analysis*. Rowley, Mass.: Newbury House.

Kristeva, Julia 1977. *Of Chinese Women*. Trans. Anita Barrows. New York: Urizen Books.

—— 1980a. *Desire in Language: a semiotic approach to literature and art*. Trans. Thomas Gora, Alice Jardine and Leon S. Roudiez. New York: Columbia University Press.

—— 1980b. Oscillation between power and denial. In Elaine Marks and Isabelle de Courtivron (eds), *New French Feminism*, Amherst: University of Massachusetts Press, 165–7.

—— 1981. Women's time. *Signs*, 7: 13–35.

—— 1982. *The Power of Horror*. Trans. Leon Roudiez. New York: Columbia University Press.

—— 1984. *Revolution in Poetic Language*. Trans. Margaret Waller. New York: Columbia University Press.

—— 1986a. About Chinese Women. In Toril Moi (ed.), *The Kristeva Reader*, New York: Columbia University Press, 138–59.

—— 1986b. A new type of intellectual: the dissident. In Toril Moi (ed.), *The Kristeva Reader*, New York: Columbia University Press, 292–300.

—— 1987. *In the Beginning Was Love: psychoanalysis and faith*. New York: Columbia University Press.

Kruks, Sonia 1988. De Beauvoir and contemporary feminist debates. Unpublished paper.

Lacan, Jacques 1968. *The Language of the Self*. Baltimore: John Hopkins Press.

—— et al. 1985. *Feminine Sexuality*. Ed. Juliet Mitchell and Jacqueline Rose. New York: Norton.

Lakoff, Robin 1975. *Language and Woman's Place*. New York: Harper and Row.

Leff, Michael 1987. Modern sophistic and the unity of rhetoric. In John Nelson et al. (eds), *The Rhetoric of the Human Sciences*, Madison: University of Wisconsin Press, 19–37.

Leibowitz, Lila 1978. *Females, Males, and Families: a biosocial approach*. North Scituate, Mass.: Duxbury Press.

Lemert, Charles 1979. *Sociology and the Twilight of Man: homocentrism and discourse in sociological theory*. Carbondale: Southern Illinois University Press.

—— and Garth Gillan 1982. *Michael Foucault: social theory and transgression*. New York: Columbia University Press.

Lerner, Gerda 1986. *The Creation of Patriarchy*. New York: Oxford University Press.

Lewontin, Richard, Steven Rose and Leon Kamin 1984. *Not in Our Genes: Biology, ideology and human nature*. New York: Pantheon.

Llwelyn, John 1985. *Beyond Metaphysics: the hermeneutic circle in contemporary continental philosophy*. New York: Humanities Press.

—— 1986. *Derrida on the Threshold of Sense*. New York: St Martins.

Llyod, Genevieve 1983. Reason, gender and morality in the history of philosophy. *Social Research*, 50 (3): 490–513.

—— 1984. *The Man of Reason: "male" and "female" in western philosophy*. Minneapolis: University of Minnesota Press.

Longino, Helen and Ruth Doell. Body, bias and behavior: a comparative analysis of reasoning in two areas of biological science. *Signs*, 9: 206–27.

Lorde, Audre 1981. The master's tools will never dismantle the master's house. In Cherrie Moraga and Gloria Anzaldua (eds), *This Bridge Called My Back*, New York: Kitchen Table Press, 98–101.

Love, Nancy 1987. Freeing the feminine: critical theory and the family revisited. Unpublished paper.

Lovitt, William 1977. Introduction. In Martin Heidegger, *The Question Concerning Technology and Other Essays*. Trans. William Lovitt, New York: Harper and Row, xiii–xxxix.

Lowe, Marian 1981. Cooperation and competition in science. *International Journal of Women's Studies*, 4: 362–8.

—— and Ruth Hubbard 1983. Introduction. In Marian Lowe and Ruth Hubbard (eds), *Women's Nature: rationalizations of inequality*, New York: Pergamon Press, ix–xii.

Lydon, Mary 1988. Foucault and feminism: a romance of many dimensons. In Irene Diamond and Lee Quinby (eds), *Foucault and Feminism: reflections on resistance*, Boston: Northeastern University Press, 135–47.

Lyons, Nona 1983. Two perspectives on self, relationships and morality. *Harvard Educational Review*, 53: 125–45.

Lyotard, Jean-Francois 1978. Some of the things at stake in women's struggles. *Sub-Stance*, 20: 9–17.

—— 1984. *The Postmodern Condition: a report on knowledge*. Trans. Geoff Bennington and Brian Massumi. Minneapolis: University of Minnesota Press.

MacCormack, Carol 1980. Nature, culture and gender: a critique. In Carol MacCormack and Marilyn Strathern (eds), *Nature, Culture and Gender*, Cambridge: Cambridge University Press, 1–24.

—— and Marilyn Strathern (eds) 1980. *Nature, Culture and gender*. Cambridge: Cambridge University Press.

MacIntyre, Alasdair 1981. *After Virtue: a study in moral theory*. Notre Dame: Notre Dame University Press.

—— 1988. *Whose Justice? Whose Rationality?* Notre Dame: Notre Dame University Press.

MacKenzie, Catriona 1986. Simone de Beauvoir: philosophy and/or the female body. In Carole Pateman and Elizabeth Gross, *Feminist Challenges*, Boston: Northeastern University Press, 144–56.

MacKinnon, Catherine 1982. Feminism, Marxism, method and the state: an agenda for theory. In Nannerl Keohane, Michelle Rosaldo and Barbara Gelpi (eds), *Feminist Theory: a critique of ideology*, Chicago: University of Chicago Press, 1–30.

Major-Poetz, Pamela 1983. *Michel Foucault's Archaeology of Western Culture*. Chapel Hill: University of North Carolina Press.

Marcil-Lacoste, Louise 1983. The trivialization of "equality." In Sandra Harding and Merrill Hintikka (eds), *Discovering Reality*, Boston: D. Reidel, 121–37.

Marcus, Steven 1985. Freud and Dora: story, history, case history. In Charles Bernheimer and Claire Kahane (eds), *In Dora's Case: Freud, hysteria, feminism*, New York: Columbia University Press, 56–91.

Margolis, Joseph 1986. *Pragmatism Without Foundations*. New York: Basil Blackwell.

Marks, Elaine and Isabelle de Courtivron 1980. Why this book? and Introduction. In Elaine Marks and Isabelle de Courtivron, *New French Feminism*, Amherst: University of Massachusetts Press, ix–xiii, 1–38.

Martin, Biddy 1988. Feminism, criticism and Foucault. In Irene Diamond and Lee Quinby (eds), *Feminism and Foucault: reflections on resistance*, Boston: Northeastern University Press, 3–19.

Martin, Jane 1985. *Reclaiming a Conversation: the ideal of the educated woman*. New Haven, Conn.: Yale University Press.

McDermott, Patrice 1985. The epistemological challenge of post-Lacanian French feminist theory: Luce Irigaray. Unpublished paper.

—— 1987. Post-Lacanian French feminist theory: Luce Irigaray. *Women and Politics*, 7 (3): 47–64.

McMillan, Carol 1982. *Women, Reason and Nature*. Oxford: Basil Blackwell.

Meese, Elizabeth 1986. *Crossing the Double-Cross: the practice of feminist criticism*. Chapel Hill: University of North Carolina Press.

Megill, Allan 1985. *Prophets of Extremity*. Berkeley: University of California Press.

Merchant, Carolyn 1980. *The Death of Nature*. San Francisco, Cal.: Harper and Row.

Mill, John Stuart 1963. *The Six Great Humanist Essays of John Stuart Mill.* New York: Washington Square Press.

—— 1971. *On Liberty, Representative Government, The Subjection of Women*. London: Oxford University Press.

—— and Harriet Taylor Mill 1970. *Essays on Sex Equality*. Ed. Alice Rossi. Chicago: University of Chicago Press.

Miller, Jean Baker 1976. *Toward a New Psychology of Women*. Boston, Mass.: Beacon Press.

Millman, Marcia and Rosabeth Kanter 1975. Editorial Introduction. In Marcia Millman and Rosabeth Kanter, *Another Voice: feminist perspectives on social life and social science*, New York: Doubleday, vii–xvii.

Mills, Patricia 1987. *Women, Nature and Psyche*. New Haven, Conn.: Yale University Press.

Mitchell, Juliet 1974. *Psychoanalysis and Feminism*. New York: Pantheon Books.

—— 1985. Introduction I. In Juliet Mitchell and Jacqueline Rose (eds), *Feminine Sexuality*, New York: Norton, 1–26.

Moi, Toril 1985a. Representation of patriarchy: sexuality and epistemology in Freud's Dora. In Charles Bernheimer and Claire Kahane, *In Dora's Case: Freud, hysteria, feminism*, New York: Columbia University Press, 181–99.

—— 1985b. *Sexual/Textual Politics: feminist literary theory*. New York: Methuen.

—— 1986. Introduction. In Toril Moi (ed.), *The Kristeva Reader*, New York: Columbia University Press, 1–22.

—— 1987. *French Feminist Thought*. New York: Basil Blackwell.

Morgan, Robin 1982. *The Anatomy of Freedom: feminism, physics and global politics*. New York: Doubleday.

Nagele, Rainer 1986. The scene of the other: Theodor W. Adorno's *Negative Dialectics* in the context of poststructuralism. In Jonathan Arac (ed.), *Postmodernism and Politics*, Minneapolis: University of Minnesota Press, 91–111.

Nails, Debra 1983. Social scientific sexism: Gilligan's mismeasure of man. *Social Research*, 50 (3): 643–64.

Nelson, John et al. (eds) 1987. *The Rhetoric of the Human Sciences: language and argument in scholarship and public affairs*. Madison: University of Wisconsin Press.

Nicholson, Linda 1983. Women, morality and history. *Social Research*, 50 (3): 514–36.

—— 1986. *Gender and History*. New York: Columbia University Press.

Nietzsche, Friedrich 1964a. *Complete Works*, vol. 2. Ed. Oscar Levy. New York: Russell and Russell.

—— 1964b: *Beyond Good and Evil*. Trans. Helen Zimmern. In *Complete Works*, vol. 12, ed. Oscar Levy, New York: Russell and Russell.

—— 1984. *Human, All Too Human*. Lincoln: University of Nebraska Press.

Noddings, Nel 1984. *Caring*. Berkeley: University of California Press.

Nye, Andrea 1986. Preparing the way for a feminist praxis. *Hypatia*, 1: 101–16.

—— 1987. The woman clothed with the sun: Julia Kristeva and the escape from/to language. *Signs*, 12 (4): 661–86.

Oakes, Guy 1984. The problem of women in Simmel's theory of culture. In George Simmel, *George Simmel: on women, sexuality and love*. trans. Guy Oakes, New Haven, Conn.: Yale University Press, 3–62.

O'Brien, Mary 1981. *The Politics of Reproduction*. Boston, Mass.: Routledge and Kegan Paul.

—— 1982. Feminist theory and dialectical logic. In Nannerl Keohane, Michelle Rosaldo and Barbara Gelpi (eds), *Feminist Theory: a critique of ideology*, Chicago: University of Chicago Press, 99–112.

Okin, Susan Moller 1979. *Women in Western Political Thought*. Princeton, N.J.: Princeton University Press.

Ong, Walter 1967. *The Presence of the Word*. New Haven, Conn.: Yale University Press.

—— 1977. *Interfaces of the Word: studies in the evolution of consciousness and culture*. Ithaca: Cornell University Press.

—— 1981. *Fighting for Life: contest, sexuality and consciousness*. Ithaca: Cornell University Press.

Ortner, Sherry 1974. Is female to male as nature is to culture? In Michelle Rosaldo and Louise Lamphere (eds), *Woman, Culture and Society*, Stanford: Stanford University Press, 67–87.

—— and Harriet Whitehead 1981. Introduction: accounting for sexual meanings. In Sherry Ortner and Harriet Whitehead, (eds), *Sexual Meanings: the cultural construction of gender and sexuality*, New York: Cambridge University Press, 1–27.

Owens, Craig 1983. The discourse of others: feminists and postmodernism. In Hal Foster (ed.), *The Anti-Aesthetic: essays on postmodern culture*, Port Townsend, Wash.: Bay Press, 57–82.

Parsons, Kathryn Pyne 1979. Nietzsche and moral change. In Martha Osborne (ed.), *Women in Western Thought*, New York: Random House, 235–48.

Pateman, Carole 1988. *The Sexual Contract*. Stanford, Cal.: Stanford University Press.

Philip, Mark 1983. Foucault on power: a problem in radical translation? *Political Theory*, 11: 29–52.

Pitkin, Hanna 1984. *Fortune is a Woman: gender and politics in the thought of Niccólo Michiavelli*. Berkeley: University of California Press.

Plaza, Monique 1978. "Phallomorphic power" and the psychology of "woman." *Ideology and Consciousness*, 4: 5–36.

Poovey, Mary 1988. Feminism and deconstruction. *Feminist Studies*, 14 (1): 51–65.

Poster, Mark 1984. *Foucault, Marxism and History*. Oxford: Basil Blackwell.

—— 1986. Foucault and the tyranny of Greece. In David Couzens Hoy (ed.), *Foucault: a critical reader*, New York: Basil Blackwell, 205–20.

Potter, Elizabeth 1988. Modeling the gender politics in science. *Hypatia*, 3: 19–33.

Rabine, Leslie 1988. A feminist politics of nonidentity. *Feminist Studies*, 14 (1): 11–30.

Rajchman, John 1985. *Michel Foucault: the freedom of philosophy*. New York: Columbia University Press.

Raymond, Janice 1981. The illusion of androgyny. In Charlotte Bunch et al. (eds), *Building Feminist Theory*, New York: Longman, 59–66.

Reed, Evelyn 1978. *Sexism and Science*. New York: Pathfinder.

Reiter, Rayner (ed.) 1975. *Toward and Antropology of Women*. New York: Monthly Review Press.

Rhode, Deborah 1986. Feminist perspectives on legal ideology. In Juliet Mitchell and Ann Oakley (eds), *What is Feminism?*, New York: Pantheon, 151–60.

Rich, Adrienne 1976. *Of Woman Born*. New York: Norton.

Ricoeur, Paul 1983. On Interpretation. In Alan Montefiore (ed.), *Philosophy in France Today*, Cambridge: Cambridge University Press, 175–97.

Riemer, Ruby 1986. Feminist theory and rational man: a tale of two crises. Unpublished paper.

Ring Jennifer 1986. MacKinnon and Marx on subjectivity, objectivity and gender: the feminist potential of dialectical method. Unpublished paper.

Roberts, Joan (ed.) 1976. *Beyond Intellectual Sexism: a new woman, a new reality*. New York: David McKay.

Rogers, Susan 1978. Woman's place: a critical review of anthropological theory. *Comparative Studies in Society and History*, 20: 123–62.

Rorty, Richard 1979. *Philosophy and the Mirror of Nature*, Princeton N.J.: Princeton University Press.

—— 1982. *The consequences of Pragmatism*. Minneapolis: University of Minnesota Press.

—— 1983. Postmodernist bourgeois liberalism. *Journal of Philosophy*, 80: 583–9.

—— 1986. Foucault and epistemology. In David Couzens Hoy (ed.), *Foucault: a critical reader*, New York: Basil Blackwell, 41–9.

—— 1987. Science as solidarity. In John Nelson, et al. (eds), *The Rhetoric of the Human Sciences*, Madison: University of Wisconsin Press, 38–52.

—— 1989. *Contingency, Irony and Solidarity*. New York: Cambridge University Press.

Rosaldo, Michelle and Louise Lamphere (eds) 1974. *Women, Culture and Society*. Stanford, Cal.: Stanford University Press.

Rose, Hilary 1983. Hand, brain and heart: a feminist epistemology for the natural sciences. *Signs*, 9: 73–90.

—— 1986a. Beyond masculine realities. In Ruth Bleier (ed.), *Feminist Approaches to Science*, New York: Pergamon Press, 57–76.

—— 1986b. Women's work: women's knowledge. In Juliet Mitchell and Ann Oakley (eds), *What is Feminism*, New York: Pantheon, 161–83.

—— and Steven Rose (eds) 1976. *The Radicalization of Science: ideology of/in the natural sciences*. London: Macmillan Press.

Rosser, Sue 1984. A call for feminist science. *International Journal of Women's Studies* 7: 3–9.

Rossi, Alice 1970. Sentiment and intellect. In Alice Rossi (ed.), *Essays on Sex Equality*, Chicago: University of Chicago Press, 3–63.

—— 1977. A biosocial perspective on parenting. *Daedelus*, 106: 1–31.

Rubin, Gayle 1975. The traffic in women: notes on the "political economy" of sex. In Rayna Reiter (ed.), *Toward an Anthropology of Women*, New York: Monthly Review Press, 157–210.

Ruddick, Sarah 1980. Maternal Thinking. *Feminist Studies*, 6: 342–67.

—— 1983. Pacifying the forces: drafting women in the interest of peace. *Signs* 8 (3): 471–89.

—— 1984. Preservative love and military destruction: some reflections on mothering and peace. In Joyce Trebilcot (ed.), *Mothering: essays in feminist theory*, Totowa, N.J.: Rowman and Allanheld, 231–62.

—— 1987. Remarks on the sexual politics of reason. In Eva Kittay and Diana Meyers (eds), *Women and Moral Theory*, Totowa, N.J.: Rowman and Littlefield, 237–60.

Russo, Mary 1986. Female grotesques: carnival and theory. In Teresa De Lauretis (ed.), *Feminist Studies/Critical Studies*, Bloomington: Indiana University Press, 213–29.

Ryan, Michael 1982. *Marxism and Deconstruction*. Baltimore: Johns Hopkins University Press.

Sagan, Eli 1988. *Freud, Women and Morality: the psychology of good and evil*. New York: Basic Books.

Sanday, Peggy 1981. *Female Power and Male Dominance*. New York: Cambridge University Press.

Saxonhouse, Arlene 1985. *Women in the History of Political Thought: ancient Greece to Machiavelli*. New York: Praeger.

Sawicki, Jana 1988. Identity politics and sexual freedom. In Irene Diamond and Lee Quinby (eds), *Foucault and Feminism: reflections on resistance*, Boston: Northeastern University Press, 177–91.

Sayers, Janet 1982. *Biological Politics: feminist and anti-feminist perspectives*. London: Tavistock.

—— 1986. *Sexual Contradictions: psychology, psychoanalysis and feminism*. London: Tavistock.

Scheman, Naomi 1983. Individualism and the objects of psychology. In Sandra Harding and Merrill Hintikka (eds), *Discovering Reality*, Boston: D. Reidel, 225–44.

Schor, Naomi 1987. Dreaming dissymmetry: Barthes, Foucault and sexual difference. In Alice Jardine and Paul Smith (eds), *Men in Feminism*, New York: Methuen, 98–110.

Schwarzer, Alice 1984. *After "The Second Sex": conversations with Simone de Beauvoir*. New York: Pantheon.

Scott, Joan 1988. Deconstructing equality – versus – difference: or, the uses of poststructuralist theory for feminism. *Feminist Studies*, 14 (1): 33–50.

Secor, Cynthia 1974. Androgyny: an early reappraisal. *Women's Studies*, 2: 161–9.

Shapiro, Michael 1980. Interpretation and political understanding. Unpublished paper.

—— 1984. Literary production as a politicizing practice. In Michael Shapiro (ed.), *Language and Politics*, Oxford: Basil Blackwell, 215–53.

—— 1987. Writing, the self and the order: rationalistic, critical and genealogical approaches. Unpublished paper.

Sherman, Julia and Evelyn Beck 1979. Introduction. In Julia Sherman and Evelyn Beck (eds), *The Prism of Sex: essays in the sociology of knowledge*, Madison: University of Winsconsin Press, 3–8.

Sichtermann, Barbara 1986. *Femininity: the politics of the personal*, trans. John Witlan, Minneapolis: University of Minnesota Press.

Silverman, Kaja 1983. *The Subject of Semiotics*. New York: Oxford University Press.

Simmel, Georg 1984. *On Women, Sexuality and Love*. Trans. Guy Oakes. New Haven, Conn.: Yale University Press.

Simons, Margaret and Jessica Benjamin 1979. Simone de Beauvoir: an interview. *Feminist Studies*, 5: 330–45.

Singer, Jane 1976. *Androgyny: toward a new theory of sexuality*. Garden City, N.Y.: Anchor Press.

Slater, Philip 1968. *The Glory of Hera: Greek mythology and the Greek family*. Boston, Mass.: Beacon Press.

Smith, Dorothy 1977. Some implications of a sociology for women. In *Woman in a Man-Made World: a socioeconomic handbook*, Chicago: Rand-McNally, 15–29.

—— 1979. A sociology for women. In Julia Sherman and Evelyn Beck (eds), *The Prism of Sex: essays in the sociology of knowledge*. Madison: University of Wisconsin Press, 135–87.

Smith, Joan 1982-2. Sociobiology and feminism: the very strange courtship of competing paradigms. *Philosophical Forum*, 13: 224–43.

—— 1983. Feminist analysis of gender: a mystique. In Marian Lowe and Ruth Hubbard (eds), *Woman's Nature: rationalizations of inequality*, New York: Pergamon, 89–109.

Smith, Paul 1988. *Discerning the Subject*. Minneapolis: University of Minnesota Press.

Smith, Steven 1985. Althusser's Marxism without a knowing subject. *American Political Science Review*, 79: 641–55.

Spender, Dale 1980. *Man-Made Language*. London: Routledge and Kegan Paul.

—— 1981. Introduction. In Dale Spender (ed.), *Men's Studies Modified*, Oxford: Pergamon Press, 1–9.

Spivak, Gayatri 1976. Translator's Preface. In Jacques Derrida, *Of Grammatology*, Baltimore: Johns Hopkins Press, ix–ixxxvii.

—— 1981. French feminism in an international frame. *Yale French Studies*, 62: 154–84.

—— 1983. Displacement and the discourse of women. In Mark Krupnick (ed.), *Displacement: Derrida and after*, Bloomington: Indiana University Press, 169–95.

—— 1984. Love me, love my ombre, elle. *Diacritics*, Winter, 19–36.

—— 1987a. Explanation and culture: marginalia. In Gayatri Spivak, *Other Worlds*, New York: Methuen, 103–17.

—— 1987b. Sex and history in *The Prelude* (1805): books nine to thirteen. In Gayatri Spivak, *Other Worlds*, New York: Methuen, 46–76.

Stacey, Judith 1983. The new conservative feminism. *Feminist Studies*, 9: 559–83.

—— 1986. Are feminists afraid to leave home? In Juliet Mitchell and Ann Oakley (eds), *What is Feminism?*, New York: Pantheon, 208–37.

—— and Barrie Thorne 1985. The missing feminist revolution in sociology. *Social Problems*, 32: 301–16.

Stanton, Domna 1980. Languange and revolution: the Franco-American dis-connection. In Hester Eisenstein and Alice Jardine (eds), *The Future of Difference*, Boston, Mass.: G. K. Hall, 73–87.

—— 1986. Difference on trial: a critique of the maternal metaphor in Cixous, Irigaray and Kristeva. In Nancy Miller (ed.), *The Poetics of Gender*, New York: Columbia University Press, 157–82.

Star, Susan Leigh 1979. Sex differences and the dichotomization of the brain. In Ruth Hubbard and Marian Lowe (eds), *Genes and Gender II*, New York: Gordian Press, 113–30.

Stern, Karl 1965. *The Flight from Woman*. New York: Noonday Press.

Strathern, Marilyn 1980. No nature, no culture. In Carol MacCormack and Marilyn Strathern (eds), *Nature, Culture and Gender*, Cambridge: Cambridge University Press, 174–222.

Strong, Tracy 1975. *Friedrich Nietzsche and the Politics of Transfiguration*. Berkeley: University of California Press.

—— 1984. Language and nihilism: Nietzsche's critique of epistemology. In Michael Shapiro (ed.), *Language and Politics*, Oxford: Basil Blackwell, 81–107.

Taylor, Charles 1984. Foucault on freedom and truth. *Political Theory*, 12 (2): 152–83.

Taylor, Mark 1987. Descartes, Nietzsche and the search for the unsayable. *New York Times Book Review*, February 1, 3, 34.

Thompson, John 1984. *Studies in the Theory of Ideology*. Berkeley: University of California Press.

Trask, Haunani-Kay 1986. *Eros and Power: the promise of feminist theory*. Philadelphia: University of Pennsylvania Press.

Trebilcot, Joyce 1982. Two forms of androgynism. In Mary Vetterling-Braggin (ed.), *"Femininity," "Masculinity," and "Androgyny': a modern philosophical discussion*, Totowa, N.J.: Rowman and Littlefield, 161–9.

Tronto, Joan 1987a. Beyond gender difference to a theory of care. *Signs*, 12 (4): 644–63.

—— 1987b. Political science and caring: or, the perils of balkanized social science. *Women and Politics*, 7 (3): 85–97.

Tuana, Nancy 1986. The unhappy marriage of alchemy and feminism. Unpublished paper.

Vickers, Jill 1982. Memoirs of an ontological exile: the methodological rebellions of feminist research. In Geraldine Finn and Angela Miles (eds), *Feminism in Canada*, Montreal: Black Rose Books, 27–46.

Wachterhauser, Brice 1986. Introduction: history and language in understanding. In Brice Wachterhauser (ed.), *Hermeneutics and Modern Philosophy*, Albany: SUNY Press, 5–61.

Walzer, Michael 1983. *Spheres of Justice: a defense of pluralism and equality*, New York: Basic Books.

—— 1987. *Interpretation and Social Criticism*. Cambridge: Harvard University Press.

Warnke, Georgia 1986. *The Hermeneutics of Gadamer*. Oxford: Basil Blackwell.

Weber, Max 1949. *The Methodology of the Social Sciences*. Trans and ed. Edward Shils and Henry Finch. New York: The Free Press.

—— 1968. *Economy and Society*. Ed. Guenther Roth and Claus Wittich. Berkeley: University of California Press.

Weedon, Chris 1987. *Feminist Practice and Poststructuralist Theory*. New York: Basil Blackwell.

Weinsheimer, Joel 1985. *Gadamer's Hermeneutics*. New Haven, Conn.: Yale University Press.

Wendell, Susan 1987. A (qualified) defense of liberal feminism. *Hypathia*, 2 (2): 65–93.

Wenzel, Helene 1981. The text and body/politics: an appreciation of Monique Wittig's writings in context. *Feminist Studies*, 7: 264–87.

Westkott, M. 1979. Feminist criticism of the social sciences. *Harvard Educational Review*, 49: 422–30.

Whitbeck, Carolyn 1984. A different reality: feminist ontology. In Carol Gould (ed.), *Beyond Domination*, Totowa, N.J.: Roman and Allanheld, 64–88.

White, Stephen 1986. Post-structuralism and political inquiry. Unpublished paper.

Wittig, Monique 1986. The mark of gender. In Nancy Miller (ed.), *The Poetics of Gender*, New York: Columbia University Press, 63–73.

Wollstonecraft, Mary 1967. *A Vindication of the Rights of Woman*. New York: Norton.

Woolf, Virginia 1984. *Three Guineas*. In *A Room of One's Own and Three Guineas*, London: Chatto and Windus, 107–310.

Young, Iris 1980. Socialist feminism and the limits of dual systems theory. *Socialist Review*, 50–1: 169–88.

—— 1984. Is male gender identity the cause of male domination? In Joyce Trebilcot (ed.), *Mothering: essays in feminist theory*, Totowa, N.J.: Roman and Allanheld, 129–46.

—— 1985. Humanism, gynocentrism and feminist politics. *Hypatia*. Special issue of *Women's Studies International Forum* 8: 173–83.

—— 1986a. The ideal of community and the politics of difference. *Social Theory and Practice*, 12: 1–26.

—— 1986b. Impartiality and the civic public sphere: some implications of feminist critiques of moral and political theory. *Praxis International* 5: 381–401.

Young, Robert 1981. Post-structuralism: an introduction. In Robert Young (ed.), *Untying the Text*, Boston, Mass.: Routledge and Kegan Paul, 1–19.

Index